D1223589

Bloom's Modern Critical Interpretations

The Adventures of
  Huckleberry Finn
The Age of Innocence
Alice's Adventures in
  Wonderland
All Quiet on the
  Western Front
As You Like It
The Ballad of the Sad
  Café
Beloved
Beowulf
Black Boy
The Bluest Eye
The Canterbury Tales
Cat on a Hot Tin Roof
The Catcher in the Rye
Catch-22
The Chronicles of
  Narnia
The Color Purple
Crime and
  Punishment
The Crucible
Darkness at Noon
Death of a Salesman
The Death of Artemio
  Cruz
Don Quixote
Emerson's Essays
Emma
Fahrenheit 451
A Farewell to Arms
Frankenstein
The Glass Menagerie

The Grapes of Wrath
Great Expectations
The Great Gatsby
Gulliver's Travels
Hamlet
The Handmaid's Tale
Heart of Darkness
I Know Why the
  Caged Bird Sings
The Iliad
Jane Eyre
The Joy Luck Club
The Jungle
Long Day's Journey
  into Night
Lord of the Flies
The Lord of the Rings
Love in the Time of
  Cholera
The Man Without
  Qualities
The Metamorphosis
Miss Lonelyhearts
Moby-Dick
My Ántonia
Native Son
Night
1984
The Odyssey
Oedipus Rex
The Old Man and the
  Sea
On the Road
One Flew over the
  Cuckoo's Nest

One Hundred Years of
  Solitude
Persuasion
Portnoy's Complaint
Pride and Prejudice
Ragtime
The Red Badge of
  Courage
Romeo and Juliet
The Rubáiyát of Omar
  Khayyám
The Scarlet Letter
A Separate Peace
Silas Marner
Song of Solomon
The Sound and the
  Fury
The Stranger
A Streetcar Named
  Desire
Sula
The Tale of Genji
A Tale of Two Cities
"The Tell-Tale Heart"
  and Other Stories
Their Eyes Were
  Watching God
Things Fall Apart
To Kill a Mockingbird
Ulysses
Waiting for Godot
The Waste Land
Wuthering Heights
Young Goodman
  Brown

Toni Morrison's
Song of Solomon
New Edition

Edited and with an introduction by
Harold Bloom
Sterling Professor of the Humanities
Yale University

BLOOM'S
LITERARY CRITICISM
An imprint of Infobase Publishing

Bloom's Modern Critical Interpretations: Song of Solomon—New Edition

Bloom's Literary Criticism
An imprint of Infobase Publishing
132 West 31st Street
New York NY 10001

Library of Congress Cataloging-in-Publication Data
Toni Morrison's Song of Solomon / edited and with an introduction by Harold Bloom. — New ed.
    p. cm. — (Bloom's modern critical interpretations)
   Includes bibliographical references and index.
   ISBN 978-1-60413-392-9
  1. Morrison, Toni. Song of Solomon.   2. Domestic fiction, American—History and criticism.   3. African American families in literature.   4. African Americans in literature.   5. Michigan—In literature.   I. Bloom, Harold.   II. Title.   III. Series.
   PS3563.O8749S638 2009
   813'.54—dc22
                                                                          2008052354

Contributing editor: Pamela Loos
Cover designed by Takeshi Takahashi

Printed in the United States of America
IBT IBT 10 9 8 7 6 5 4 3 2 1

This book is printed on acid-free paper.

All links and Web addresses were checked and verified to be correct at the time of publication. Because of the dynamic nature of the Web, some addresses and links may have changed since publication and may no longer be valid.

Contents

Editor's Note

My introduction pays aesthetic tribute to *Song of Solomon*, while refraining from endorsement of Morrison's cultural politics.

Trudier Harris proceeds to cheer for that cultural uplift, while Patrick Bryce Bjork also joins in the communal spirit, as does J. Brooks Bouson in his reflections on "black masculinity."

Faulkner, as the intertextual father, is transcended, in the true belief of John N. Duvall, after which Dana Medoro summons the ghost of Senator Theodore Bilbo of Mississippi, who scarcely seems relevant in the era of President Barack Obama.

Wes Berry meditates on a possible ecological Morrison, while Faulkner is restored to something like his relevance by Lorie Watkins Fulton.

Biblical names in *Song of Solomon* are usefully studied by Judy Pocock, after which Judith Fletcher concludes this volume with a Circean account of the quasi-Homeric theme of naming in what continues to be, for me, Morrison's best novel.

HAROLD BLOOM

Introduction

Toni Morrison's third novel, *Song of Solomon* (1977), seems to me her masterwork to date, though *Beloved* (1987) has even more readers. A superb, highly conscious artist from her beginning, Morrison is also a committed social activist. Exemplary as it is, her African-American feminist stance is the prime concern of nearly all her critics, which makes for a certain monotony in their cheerleading. Morrison is scarcely responsible for them, though I detect an intensification of ideological fervor when I pass from rereading *Song of Solomon* to rereading *Beloved* and then go on to *Jazz* and *Paradise*, the novels that followed. A novelist's politics are part of her panoply, her arms and armor. Time stales our coverings; fictions that endure do so despite the passionate commitments of their authors, while claques, however sincere, do not assure literary survival. The very titles of many of the essays in this volume testify to political obsessions: "black cultural nationalism," "myth, ideology, and gender," "race and class consciousness," "political identity," "competing discourses." Morrison, far cannier than her enthusiasts, at her most persuasive transcends her own indubitable concerns. Her art, grounded in African-American realities and concerns, is nevertheless not primarily naturalistic in its aims and modes.

Morrison has been vehement in asserting that African-American literature is her aesthetic context: she has invoked slave narratives, folklore, spirituals, and jazz songs. So advanced a stylist and storyteller is not likely to celebrate Zora Neale Hurston as a forerunner, or to imagine a relation between herself and Richard Wright, or James Baldwin. Her authentic rival is the late Ralph Waldo Ellison, whose *Invisible Man* remains the most extraordinary achievement in African-American fiction. Morrison subtly wards off

1

Invisible Man (1952), from *The Bluest Eye* (1970) on to *Paradise* (1999). Though she has deprecated the "complex series of evasions" of modernist literature and its criticism, no one is more brilliant at her own complex series of evasions, particularly of Ralph Ellison, unwanted strong precursor. This is not to suggest that Ellison is her prime precursor: William Faulkner shadows Morrison's work always, and inspires even more creative evasions in her best writing.

I am aware that I am at variance with nearly all of Morrison's critics, who take their lead from her *Playing in the Dark: Whiteness and the Literary Imagination,* one of her most adroit evasions of the central Western literary tradition that, in mere fact, has fostered her. But then, as a professional literary critic, I must declare an interest, since my argument for the inescapability of what I have termed "the anxiety of influence" is contested by the culturally correct. There is no anguish of contamination or guilt of inheritance for black women writers in particular, I frequently am admonished. Patriarchal, capitalistic, phallocentric notions must be swept aside: they are racist, sexist, exclusionary, exploitative. If even Shakespeare can become Alternative Shakespeare, then Toni Morrison can spring fullgrown from the head of Black Athena.

Every strong writer welcomes the opportunity to be an original, and Morrison's literary achievement more than justifies her sly embrace of African-American cultural narcissism. Her critics seem to me quite another matter, but my Editor's Note is an appropriate context for commenting upon them. Here I desire only to discuss, rather briefly, the genesis of *Song of Solomon*'s authentic aesthetic strength from the creative agon with Faulkner and with Ellison. Morrison deftly uses Faulkner while parrying Ellison: out of the strong comes forth sweetness. *Song of Solomon* exuberantly is informed by the creative gusto of Morrison's sense of victory in the contest that is inevitable for the art of literature. Jacob Burckhardt and Friedrich Nietzsche both pioneered in reminding us that the Athenians conceived of literature as an agon. Nietzsche admirably condensed this insight in his grand fragment, "Homer's Contest":

> Every talent must unfold itself in fighting . . . And just as the youths were educated through contests, their educators were also engaged in contests with each other. The great musical masters, Pindar and Simonides, stood side by side, mistrustful and jealous; in the spirit of contest. The sophist, the advanced teacher of antiquity, meets another sophist; even the most universal type of instruction, through the drama, was meted out to the people only in the form of a tremendous wrestling among the great musical and dramatic artists. How wonderful! "Even the artist hates the artist." Whereas

modern man fears nothing in an artist more than the emotion of any personal fight, the Greek knows the artist only as engaged in a personal fight. Precisely where modern man senses the weakness of a work of art, the Hellene seeks the source of its greatest strength.

Probably Morrison would dissent from Nietzsche, but that would be Morrison the critic, not Morrison the novelist, who is engaged in a personal fight with *Invisible Man* and with Faulkner's *Light in August*. Morrison's career is still in progress; it is too soon to prophesy whether she will yet surpass *The Song of Solomon*. Again, I am aware that admirers of *Beloved*, a highly deliberate work of art, believe that Morrison has transcended her earlier work. Since I find *Beloved* ideologically overdetermined, and therefore in places somewhat tendentious, I prefer *Song of Solomon*. Highly conscious as she is of the American romance tradition, from Hawthorne and Melville through Faulkner and Ellison, Morrison wonderfully subverts that tradition in *Song of Solomon*. This subversion is not primarily ideological, but properly imaginative and revisionary. Great solitaries—Hester Prynne, Captain Ahab, Joe Christmas, Invisible Man—are joined by a different kind of solitary, Milkman Dead. Milkman, like his precursors, quests for the restoration of his true self, lest he remain a Jonah, but Morrison shapes her protagonist's quest so that it is communitarian despite itself. She does the same in *Beloved*, yet with an inverted sentimentalism that may be the consequence of too overt a reliance upon the political myth of a social energy inherent in the souls of Southern blacks. In *Song of Solomon*, a work of more individual mythopoeia, the refining of community is aesthetically persuasive.

Ellison's nameless Invisible Man is massively persuasive in his final judgment that there is *no* community for him, black or white:

> Step outside the narrow borders of what men call reality and you step into chaos ... or imagination. That too I've learned in the cellar, and not by deadening my sense of perception; I'm invisible, not blind.

Morrison's Milkman Dead reaches a conclusion radically revisionary of Ellison's nameless man:

> How many dead lives and fading memories were buried in and beneath the names of the places in this country. Under the recorded names were other names, just as "Macon Dead," recorded for all time in some dusty file, hid from view the real names of people, places, and things. Names that had meaning ... When you know

your name, you should hang to it, for unless it is noted down and remembered, it will die when you do.

The Invisible Man, who will accept no name whatsoever, has stepped into chaos *or* imagination, two words for the same entity, or are they antithesis? Ellison, as an Emersonian, allows for both readings. Morrison, born Chloe Anthony Wofford, has held on to her original middle name as the "real" one. Milkman loses the false name, "Dead," to acquire the ancestral real name, Solomon or Shalimar. Ellison perhaps would have judged that Morrison had kept within narrower borders than she required; I never discussed her work with him, so I do not know, but African-American nationalism, or any sort, was what he had rejected in his poignant and deluded Ras the Exhorter. Milkman's superb poignance is that he is anything but an Exhorter.

Faulkner I find everywhere in Morrison, generally transmuted, yet never finally transcended. In our century, Wallace Stevens wrote the poems of our climate, and Faulkner wrote the best of our novels, particularly in *As I Lay Dying* and *Light in August*. Returning to a fictive South, Milkman also returns to Faulkner, primarily to "The Bear" and its rituals of initiation. I dislike going against Morrison's own passionate critical pronouncements, yet I hardly am attempting "to *place* value only where that influence is located." Joseph Conrad does not crowd out Faulkner, nor does Faulkner render Morrison less gifted, less black, less female, less Marxist. Even the strongest of novelists cannot choose their own precursors. Hemingway wanted to assert *Huckleberry Finn* as his origin, but the ethos and mode of *The Sun Also Rises* are distinctly Conradian. "Africanism is inextricable from the definition of Americanness," Morrison insists. She ought to be right, and as a nation we would be better if she were right. One learns the truth about American Religion, I am convinced, if we trace its origin to the early black Baptists in America, who carried an African *gnosis* with them, in which "the little me within the big me" was the ultimate, unfallen reality. Morrison, like Faulkner, has a great deal to teach us about both "white" American and African-American identity. In a long enough perspective, Faulkner and Morrison may be teaching the same troubled truths.

TRUDIER HARRIS

Song of Solomon

Milkman Dead: An Anti-Classical Hero

Many scholars approaching Toni Morrison's *Song of Solomon* (New York: Knopf, 1977) have tried to explain the novel in traditional mythological terms. They place Milkman's birth in the company of those of Moses, King Arthur, Achilles, Prometheus, and other legendary figures treated by Lord Raglan in *The Hero* and by Joseph Campbell in *The Hero With A Thousand Faces*.[1] When parallels to these leave off, they turn to heroic patterns derived from classical Greek and Roman mythology in an effort to identify and incorporate the various allusions Morrison draws upon in the novel.[2]

These approaches lead to focusing upon the dangerous circumstances surrounding Milkman's conception and birth as explanations for his difference. There is magic in Pilate giving Ruth a potion to administer in Macon Dead's food in order to ensure Milkman's conception, and there is the added trauma of Macon trying to force an abortion once he learns that his four-day renewed sexual attraction for his wife has led to her pregnancy. To minimize the danger, Pilate, the witchlike godmother, watches over Milkman's advent into the world with all the care of one of the wise men anticipating the birth of Christ.

The mythical connections continue in Milkman's adult life in the quest he undertakes in search of gold. Comparable to Jason's search for the golden fleece, or to Odysseus's journey home, Milkman's travels eventually lead to his

From *Fiction and Folklore: The Novels of Toni Morrison*, pp. 85–115, 201–206. © 1991 by Trudier Harris.

salvation as well. Helpers and hinderers on that journey are also comparable to those peopling the myths of the world. The classical Circe immediately comes to mind in the episode where Milkman meets a woman with the same name, a strange being in an unkempt house full of dogs. And who can fail to think of Icarus throughout the book as Morrison focuses upon Milkman's desire to fly?

Other critical mythology-seekers concentrate on smaller connections in the novel, such as the ghost of Pilate's father and rituals of scapegoating, which indicate Morrison's familiarity with a variety of cultural myths. Such symbol mongers seek in vain for some pattern that will explain the whole of the novel, but they are left with the bits and pieces of the myths and mythological characters Morrison has alluded to in her work. They quickly discover puzzling loose ends. The Icarus myth might be relevant, but that is not what the novel is ultimately about, and it does not serve to account wholly for Milkman's actions. Milkman may be in search of something, but he also carries "something" within himself that he must uncover as he makes his geographical and psychological journey. The pieces of those familiar patterns, therefore, in the final analysis do not add up to a wholeness of approach to the novel. They leave the myth hunters pleased with their recognition of the various myths, but dissatisfied that such myths do not bring them to a single, complete understanding of the novel—not to mention the various multiple strands of understanding.

The problem with such approaches is the refusal by critics to see the classical allusions as additional layers that enhance but are not designed to explain the novel. Morrison recognizes that the use of such stories to explain African-American culture would amount to a grossly ineffective superimposition of an alien world view on a culture that she has consistently shown to be resistant to such externally imposed concepts. Trying to explain Milkman Dead solely in terms of Greek myth is just as erroneous as trying to explain the Breedlove family in *The Bluest Eye* in terms of the tale of Dick and Jane.[3]

There is undoubtedly mythology in *Song of Solomon*, but it does not derive solely from outside the black community. Morrison herself has said of "the flying myth" in *Song of Solomon*: "If it means Icarus to some readers, fine; I want to take credit for that. But my meaning is specific: it is about black people who could fly. That was always part of the folklore of my life; flying was one of our gifts. I don't care how silly it may seem. It is everywhere—people used to talk about it, it's in the spirituals and gospels."[4] Those who insist exclusively upon traditional mythological approaches to the novel, therefore, fail to realize that the African-American world view will not align itself wholly with Greek myth.

The Greek and Roman world views are ones in which the dichotomies between good and evil are usually fairly clearly delineated—Odysseus is good; the Sirens are bad. Jason finally merits our approval; Medusa is expendable. The fickleness in that world belongs more to the gods than to the characters on earth who are acting out or against the wishes of the gods. Characters who earn our sympathy do so in unambiguous ways. We never stop to think that the Harpies may have some legitimate complaints, or that Circe may have her reasons for turning men into swine. We are asked simply to see the world in an either/or relationship to the events, issues, and characters presented.

Such an approach to *Song of Solomon* is impossible. A complex world, the one Morrison has created draws upon a dualism as old as African-American existence in the New World. That world view presupposes an intertwining of the secular and sacred realms of existence. Individuals who worked all week and went to root doctors on Saturday could just as easily shout in ecstasy through calling upon the name of the Lord on Sunday. Such a history sets the stage for a dualistic world view, but it does not inform exactly the world Morrison has created. Few characters in Morrison's novels are religious; in fact, those like Soaphead Church in *The Bluest Eye* are parodies of religious fervor, and Pauline Breedlove, though she clings to the church, worships a god more of her own creation than one reflecting an absolute morality beyond herself. Eva Peace and her daughters loved men, not God; indeed, Eva sets herself up as a goddess. Only Ruth in *Song of Solomon* practices conventional religion; then, she perverts the very notion of Christianity by worshipping her dead father.[5]

Morality, then, or any code of ethics based on how other human beings should be treated in *Song of Solomon*, does not grow from roots of Christianity. Yet we can conclude that certain actions are right and others wrong. The dualism develops when Morrison continues to blur the line between one person's right and another persons wrong. She refuses to allow us to be comfortable in our conclusions because the evidence for such evaluations keeps shifting. The circumstances surrounding the death of Ruth Foster Dead's father are a prime example of this. Did she caress his corpse, as Macon Dead claims? Did Macon kill her father, as Ruth claims? Who is right or wrong? Both and neither. When we consequently try to fit the actions of Milkman Dead into a pattern, we arrive at the same ambiguous conclusions. Should all of his former trespasses be forgiven just because he learns to fly? Was he right in emotionally abusing and neglecting Hagar? Wrong in telling Macon about Corinthians's affair with Porter? As Joseph T. Skerrett, Jr., has pointed out, stories of various kinds are key to the structuring of the novel, and the presentation of everybody's versions of events about themselves and others—frequently contradictory—reflects the essence of the African-American storytelling tradition.[6]

Morrison ultimately intends Milkman as a heroic figure whose heroism can only be defined through dualistic, sometimes ambiguous action and whose qualifications for heroism do not depend upon his goodness. As folklorist John W. Roberts has illustrated clearly, definitions for heroism vary with cultures and with circumstances within cultures: "figures (both real and mythic) and actions dubbed heroic in one context or by one group of people may be viewed as ordinary or even criminal in another context or by other groups, or even by the same ones at different times."[7] Milkman's deviation from classical western perceptions of heroism, therefore, do not in themselves preclude his eventual elevation to that status. Milkman's childhood is not shadowed in a mood of anticipation that he will perform some great act for the community, as is Jimmy's in Ernest Gaines's *The Autobiography of Miss Jane Pittman*.[8] Milkman is not chosen; rather, he is roused from his inconsequential state only as long as it takes Ruth to satisfy her desperate mothering urges. During his early years, Milkman does not do or think; he simply *is*—frequently a shadowy figure, sometimes an embarrassment, but never of any real consequence to anyone in his family.

His lack of development under any clear-cut moral strictures begins his erratic bouts with traditional notions of right and wrong. He sees his father disrespect his mother and dispossess tenants, and Macon early teaches him that material values are preferable to spiritual ones; certainly no dictum such as "love thy neighbor as thyself" guides his actions toward strangers or family. As a teenager, therefore, it is easy for Milkman to disobey Macon and go to Pilate's house because that environment represents a new thrill for him. He can also sense his future value to Macon and thereby gauge the limits to which he can take disobedience. He can dismiss his sisters as inconsequential, dead replicas of his mother, and he can dismiss his mother as a mere shadow of a woman. However, he may use his difference from the women, his maleness, to direct his straying from the straight and narrow path Macon sets down to govern his actions toward Pilate.

Milkman's underdeveloped moral sense also accounts in part for his unkind treatment of Hagar. His rent collecting for Macon has instilled more of a sense of power than one of responsibility toward other human beings. Hagar, just another thrilling convenience, can be dismissed with impunity when Milkman tires of her. Yet it is Milkman's rather than Hagar's perspective that Morrison follows through most of the relationship. She forces us to wait and wait through it, to consider Hagar expendable even if we do not consider Milkman innocent. She urges us to accept the *possibility* that something great is in the making and to tolerate Milkman's destructiveness until he, like Velma Henry in Toni Cade Bambara's *The Salt Eaters* (1980), discovers his mission on earth.

A spoiled brat, Milkman becomes a trial to our sympathies during this waiting process. Why doesn't this thirty-year-old man hurry up and find himself, we ask, and quit being so inexcusably and repulsively childish? Uneasiness notwithstanding, we do sense that Milkman has a special relationship to Pilate, and that is the direction from which the measure of tolerance we feel for him comes. If Milkman can be saved from his spiritual inertia and his human detachment, then Pilate is the course through whom that saving must come.

A helper in the tradition of those recognized by Vladimir Propp in his *Morphology of the Folktale*, Pilate becomes a surrogate mother for Milkman—for he barely has a relationship with Ruth—and she also becomes his spiritual guide into a world where commitment replaces detachment and where materialistic pursuits are dwarfed by inner fulfillment.[9] The dualism in Milkman's life, then, can be measured by his interaction with members of his family as well as by his relationship to Guitar and the Seven Days.

For Milkman, the murderous activities of the Seven Days mean little in comparison to his own seeking after thrills. The eye-for-an-eye rationale for the murders of white people in retaliation for the deaths of blacks is inconsequential to Milkman. We condemn the murders precisely because of the rationale, for it leads to the kind of predicament Bigger Thomas finds himself in with the murder of Bessie Mears: murder of the oppressor eventually leads to murder of the oppressed. Because Milkman has no political consciousness, he does not care that Guitar's actions are psychologically warping—until he becomes the prey in Guitar's predatory hunt. Before this, he neither applauds nor condemns Guitar; the activities of the group are simply not incorporable into his lifestyle or into his limited moral vision. He is content to exist with any ugliness in the world as long as it does not directly injure him—even when he has had a hand in creating the ugliness, as with Hagar.

Actions contrary to those expected in the traditional hero are apparent in Milkman's conspiring, with Guitar, to steal from Pilate's house what they believe is a bag of gold. The robbery is a violation comparable to rape. Pilate, Reba, and Hagar have welcomed Milkman into their home. They have fed him and given him spiritual sustenance, and Hagar has welcomed him into her bed. Without compunction, Milkman robs them of what he believes is their most valuable possession. Traditional heroes who steal, such as Jack and Prometheus, do so for altruistic purposes—to save a starving family, to find the way home, to rescue a captured princess, to aid humanity in general. A larger moral purpose guides their small infractions of morality. Milkman has no redeeming purpose or qualities during this incident; it is only our hope that he may one day be redeemed that saves him from utter dismissal.

Warped values, inadequate character formation, and self-centeredness all define Milkman's incomplete vision of the world. He treats Pilate's house, which we have come to view as tranquil, invigorating, almost sacred, as a lair of monsters through whom he must negotiate safe passage with his stolen gold. While it may be viewed as a prank, the robbery nonetheless has the overtones of greed and self-aggrandizement that have characterized Milkman in relation to Macon. Instead of condemning or excusing the action at this point, we are encouraged to wait for whatever outcome Morrison has in store for Milkman and for us. That response is taught in part from our experiences with Morrison's earlier novels, but also from the shades of gray that permeate this novel.

And why does Morrison ask us to withhold judgment on Milkman for so long? The answer lies in part in the paradoxical elements of his nickname. The name suggests dependence and immaturity that will eventually lead to strength. It suggests nurturing by the women in his life, and it anticipates the time he will move beyond the need for that nurturing; the dualism in the name is symbolic of the dualistic world view in the novel.[10] Nurtured initially by Ruth, his biological mother, Milkman is nursed far beyond the time during which suckling is appropriate. Seeking through this act to become almost an extranatural influence upon Milkman in order to alleviate her dissatisfaction with her own life, Ruth instead delays Milkman's maturity and leaves him in a state of underdevelopment that she does not have the skills to rectify. Milkman thus hangs in limbo until Pilate enters his life to take over the nurturing function as the true extranatural mother. Ruth is too bound by her father's memory and Macon's oppression to develop the imagination or acquire the freedom that Pilate has. It is this new mother, who spiritually attended at Milkman's birth, who must guide him beyond the peacock plumage of materialism that binds him to earth and teach him how to fly.[11]

Ruth and Pilate are contrasting nurturers who reflect the dualistic world view in the novel. Ruth represents the sacred part of the traditional secular/sacred dichotomy in African-American cosmology. She respects tradition, is understandably conventional, and worships at the altar of her father's memory. While these things may be of an un-Christian, untraditional religious nature, in the *forms* they take, they nevertheless tie Ruth to rules carefully observed in religious environments. Such connections show strictures almost as tangible as the house in which the Dead family is trapped, and they ensure that Milkman can never achieve his potential as long as he is in the environment where his mother can influence him. Ruth's brand of obsession, no matter its origins or extenuating circumstances, can only mean closure and heaviness for Milkman, not freedom and flight. Unable, however, to push Milkman beyond her influence willingly, Ruth can only watch as he discovers Pilate's world. She has no ultimate redress against her role being usurped by Pilate, the surrogate mother, for Milkman must escape the Dead house, must go into that world, if he is to grow.

Pilate represents the secular side of the traditional dichotomy—nonconformity, freedom to explore, ties to history that transcend written records, and the extranatural quality that Ruth's limited imagination can barely glimpse. Her lack of a navel symbolizes her extranatural mothering role, as well as the mythical connotations of an individual who, as Morrison has observed, had to "literally invent herself."[12] Such a distinguishing feature, along with her height, ties her to M'Dear in *The Bluest Eye* and to Sula in suggesting that she has more than human power. And indeed others view Pilate as having the traits of voodoo doctors and conjurers: "Pilate, who never bothered anybody, was helpful to everybody, but who also was believed to have the power to step out of her skin, set a bush afire from fifty yards, and turn a man into a ripe rutabaga—all on account of the fact that she had no navel" (94). Milkman and Guitar heighten this perception of her extranatural qualities by being "spellbound" by the stories she tells (36). Unlike most people, she is not afraid of death, and she carries on conversations with her "mentor," her dead father (147, 151). This breaking down of planes of existence anticipates *Beloved*, where the living not only talk to the dead, but the dead dwell with the living.[13] Pilate is also a "natural healer" (150), perhaps through her receptivity and sensitivity to the physical world around her. Though her absent navel leads people to designate her "mermaid" or "witch," she is incapable of holding malice against anyone.[14] She has a special "way of being in the world," one that highlights her ability to make contact beyond this world. Her flat stomach becomes the metaphor for her "otherness," as Sula's birthmark and Pecola's ugliness have been in Morrison's earlier novels, though certainly Pilate's persecution is not as consistently dramatized as theirs.

Absence of that physical bond between mother and child in this world makes Pilate the only appropriate guide and nurturer for Milkman to extranatural perception. We must recognize, then, that Milkman's period of confusion, during which so many of his traditionally immoral actions occur, is linked to the time in his life when he is essentially "motherless," before he accepts enough of Pilate's influence to arrive at his long-delayed manhood. The period of Pilate's influence is made up of incidents from which Milkman could gather the values necessary to know himself and his family. The lessons Pilate subtly offers, if Milkman is sensitive to them, could provide the solid perch from which he can fly. Her lessons also show, sometimes by negative example, how he can shape responses to the world; those responses will enable him to become Pilate's successor as the keeper of family honor and believer in family traditions.[15]

As one of Milkman's lessons, consider the incident with Reba's lover. Pilate rescues her daughter from a man stupid enough to beat a woman who has been more than generous to him. Milkman watches as Pilate, grasping the man around the neck with one hand and wielding her knife over his heart with the other, placidly lectures him on the limits of motherly tolerance. Milkman is impressed by the showmanship of the incident without realizing its greater value: Pilate shows a commitment to family first of all, and she shows it without a destructive outcome. She controls her temper, and she controls the man who has harmed Reba. Such actions are in contrast to Milkman, who, despite his more than six feet of height, is still immature; when a potentially violent scene develops in the Dead house, Milkman responds to it by threatening more violence to Macon in retaliation for Macon slapping Ruth. Pilate's patient settling of the dispute, her generous response to the stranger, is in marked contrast to Milkman's self-centered attitude. Her actions are also a contrast to Milkman's treatment of Hagar.

Pilate and Reba's caring for Hagar, though sometimes extreme in its tolerance, nevertheless indicates that they are basically self-sacrificing where family is concerned. They are both appalled when Hagar maintains that there have been days when she was hungry, because they are committed to taking care of all of her physical needs. Once they realize that she refers to a different kind of hunger, their anxiety subsides. Their treatment of Hagar, which Milkman witnesses for a time before he becomes her sexual partner, is in direct contrast to his later abuse of Hagar. He has learned nothing from them about human relationships of an altruistic nature; instead, he keeps the women in a corner of his mind marked "other" and continues on his self-destructive, materialistic ways.

Pilate also provides him with the opportunity for reevaluating his relationship to his parents, especially his father. Although Pilate and Macon have been estranged for years, she nevertheless finds her way, finally, to her only other living relative. That means more to her than remembering whatever it was that initially separated them. She and Macon are not completely reconciled, but she has at least made the effort to find him and to move near him. That kind of geographical, spatial support portends a commitment to kin that Milkman cannot begin to fathom. Pilate and Macon may not be on regular speaking terms with each other, but in some ways she is closer to him than Milkman could ever be, and she is similarly closer to Ruth than Milkman is to his mother. Macon and Pilate, and Pilate and Ruth, have shared traumas of existence that make failures to socialize or petty squabbling inaccurate measures of the depth of their relationships. Milkman superficially chooses Pilate's license and freedom over his father's strictures without realizing that the two are complementary, inseparably bound in their meaning for his destiny.

These specific lessons that Milkman fails to learn are but the fractional representations of the philosophy of wholeness that Pilate practices. When Milkman goes into her home, he goes into a peaceful environment, one unmarred by the shadowy figures of his sisters or the blistering hatred his parents have for each other. He finds a soothing place, one in which nothing is required of him, except perhaps that he give himself wholly to its influence. It is an oasis in a world where the sands of materialism promise to smother even the most altruistic soul. Here, the love of money has no meaning. Middle-class dress and fancy whatnots are just as alien as Milkman is initially in Danville, Pennsylvania, and Shalimar, Virginia. Pilate, Reba, and Hagar have allowed the world to pass them by, at least the world in which most people find themselves trapped. In their voluntary retreat, however, they have managed to salvage more valuable things—a leisurely appreciation of life, joy in each other's company, a love of music, and the simple, credulous wonder in things as they are, with which most adults have lost contact. Most important, Pilate has a security in, and a comfort with, herself that Milkman will perhaps never achieve; contentment with being, and with being without encumbrances, are Pilate's forte. What others judge to be her disrespect for progress can also be viewed as her hold onto sanity in a world content to drive itself mad.

This philosophy is what she offers to Milkman, but he is so intent upon marveling at her difference that he fails to meditate upon its intrinsic healthy qualities. Pilate is herself a living example, as walking metaphor, for Milkman, but his vision, too coated with his father's materialism and the narrowness of the world on Not Doctor Street, cannot penetrate the surface of Pilate's existence to stare upon its life-saving depths.

When Milkman learns to fly, we evaluate his success as a testament to Pilate's piloting. He emerges as a heroic personality precisely because he has been more human than superhuman, more sinning than saved. Like Brer Rabbit, he has experienced the flexibility of morality. Like John the slave, he has been as much manipulator as manipulated. He has survived a lifestyle comparable to that many black preachers reject in their bids to become representatives of their people.[16] And he has shown that goodness alone is not the major prerequisite for heroism. Through him, Morrison illustrates that a simplistic approach to the evaluation of heroic deeds will not suffice for the complexity so integral to her novel. Her blurring of the lines of absolute values is characteristic of the trends in African-American folk culture that help to define Milkman and that give Morrison's writing such a distinctive flavor.

A Journey That Works

The Bluest Eye and *Sula* depicted characters in search of something they could never achieve, on journeys of seeking that left them insane, complacent, or dead. Pecola's search for blue eyes shows that the archetypal fairy tale pattern of seeking is antithetical to, and ultimately cannot allow fulfillment for, members of black communities. Pauline Breedlove's search for an identity outside of her blackness and her black heritage also ends in disaster, for that reversal is similarly antithetical to her true existence. The journey north for Pauline and the journey inward for Pecola both backfired. Sula's wandering can also be viewed as an aborted attempt to find meaning in her existence; unable to do so on southern or northern soil, she returns to her home in the North, more out of resignation than accomplishment. In her first two novels, therefore, Morrison depicts no pattern of seeking that leads to contentment for her characters. They are driven, disturbed, unsettled from the beginnings to the ends of their journeys. With Milkman Dead in *Song of Solomon*, Morrison culminates her pattern of reversal and simultaneously allows Milkman to find meaning in a territory that her previous characters have shunned or escaped.

Few characters in African-American literature chart their courses from north to south, for the myth informing their actions invariably pictured the North as the freer place, where money was plentiful and liberty unchallenged. So they usually went north, to that earthly land of milk and honey.[17] In *Song of Solomon*, therefore, Morrison debunks one myth and creates another. Born in the North, and heir to the material advantages that generations of blacks identified with that territory, Milkman Dead must find meaning for his life by reversing the pattern, by going south, back into the territory of his ancestors. There must also be a reversal in his expectations on that soil. Initially, he goes searching for gold, as many generations of blacks came north in hopes of improving their material wealth. But the South is not the land of riches, of physical, tangible goods waiting for those seeking their fortunes. It is the land of blood and death, of slavery, of countless generations of Africans tied to brutal and unrewarding labor, of intangible instead of tangible wealth. Milkman ultimately returns to the South for things that he can carry away only in his mind, in his conception of self, in his contentment with communal and familial history, and in his satisfaction with knowing and being who he is.

Milkman's journey is one that works because he forges out of it a blueprint for knowing himself. By going against the traditional archetypal movement and structuring a more personally rewarding one, Milkman earns our respect as he discovers his identity. Though his journey may share certain features with some of the mythological quests, it is nevertheless more distinctive than imitative.

Milkman's major problem is that he has been too complacent in his northern, middle-class existence, far removed from the stock of black people in the South who were tied to his ancestors who moved north. In order for Milkman to appreciate those roots, to become receptive to his past, he must be stripped of external symbols of separation. His city ways and attitudes have to change; Morrison effects the change by showing their uselessness on southern soil. Milkman undergoes a devolution from which he can be reborn as a sensitive human being. The stripping process begins with his arrival in Danville, Pennsylvania, where he hopes to find leads on where Pilate has left the gold. His emotions, clothing, accessories, and manners are all signs of the distance between him and the people whose help he needs.

Emotional readjustment signals the onset of many changes. For the first time he is put in the position of trying "to make a pleasant impression on a stranger" (229) when he goes to Reverend Cooper's house asking about Circe. That slight discomfiture gives way to tale swapping when Milkman discovers that Cooper has known his father, yet it is nonetheless a prediction of the adjustments Milkman will have to make on his journey.

His trip to Circe's house and to the cave induce physical discomfiture to match the earlier emotional one; the literal stripping process begins. His city hat gets ripped off by tree branches. He must take off his shoes and socks in crossing the stream to the cave, and his bare feet are "unprepared for the coldness of the water and the slimy stones at the bottom" (249). He soaks his fancy pants and cigarettes, and breaks the "gold Longines" watch his mother had given him: "the face was splintered and the minute hand was bent" (250). His fancy shirt becomes soaked with sweat, as does his face, for which he uses his tie as a handkerchief. Upon discovering no gold in the cave, he screams in anger, and the bats in the cave startle him into a run, "whereupon the sole of his right shoe split away from the soft cordovan leather" (252). He uses his tie to strap the shoe together and lashes his way through branches and weeds back to the stream and the highway where he has been scheduled for a pickup. His watch now gone, he can only gauge by the sun that his ride has probably come and gone.

Although he has been stripped of several items of his city clothing, Milkman has not learned much from his adventures. His disrespectful manners show that he is still insensitive to Southern hospitality. The man who prides himself on being able to give the worn and tattered Milkman a ride back into Danville has his gesture thrown in his face when Milkman tries to pay him for one of his Cokes. The man's face "changes" as he insists that, he "ain't got much," but he "can afford a Coke and a lift now and then" (255). His love for gold has blinded Milkman to the little courtesies of life, to the small favors that poor people relish performing for one another. His greed is his only motivation: "The fact was he wanted the gold because it was gold and he wanted to own it. Free" (257). A long way from the changes that will be necessary for his growth, Milkman has at least begun the physical movement that will eventually be matched by an emotional and spiritual change.

Milkman's sojourn in the wilderness of Danville has been difficult for him emotionally and physically, almost as if the very environment thwarts the unhealthy motives he has in looking for the gold. At this stage, the journey backfires more than it moves forward. Yet Milkman discovers some things in the process. He knows that the gold is no longer in the cave, and he surmises that Pilate had probably returned with it to her ancestral home in Virginia. Though he moves in that direction without a clear sense of where he is going or a significantly altered psyche, his willingness to continue the journey is itself noteworthy, for he has at least not been deterred by the obstacles he has encountered. They are mere preludes to what he must overcome the closer he gets to the object of his quest.

Journeys, by their very nature, pose obstacles for questers. There must be some test to gauge that the seeker is worthy of reward, as well as to determine if he or she has the stamina and the will to continue the quest. Whether posed by humans or gods, the tests, if passed successfully, earn respect for the seeker and enable him or her to make progress on the journey. For Milkman Dead, northern black rich man, the tests involve humiliation designed to teach him that his status does not separate him from the national corpus of black humanity. They show that his pride is disproportionate to his achievements, that he must learn to value those toward whom he is disdainful, and that he needs more assistance than his previous independence has allowed for. Because of the extent of his arrogance and the height of his separation from the blacks he meets, his tests have to be especially humbling. The black men in Shalimar, Virginia, are more than willing—and able—to effect his reassessment of his position in the world.

Milkman insults their ways and denies their humanity within a few minutes of his arrival in town. Bred to insensitivity concerning the customs of the South, his very ignorance is a weapon he wields against the men. He casually mentions that he will buy a new car if the old one cannot be repaired, thereby making the men dwell intensely upon their poverty and limited abilities to take care of their families. "He hadn't bothered to say his name, nor ask theirs, had called them 'them' . . . his manner, his clothes were reminders that they had no crops of their own and no land to speak of either" (266). His money highlights their poverty, and his easy survey of their women threatens the fragile bonds they can still use to claim their manhood. When he locks his car, in a town "where there couldn't be more than two keys twenty-five miles around," they know he is like the white men for whom they sit and hope for a day's work: "They looked at his skin and saw it was as black as theirs, but they knew he had the heart of the white men who came to pick them up in the trucks when they needed anonymous, faceless laborers" (266).

A man whose mere presence calls into question their own claims to manhood can only be tested in the same arena. Milkman has the power, manner, clothes, and money the black men identify with white men; therefore, they focus their first test on his sexual capacity—is he as much a man in sexual matters as the signs suggest, or can he be a "faggot"? If they can humiliate him with insinuations about homosexuality, and perhaps embarrass him or drive him away, they can restore to themselves some of the lack of manhood his presence makes them feel. The ritual of transference is old, though its specific manifestations may be unique. If Milkman leaves the scene, then the men will feel justified in not helping or accepting him. If he can hold his own and somehow survive their insults, then they will stop the ritual testing and tolerate him, perhaps even accept him into the community.

The men in Solomon's General Store begin their test with a verbal assault, in the tradition of one of the oldest forms of contest within black communities. Rather than playing the dozens, which would reflect subtle, less direct attacks, they confront Milkman with insults aimed not at his mother but specifically at him. From the assertion that "pricks is ... wee, wee little" in the North, they seek confirmation from Milkman and move on to insults about homosexuality and sexual perversion:

"That true?" The first man looked at Milkman for an answer.

"I wouldn't know," said Milkman. "I never spent much time smacking my lips over another mans dick." Everybody smiled, including Milkman. It was about to begin.

"What about his ass hole? Ever smack your lips over that?"

"Once," said Milkman. "When a little young nigger made me mad and I had to jam a Coke bottle up his ass."

"What'd you use a bottle for? Your cock wouldn't fill it?"

"It did. After I took the Coke bottle out. Filled his mouth too."

"Prefer mouth, do you?"

"If it's big enough, and ugly enough, and belongs to a ignorant motherfucker who is about to get the livin shit whipped out of him." (267)

More mouth than ability, Milkman pleases the spectators by succumbing to the physical battle they have all anticipated, but he is little match for his knife-flashing opponent: "Milkman did the best he could with a broken bottle, but his face got slit, so did his left hand, and so did his pretty beige suit, and he probably would have had his throat cut if two women hadn't come running in screaming . . ." (268). Having given his adversary a "jagged cut" over his eye, sufficient to induce profuse bleeding, Milkman is left in the hot sun, tending his wounds and reflecting on the incident as the others casually go their way.

Milkman's ability to hold his own with the bottle earns him a tinge of respect, but not enough for the fun to end. The measure of his worthiness continues in the older men's invitation to him to join them in a night hunt. Milkman cannot walk away from the challenge and still claim superiority, so he boasts that he is the "best shot there is" (269). The claim is a vestige of pride held on to in an impossible situation. The pride has to be tempered at the same time that the men must reevaluate their feelings toward Milkman. Change on his part will bring him closer to them and, on theirs, will encourage them to respect him at a mutual, horizontal level rather than a hierarchical one. As Dorothy H. Lee comments, "the older men take over the initiation rite from the youths. The names of the men—Omar, King Walker, Luther Solomon, Calvin Breakstone, and a giant called Small Boy—seem to indicate that Milkman has entered the circle of village elders, of poets, kings, and men of God."[18]

The coon hunt tests Milkman's courage and endurance, simultaneously forcing him to be dependent upon individuals he has scorned. Their familiarity with the territory, equipment, and procedures highlights Milkman's greenness. He does not foresee the noise that loose change in his pocket would make during a hunt, and he shows his lack of night sight by bumping into Calvin as they walk along a trail listening for the dogs. Milkman's city body, worn down by the earlier testing and his general fatigue, eventually gives out, and he finds himself alone in the dark woods, too weak to do anything but sit and reflect upon the circumstances that have brought him to that point. The hunt therefore assumes a triple purpose. It is a part of Milkman's journey south, a part of the ritual testing, and most important, a part of his journey inward, his "hunt" for the best within himself. His reflections show some of the strongest signs of growth, among them his recognition that he has treated his family and Pilate's badly. He literally experiences a dark night of the soul in which he realizes that none of the things separating him from the men hunting with him are of any use to him:

> There was nothing here to help him—not his money, his car, his father's reputation, his suit, or his shoes. In fact they hampered him. Except for his broken watch, and his wallet with about two hundred dollars, all he had started out with on his journey was gone: . . . His watch and his two hundred dollars would be of no

help out here, where all a man had was what he was born with, or had learned to use. And endurance. Eyes, ears, nose, taste, touch— and some other sense that he knew he did not have: an ability to separate out, of all the things there were to sense, the one that life itself might depend on. (277)

Milkman is learning lessons that he will not truly be able to value until later, but his current predicament has caused a previously unmatched reflection on his part. Guitar's attempt to strangle him to death shortly after these reflections makes Milkman realize even more the fragile nature of the material goods he has clung to throughout his life.[19]

That brush with death seems to sharpen Milkman's desire to live. He is able to find his way in the darkness to the spot where Calvin and the other men have treed a bobcat. A more expansive symbol of Milkman's newfound awareness than a coon would perhaps be, the bobcat becomes a measure of Milkman's acceptance into the group of hunters, into the kind of courage that has taken him through his path in the woods. The bobcat also culminates the ritual of acceptance; by allowing Milkman, the initiate, to pull out its heart, the men incorporate him into their fraternity and forgive him his former superiority over them.[20] He can now joke easily with them, admit that he was "scared to death" (280), describe that condition graphically for them, and enjoy becoming the butt of their jokes.

This coon-turned-bobcat hunt has additional significance from the perspective of African-American folklore and culture. "Coon," like "nigger," is a derisive name for blacks, one of which most insiders to the culture are aware. To be called a coon is to be reduced in value, made more thing than human. The pattern of Milkman's life has been one in which he has not lived up to anyone's conception of manhood—not his father's or Guitar's or Pilate's or even his own. Going on the coon hunt, then, is a metaphorical way for him to shed the negative connotations of his lack of manliness, the negative connotations of his lack of commitment to black community and black people, and to gain a victory from that confrontation with absence.

His position is not unlike that of the black man in the folktale, "Coon in the Box."[21] John the slave convinces his master that he can tell fortunes, after which the master bets his entire plantation on John's skill. The bettors test John by putting a raccoon under a box and guarding it until the time he is scheduled to reveal the contents. Knowing that he has listened outside his master's bedroom to predict previous events, and knowing that he has no knowledge of what is under the box, John is in a predicament when the time comes for him to show his clairvoyance. After much posturing, puzzling, and head-scratching, he accepts his presumed fate by simply saying: "Well, master,

I guess you got the old coon at last." Having been reduced to relying on nothing but their natural wits, John and Milkman make the right choices, utter the right words, and survive. And survival is all that matters at the test point, for the game for both characters (Milkman bragging that he knows hunting, and John bragging that he can tell fortunes) has become more dangerous than either intended. John turns the potentially negative situation positive by equating himself with the derisive epithet for blacks, and Milkman eludes his course of self-destruction by realizing that he has indeed been "niggerish" in his treatment of all the people in his life. Both survive by arriving at the point of vulnerability and *accepting* that potentially destructive condition.

At the literal level of the hunt, however, Milkman has again held his own, and the men are fair-minded enough to recognize it; they now share food and company with him and provide him with the first lead to finding information about his grandmother, Singing Bird. Finally, they send him to a woman who completes his process of initiation into their community.

Sweet, as she is more than appropriately named, is one of the "pretty women" Milkman has been brash enough to observe upon his arrival in Shalimar. Now that he has proved his manhood on their terms, the men judge him to be ready to sleep with one of the local women. She becomes one of the rewards for the quester having successfully completed his quest. Hers is a ritual of reclamation for him, which involves purification before lovemaking. She washes away the blood of the fight and the dirt and grime of the evening's hunt, thus formally baptizing him into official acceptance in Shalimar. And she willingly presents herself as the prize he has won for battles endured. Such a formulaic analysis, however, is mitigated by Sweet and Milkman thoroughly enjoying their sharing, especially Milkman, who is awakened to a new sense of awe in physical contact with a woman. "What she did for his sore feet, his cut face, his back, his neck, his thighs, and the palms of his hands was so delicious he couldn't imagine that the lovemaking to follow would be anything but anticlimactic" (285). It so far exceeds his expectations that he offers to give her a bath in return, an action far removed from anything he has done for Hagar and, in its sharing, anything he has done for any of the women in his life.

Having been tested verbally, physically, emotionally, and sexually, Milkman is better prepared, more sensitized to recognize that his family history is more important than any gold he could seek. His tests have taught him that human beings are not to be dismissed or ill treated with impunity. As a part of the tie that binds him to all living beings, especially people of African descent, he can no longer use his money to separate himself from the Sauls of Shalimar, or his city-slicker shoes to separate him from the Calvins, or his condescension from the Sweets of the world. They all tie him to a communal and familial heritage that goes back to Africa, and they represent, in their various states of development, some portion of his grandfather's journey from Virginia to Pennsylvania. The first Macon Dead's hope for better things drove him from the stifling South, a hope shared by the people who are still living there and being similarly stifled by poverty. And his travel on a wagon, so far distant psychologically and economically from Milkman Dead, reflects the very soil and work to which the people of Shalimar are rooted. Milkman has been shocked into the recognition that he will not be allowed to break the circle of connectedness extending generations before his own existence.

His rediscovery of his humanity makes him sensitive enough to Susan Byrd's information to realize that the children in Shalimar are singing about his great-grandmother, Ryna, and his great-grandfather, Solomon. He deciphers names and connects their songs to Pilate's blues song about Sugarman. The puzzle of family history becomes more engaging than searching for gold. Knowing one's name, being able to call it in spite of personal or institutional distortions, becomes all important to Milkman. He understands that names have "meaning," as Pilate has understood by putting hers in her ear. He comes to understand why people in Michigan insist upon calling the street on which he lives Not Doctor Street, why they value the nicknames he has heard in the pool halls and barbershops all his life. The names, taken "from yearnings, gestures, flaws, events, mistakes, weaknesses" (330), all "bear witness" to the concreteness, the reality of black people's lives in spite of the census bureau or the post office or drunk recorders. Inherent in the tradition of which the names are a part is the penchant of black people to adhere to their own reality in spite of almost insurmountable obstacles. By arriving at this state of awareness, Milkman can link his own family names to others representing black history and struggle. The golden threads tying him to his family history are far more valuable than the original gold he has sought.[22]

Milkman's growth on his journey is measurable. He changes from a self-centered, middle-class bore to a man genuinely able to share in a physical relationship as well as in societal and communal interchanges. He realizes how wrongheaded he has been about his father and mother and how he has used all the women in his life, especially Hagar. He had put his whims and desires before those of his sisters and had discounted their needs to be more than the older siblings of Macon Dead's chosen offspring. He had judged his mother harshly and had ignorantly tried to chastise his father. He had violated Pilate's home by stealing from her and continued that violation by journeying hundred of miles to find gold he believed she had hidden. Yet in the darkness on the coon hunt and in later scenes, Milkman comes to know many of his limitations and faults, in human relationships. He has been especially abusive to Hagar:

He had used her—her love, her craziness—and most of all he had used her skulking, bitter vengeance. It made him a star, a celebrity in the Blood Bank; it told men and other women that he was one bad dude, that he had the power to drive a woman out of her mind, to destroy her, and not because she hated him, or because he had done some unforgivable thing to her, but because he had fucked her and she was driven wild by the absence of his magnificent joint. His hog's gut, Lena had called it. Even the last time, he used her. Used her imminent arrival and feeble attempt at murder as an exercise of his will against hers—an ultimatum to the universe. "Die, Hagar, die." Either this bitch dies or I do. And she stood there like a puppet strung up by a puppet master who had gone off to some other hobby. (301)

In his egotistical focus on self, he had "gone off and left" Hagar in the same way that his great-grandfather had gone and left Ryna. In fact, Milkman's reflections upon Hagar spur his recognition of his family in the song sung by the children. In his remorse over Hagar, he begins to feel a sense of family responsibility and commitment negated in his great-grandfather's action of flying away from his family.

Throughout his life, Milkman has been "leaving" his family—through his disdain and hatred for his mother and father, through his condescension toward his sisters, and through his now recognized mistreatment of Hagar. He has left a string of bodies like his great-grandfather left Ryna and Jake, Milkman's grandfather. Where the paths converge signals a new beginning for Milkman, but it may be an ambiguous one. The exhilaration he feels upon learning that Solomon could fly is matched by the tragic circumstances surrounding that fantastic event. The celebration of flying simultaneously highlights Ryna's insanity and the fatherlessness of Solomon's twenty-one sons. Happiness in the knowledge of flight leads to the enigma of unhappiness in the consequences of the flight. Flying, then, becomes a selfish celebration of the freedom of an individual judged against the enslavement of twenty-two people.[23] The selfish path Milkman has followed throughout his life parallels the flight of his great-grandfather and its symbolic implications.

When Milkman arrives at the discovery of his great-grandfather's flying abilities, he has two options. He can continue the path of Solomon (celebration without commitment), or he can use the kinship as a sign to renew his ties to his family. The journey cannot work for Milkman unless some reversal occurs; flight itself must be made secondary to commitment. If he merely celebrates flight, then he runs the risk of separation and of continuing to follow in his great-grandfather's flight pattern. If he puts commitment first, then he will show allegiance to Pilate, who has repeatedly maintained that "You cant just fly on off and leave a body" (147, 332, 333). Emotionally, it is clear that Milkman, through his reflections and seeming changes of attitudes, follows Pilate. But the attraction to flying makes him confront Guitar in what may be a fatal end to the lessons he has just learned.

In confronting Guitar, Milkman may be flying off and leaving a body again (Pilate has specifically asked him to look after Reba), but he does so with a desire for commitment, an understanding of what his role should now be in his family. And perhaps he understands his communal role as well, if we view his soaring toward Guitar as an act of love. He does take Guitar with him; if their flight ends in death, it can be viewed as Milkman having saved Guitar from himself and from the gradually warping executions he carries out. The death could also be viewed as vengeance, thereby creating a situation in which Milkman acts for family—because Guitar has killed Pilate—instead of neglecting them. The problem with this latter view is that it would mean that Milkman has adopted Guitar's eye-for-an-eye philosophy, which is unacceptable under any circumstances.[24] What is clear from the final scene is that Milkman is thoroughly changed from the selfish little creature he started out to be; he has reevaluated himself and his relationship to his family, and he has progressed in healthy ways.

The transfer of value from material to immaterial things, from things to people, and from directionless activity to purposefulness all suggest that Milkman's journey has worked for him in ways that no other journey in Morrison's novels has worked for any other character. He finds in the South, in the land of his African forebears, the key to appreciating his family and to understanding how he came to be. His enlightenment, no matter the cost, is well worth the trip.[25]

Female Sacrifices for Male Identity

The success of Milkman's journey depends in large part on the string of female bodies, figuratively and literally, that he leaves along his path. The women form a long line of mothering and nurturing that culminates in Milkman's renewed sense of himself; they become sacrifices on the altar of his possibilities. Comparable to the blood sacrifices in *Sula*, those in *Song of Solomon* are striking in that female characters are consistently the victims. That victimization begins with Ruth, whose deviant actions to get pregnant are not enough to save her future relationship with her husband or her son. In order to give birth to Milkman, Ruth must forever give up physical relations with Macon. In order to keep Milkman alive, she must intensify her role as mother, only to relinquish it forever when he becomes an adolescent.

Ruth's primary function in the novel is to give birth to Milkman, not to establish a relationship with him—certainly not beyond the long period of nursing. She is important to his story only as long as her body serves his needs (or as long as she can nurse him without discovery); once those needs are served, he casts her aside emotionally, as he will later similarly discard Hagar. Ruth has very little reality for Milkman, and she is not drawn so that our sympathies are overly aroused in favor of different treatment. Yet here is a woman who lives somewhat of a martyred life, or certainly a cloistered one, for Macon's rejection of her after Milkman's death essentially turns her into a nun. She has given her all on the altar of her male offspring, whose future, set beside hers, is judged to be significantly more worthy of consideration. Not exactly a pathetic figure, Ruth is nonetheless a sacrificial one, for her life must fade into the background as Milkman's rises to the forefront.

In the language of fairy tales, she becomes an expendable helper who gives safe passage to Milkman from conception to birth, but whose importance lessens as Milkman learns to fend for himself.[26] Her emotional sacrifices for her son are perhaps more stultifying than those of Corinthians and Magdalene, but the sisters nonetheless find their futures compromised to Milkman's. Their father becomes bored with them when he gets the opportunity to begin shaping Milkman in his image of entrepreneur. Though Macon sends Corinthians to college, that does not signal any intrinsic evaluation of her worth on his part; it is simply what a man of his means can do for his children, even if they are female. He sees the image of what being middle class means; he is unconcerned about his daughters as girls or as women. He will continue to take care of them, as the weaker, more useless sex, but they do not spark his interest, and they hold out to him no promise of the family line being continued. Also, as an extension of the war with his wife, he would more naturally identify with Milkman, a potential convert to his viewpoint, than with his daughters.

From the time Milkman urinates on Lena's dress during the family's customary Sunday drive, his desires take precedence over those of his sisters. Even before he is consciously aware of his power as male, he is able to get his way as the youngest child in the family. When he learns that his father wants him to collect rents and become his apprentice, he quickly adopts the same attitude toward his sisters that Macon has. He allows them to wash, cook, clean, and care for his other housekeeping needs without any consideration for them as individuals who may wish to do something else with their lives. When Milkman knocks Macon down for hitting Ruth, and when he tells of Corinthians's affair with Porter, he is not doing so out of love for his mother or his sister. As Lena says of the fight with Macon, Milkman was not protecting his mother: "You were taking over, letting us know you had the right to tell her and all of us what to do" (216). On the night of their conversation, when she is thirty-one, Milkman finds himself talking to a sister "to whom he had not said more than four consecutive sentences since he was in the ninth grade" (211).

Another set of Morrison's "twins," Lena and Corinthians are almost as ineffectual as the deweys. Corinthians is unable to determine her destiny until she is well into middle age, and Lena is never able to determine hers. Buffeted by external forces, they are unwilling helpers in the destiny that awaits Milkman, but helpers nonetheless.[27] Without the vividness of their deprivations and constrictions, we would have less of a sense of Milkman being his father's chosen one. Either to win their father's approval, or his tolerance, or because they have no choice, Corinthians and Lena are trapped in the house on Not Doctor Street. Their entrapment leads in part to Milkman's growth and freedom; they therefore become other victims symbolically and literally sacrificed on the altar of Milkman's quest for manhood and identity. Like Florence Grimes upon the arrival of Gabriel in James Baldwin's *Go Tell It on the Mountain* (1953), Lena and Corinthians must be sacrificed to the future that only the male offspring can have. Though Corinthians escapes in middle age, the little happiness she may now find has been undermined by years and years of subservience to someone else's definition of reality.

Milkman meditates at one point upon what he has "deserved" (276) or not as his lot in life, and he has acted throughout as if his mother and sisters were put upon earth because he deserved their services. They are almost nonentities, except when he needs a clean towel or fresh linen. Servants more than sisters in the height from which they are condescendingly viewed, Lena and Corinthians content themselves for most of their lives with existing in the tiny spaces into which Macon and Milkman have shoved them. Without value to brother or father, and without any animating love for their mother, Lena and Corinthians exist as shadows whose substance can be measured only by its fading from them into their brother's future.

Of all the female sacrifices made for Milkman's growth and development, Hagar's is the most pathetic and Pilate's the most tragic. Milkman essentially destroys Pilate's family, for once Hagar and Pilate are dead, Reba is lost; unable to care for herself, she will probably be institutionalized. Still, the women make no effort to stop the destruction of their family, which begins with Hagar. Their leniency and desire to give Hagar whatever she wants combines with Milkman's selfishness to ensure her downfall. While her desires might be simple enough to see Milkman as her quintessential fulfillment, Hagar fails to recognize that he cannot be counted on to reciprocate her passion or her love. She is an adventure for him, a toy he is content to play with over the nearly twenty complacent years of his adult adolescence. When he tires of the toy, he dispassionately tosses it aside. His proclivity for white women and for black women of his own social standing relegates Hagar to a small niche in Milkman's life; "she became a quasi-secret but permanent fixture" (97–98). The relationship of the two families to each other also dictates the quasi-secret status. Certainly Ruth would be appalled to know that Milkman is sleeping with his first cousin's daughter, and Macon would be livid not only about this son having gone into Pilate's house but having become Hagar's lover. By contrast, Reba and Pilate simply accept life as it is. Though coquettish at first, Hagar shortly becomes Milkman's for the taking, a priceless jewel diminishing its own value by its failure to value itself. She is one of the reasons Milkman is able to "stretch" "his carefree boyhood out for thirty-one years" (98). Hagar is his expected sexual outlet in the way that his sisters are his maids—convenient and exploitable. When she centers her whole life upon Milkman, placing "duty squarely in the middle of their relationship" (98), he tries "to think of a way out."

Like Plum, Hagar has acquiesced in the ritual of destruction in which she is victim. Having granted to Milkman total control of her life, she similarly grants him control of her death, which his termination of the affair amounts to. His decision to remind her that they are cousins, that "she needed a steady man who could marry her" because "he was standing in her way," is the pouring of kerosene on an already burning mind. His hypocrisy disguised as concern is a transparent rationalization designed to effect his own freedom, which he does by sending Hagar a dismissal letter:

> He went back to his father's office, got some cash out of the safe, and wrote Hagar a nice letter which ended: "Also, I want to thank you. Thank you for all you have meant to me. For making me happy all these years. I am signing this letter with love, of course, but more than that, with gratitude." (99)

Guaranteed to gall any self-respecting woman, the letter reeks of distance and emotional coldness; Milkman can send it to Hagar only because he does not value or respect her. In the absence of any sense of family or communal commitment, Milkman dismisses Hagar as easily as he perhaps dispossesses his father's tenants.

Macon Dead has put Milkman in training to be callous, and Reba and Pilate have unconsciously assured Hagar's victimization:

> Neither Pilate nor Reba knew that Hagar was not like them. Not strong enough, like Pilate, nor simple enough, like Reba, to make up her life as they had. She needed what most colored girls needed:

a chorus of mamas, grandmamas, aunts, cousins, sisters, neighbors, Sunday school teachers, best girl friends, and what all to give her the strength life demanded of her—and the humor with which to live it. (307)

Without encouraging her to see some reality outside of Milkman, some reality outside of their taking care of her, she is destined to acquiesce in her own destruction just as Milkman is destined to execute that destruction. Her "graveyard love" ("Anaconda love," Morrison calls it) for Milkman literally becomes that. As sacrificial victim, her fate is sealed. As victimizer, Milkman has other choices. Certainly Macon has taught him to value money above people, but he and Guitar, who is concerned about people, have been friends for more than twenty years by the time Milkman dismisses Hagar. Guitar's concern and the antimaterialistic philosophy he has spouted off to Milkman for years have at least ensured his exposure to something other than his father's sentiments. While Hagar has little choice in the path she follows, Milkman does not wish to make the choice that would suggest responsibility and caring. He continues carefree and unattached, finding and taking sexual favors wherever he pleases. His immaturity contains an inherent viciousness antithetical to Hagar's desire for a more committed relationship.

Hagar's sacrifice is complete when she makes Milkman's will superior to her own. As Milkman lies in Guitar's apartment, unmoving as Hagar approaches with the knife, she knows at last that she can no longer evoke any emotion from him, not even the fear that has driven her to pursue him month after month, and certainly not the pity she deserves. Yet the insensitive Milkman can only see her failure to kill him as a triumph of masculinity over femininity, of his incredible sexual powers over the susceptible Hagar. His final words to her are striking in their utter callousness:

> "If you keep your hands just that way," he said, "and then bring them down straight, straight and fast, you can drive that knife right smack in your cunt. Why don't you do that? Then all your problems will be over." He patted her cheek and turned away from her wide, dark, pleading, hollow eyes. (130)

It is ironic that Guitar, the executioner, is more sympathetic to Hagar than Milkman. When he takes the nearly comatose woman from his apartment after her attempt on Milkman's life, he maintains that Hagar has been "pitiful. Really pitiful" and asserts that "it had to be something more" that Milkman has done to her, because "that girl's hurt—and the hurt came from you" (152). Incapable of feeling the pity that Guitar does, Milkman claims that his friend is "meddling" and "criticizing" him unfairly.

By the time Milkman pauses in those dark woods to think about Hagar, many emotional light years and hundreds of miles away, she is already bringing her ritual of death to an end. He concedes that "if a stranger could try to kill him, surely Hagar, who knew him and whom he'd thrown away like a wad of chewing gum after the flavor was gone—she had a right to try to kill him too" (276–77). The accurate image of having thrown her away like chewing gum comes too late to help Hagar, but it serves its purpose in pushing Milkman toward maturity. The pattern is set in a way that Milkman thrives in direct proportion to Hagar's demise. As he learns more about his relationship to her and the rest of his family, her physical essence decreases in value. For each stage on the journey that brings enlightenment to Milkman, that enlightenment comes directly from Hagar's lifeline. When he discovers—in Shalimar, Virginia, sitting in front of Solomon's General Store—that the children are singing about his great-grandfather, he moves into a realm of self-awareness that makes it impossible for him to treat anyone else as he has treated Hagar. Almost in keeping with that progression, Hagar dies. Another victim on his search for self, she has helped Milkman in substantial ways by being an outlet for his negative emotions and a symbol around which he gathers his reflections. Once he truly understands and accepts that people cannot be ill treated with impunity, then she is no longer needed. Her purpose served, she dies before Milkman can return to act out any of his newfound knowledge about how to deal with his family and with people in general.

A helper who has not known the extent of her assistance, and whose giving leads to her own death, Hagar presents her body as one of the bridges over which Milkman walks into his own humanity and manhood. Her physical sacrifice is the culmination of Pilate's prophetic prediction on the occasion when Ruth has come to her house to ensure that Hagar would not attempt to kill Milkman again. As Hagar and Ruth stood arguing about their value to Milkman, Pilate has said: "And he wouldn't give a pile of swan shit for either one of you . . . He ain't a house, he's a man, and whatever he need, don't none of you got it" (137, 138). More specifically related to Hagar's death, Pilate comments to Ruth: "Ain't nothin goin to kill him but his own ignorance, and won't no woman ever kill him. What's likelier is that it'll be a woman save his life" (140). Her comment needs some modification, for it is not a woman, but several who save Milkman's life.[28] Hagar is one of them; she dies in order that he might grow—and perhaps, too, because there is no realistic place for her. Even if Milkman returns to the North, enlightened, with a proposal of marriage to Hagar, chances are they would not be able to execute that desire. Also, the extent of Milkman's transgressions warrants a more striking lesson than a mere forgiving and making up. Hagar's death points out the emotionally destructive binge Milkman has been on all his life. Morrison does not spare him from having to confront the trauma resulting from that crime.

Hagar, another body Milkman has left in his "flying" pursuit of his great-grandfather, is like Ryna or one of the twenty-one children Solomon left on his flight to Africa. Like Ryna, the desertion leads to insanity and death. But, also like Ryna, who lives on in the tales of Ryna's Gulch, Hagar will live on in the lessons she has taught and in the box of her hair Pilate gives to Milkman as an indication that he must take responsibility for "the life he had taken" (332). Victims in the examples of their fates, both Hagar and Ryna enable Milkman to transcend the possibility for future victimization.[29]

These pathetic women and the losses do not measure up, in the final balance, to the loss of Pilate's life in Milkman's quest for identity, family, and value beyond gold. Teacher, nurturer, surrogate mother, keeper of the blues tradition, Pilate has always placed value on altruistic human relationships. In all of these roles, she gives voice to the value of human connectedness. In singing "O Sugarman," she serves as the herald for Milkman's birth. In singing with Reba and Hagar, she articulates the pain Macon feels and soothes his wounds. In singing at Hagar's death, she voices the pain of loss in sound rather than lyrics. And in singing the "Song of Solomon," she places stress on the intricate ties to African and black American history that unite all generations of those scattered in the Diaspora. In her voice is the blending of secular and sacred traditions, natural and supernatural concerns.[30]

She values human relationships, but she recognizes human limitations. When the absence of a navel finally "isolates" Pilate, "she gave up, apparently, all interest in table manners or hygiene, but acquired a deep concern for and about human relationships" (149). When Guitar shoots her, her only regret is: "I wish I'd a knowed more people. I would of loved 'em all. If I'd a knowed more, I would a loved more" (336). That this tower of selflessness should fall, even for an enlightened Milkman, is difficult to acquiesce to. Yet it is consistent with Pilate's prediction about who would save Milkman's life, and it is consistent with the traditional demise of the helper/guide once the initiate has learned all the helper has to teach. Milkman has definitely learned the value of family and of human relationships, and he has learned that escape from a situation does not lessen responsibility for it: he is as guilty for Hagar's death as Solomon has been for Ryna's insanity and for whatever happened to his twenty-one sons. He can now effectively take his teacher's place, become the guru rather than the seeker after knowledge held by the guru.

Such a refined interpretation, however, does not alter the evaluation that Pilate joins the other women in Milkman's life in being made a victim to his health, to his growth into a positive sense of self. Milkman's inability to convince Guitar that there is no gold, combined with Guitar's warped sense of community commitment, brings about the ironic circumstances surrounding Pilate's death. Pilate and Guitar have believed in essentially the same things, in commitment and human relationships. Guitar has approached the motherly in his feelings for Hagar, and he has deeply sympathized with the destruction wrought upon her. That he should kill Pilate in his effort to shoot Milkman makes her the victim of communal, familial, and individual values, brought together in the man who loves community enough to kill for it and the one who loves family enough to die for it.

A free spirit whose body has never weighed her to the earth, Pilate is triumphant in that, by sacrificing her own life, she will bring to an end the sequence of events, both historical and contemporary, that have divided her family and caused so much grief in it. And by setting in motion the events in which Guitar is ready to die for his cause, she also succeeds in eliminating the driving force behind the hatred practiced by the Seven Days. Her victimization, therefore, might have its worth in the larger picture of familial and communal good. And in the folk patterns that inform the novel, it is frequently a good, much-to-be-missed person whose sacrifice has the power to renew. Thus Pilate can do for Milkman what no one in *The Bluest Eye* could do for Pecola Breedlove and Lorain, Ohio. Not only does she sing the lore of her culture, she lives it as well.

NOTES

1. Baron FitzRoy Richard Somerset Raglan, *The Hero: A Study in Tradition, Myth, and Drama* (1956; rpt. Westport, Conn.: Greenwood Press, 1975); Joseph Campbell, *The Hero with a Thousand Faces* (London: Abacus, 1975).

2. Some of these articles include Jacqueline de Weever, "Toni Morrison's Use of Fairy Tale, Folk Tale, and Myth in *The [sic] Song of Solomon*," *Southern Folklore Quarterly* 44 (1980): 131–44; A. Leslie Harris, "Myth as Structure in Toni Morrison's *Song of Solomon*," *MELUS* 7 (1980): 69–76; Wilfred D. Samuels, "Liminality and the Search for Self in Toni Morrison's *Song of Solomon*," *Minority Voices* 5 (1981): 59–68 (expanded in Samuels and Hudson-Weems, *Toni Morrison*, 53–78); Cynthia A. Davis, "Self, Society, and Myth in Toni Morrison's Fiction," *Contemporary Literature* 23 (1982): 323–42; Dorothy H. Lee, "*Song of Solomon*: To Ride the Air," *Black American Literature Forum* 16 (Summer 1982): 64–70; and Jones and Vinson, *The World of Toni Morrison*. Although Gerry Brenner, in "*Song of Solomon*: Rejecting Rank's Monomyth and Feminism," in *Critical Essays on Toni Morrison*, ed. McKay, 114–25, notes Morrison's rejection of the superimposition of "other kinds of structures" on her works, he nonetheless illustrates briefly how Otto Rank's monomyth applies to *Song of Solomon*; however, he asserts that Morrison "undercuts its conventional celebration of the role of the hero in our culture" (117). He also points out the shortcomings in the work of some of the other scholars who have discussed myth in connection with the novel and spends the bulk of his discussion arguing that the "subtext" for Milkman's journey "is satiric" (118).

3. For an example of an article that tries to resolve this problem by discussing Morrison's first three novels as larger than the black community, but solidly grounded in it and its aesthetic, see Norris Clark, "Flying Black: Toni Morrison's *The Bluest Eye, Sula* and *Song of Solomon,*" *Minority Voices* 4 (1980): 51–63.

4. Thomas LeClair, "'The Language Must Not Sweat': A Conversation with Toni Morrison," *The New Republic* 184 (21 Mar. 1981): 26–27.

5. Perhaps a case could be made for Pilate being religious—she keeps a faith, but one created out of the mythmaking circumstances of her personal history.

6. See Joseph T. Skerrett, Jr., "Recitation to the *Griot*: Storytelling and Learning in Toni Morrison's *Song of Solomon,*" in *Conjuring: Black Women, Fiction, and Literary Tradition,* ed. Pryse and Spillers, 192–202. See also Valerie Smith's "Toni Morrison's Narratives of Community," in her *Self-Discovery and Authority in Afro-American Narrative* (Cambridge: Harvard Univ. Press, 1987), 122–53.

7. John W. Roberts, *From Trickster to Badman: The Black Folk Hero in Slavery and Freedom* (Philadelphia: Univ. of Pennsylvania Press, 1989), 1.

8. Questions as to whether Milkman was born "with a caul" (10) to account for his seeming early "mysterious" nature do not lead to any tangible later result and thus do not select him in any particular way.

9. In *Morphology of the Folktale,* Propp asserts that seeker heroes on various journeys are assisted by helpers who may show them the way to a particular objective, provide them with a talisman that will help them in their quest, or travel along with them for a period of time (39–51).

10. Keith E. Byerman has also pointed out the ambiguity in Milkman's name and how it gets clarified in direct proportion to his finding a purpose in life. See *Fingering the Jagged Grain: Tradition and Form in Recent Black Fiction,* 207.

11. Philip M. Royster argues that Milkman is a scapegoat in the circumstances surrounding his birth, which take on legendary overtones as well. Such an approach provides an additional direction for folkloristic commentary in the novel. See "Milkman's Flying: The Scapegoat Transcended in Toni Morrison's *Song of Solomon,*" *CLA Journal* 24 (June 1982): 421.

12. See Tate, ed., *Black Women Writers at Work,* 128. This idea of the black woman inventing herself is not new for Morrison. As early as 1971, she commented that the pressures of romantic relationships, children, and jobs let the black woman know that there was no place and no one to whom she could pass her burdens: "And she had nothing to fall back on: not maleness, not whiteness, not ladyhood, not anything. And out of the profound desolation of her reality she may very well have invented herself"; Morrison, "What the Black Woman Thinks About Women's Lib," *New York Times Magazine* (22 Aug. 1971): 63. This idea is echoed almost verbatim in *Sula* (52).

13. Ruth also talks with her dead father, but he does not appear to her, as Pilate's father appears to her. Morrison has also commented on the special, almost extranatural relationship she has with her own father, who died before she started work on *Song of Solomon.* See Jean Strouse, "Toni Morrison's Black Magic," *Newsweek* (30 Mar. 1981): 57.

14. For a discussion of Pilate's witch-like, extranatural, and supernatural powers, see Jones and Vinson, *The World of Toni Morrison,* chap. 5, "Pilate Dead: Conjuress," and chap. 6, "Pilate Dead: A Symbol of the Creative Imagination."

15. In contrast to this view, Jane S. Bakerman asserts that Pilate's life is a "failure" ("Failures of Love: Female Initiation in the Novels of Toni Morrison," *American*

Literature 52 [1981]: 556), and Gerry Brenner notes that "her mission is exemplary, because it is nothing less than to live her life in manifest repudiation of the grasping ambitiousness and obsessive desires of those around her who end up as grotesques, fanatics, neurotics, or fantasists" (*"Song of Solomon*: Rejecting Rank's Monomyth and Feminism," 123). Both positions fail to see the complexity of the African-American world view animating Pilate's portrayal.

16. For a discussion of one such transition from devil to disciple, see William Ferris's film, *Two Black Churches* (New Haven: Yale Univ. Design Studio, 1975); the minister in the New Haven church recounts what his life was like before he was called to preach and explains how he will not go back to that manner of ungodliness. Perhaps the most famous of these instances is the transformation of Malcolm X, which he recounts in *The Autobiography of Malcolm X* (1965); I am grateful to Mary Hoover of San Francisco State Univ. for suggesting this comparison.

17. A striking exception to this general trend of charting the course north is John Walden in Charles W. Chesnutt's *The House Behind the Cedars* (1900). John migrates from North Carolina to South Carolina to pass for white and pursue a career as a lawyer.

18. Dorothy H. Lee, *"Song of Solomon*: To Ride the Air," 69.

19. Jane Campbell views this devolutionary process in Milkman's journey as a return to the pastoral, where he can he prepared to show kinship to nature and appreciate the "lessons of a rural setting"; *Mythic Black Fiction: The Transformation of History* (Knoxville: Univ. of Tennessee Press, 1986), 142. Campbell also explores the heroic/mythic nature of Milkman's quest "for selfhood" and how it awakens him to his "heritage: ancestor worship, the supernatural, and African religion and folklore" (137).

20. As Genevieve Fabre correctly points out, "the tests and trials become necessary rites of passage. They further purify him and initiate him back into the tribe" ("Genealogical Archaeology or the Quest for Legacy in Toni Morrison's *Song of Solomon*," in *Critical Essays on Toni Morrison*, ed. McKay, 112–13). Allowing Milkman to pull out the bobcat's heart, and later, pointing him to Sweet, are the obvious signs of his incorporation into the tribe.

21. Dorson, *American Negro Folktales*, "Coon in the Box," 126–29, and Hurston, *Mules and Men*, 87–88.

22. Any number of scholars have discussed naming in the novel, including Genevieve Fabre in "Genealogical Archaeology or the Quest for Legacy in Toni Morrison's *Song of Solomon*," 108–10; Jacqueline de Weever in "Toni Morrison's Use of Fairy Tale, Folk Tale and Myth in *The [sic] Song of Solomon*"; Dorothy H. Lee in *"Song of Solomon*: To Ride the Air" (Lee also includes commentary on biblical names); Cynthia A. Davis, "Self, Society, and Myth in Toni Morrison's Fiction"; and Ruth Rosenberg, "'And the Children May Know Their Names': Toni Morrison's *Song of Solomon*," *Literary Onomastics Studies* 8 (1981): 195–219. Although I disagree with Rosenberg's assessment of the value of nicknames in the novel (204–5), her study is nonetheless engaging.

23. For a discussion of Morrison's use of the folktale of the flying Africans, see Susan L. Blake, "Folklore and Community in *Song of Solomon*," *MELUS* 7 (1980): 77–82, and Dorothy H. Lee, *"Song of Solomon*: To Ride the Air," 64–70. Lee also traces patterns of the monomyth identified by Joseph Campbell and others in her discussion of the novel, but she weaves in African-American connections as well. For versions of the tale of the flying Africans, see Georgia Writers Project, *Drums*

and Shadows (1940; rpt. Westport, Conn.: Greenwood Press, 1973); Julius Lester, *Black Folktales*, 147–52; and Virginia Hamilton, *The People Could Fly: American Black Folktales* (New York: Knopf, 1985), 166–73. Karla Holloway notes that the flying motif in the black folk spiritual tradition also informs the novel; *New Dimensions of Spirituality*, 101–2.

24. Ralph Story provides an intriguing and provocative discussion of the historical and political background informing the creation of Guitar and the Seven Days in "An Excursion into the Black World: The 'Seven Days' in Toni Morrison's *Song of Solomon*," *Black American Literature Forum* 23 (Spring 1989): 149–58.

25. For a striking contrast to my emphasis on the positive value of the folk culture in the novel, see James W. Coleman, "Beyond the Reach of Love and Caring: Black Life in Toni Morrison's *Song of Solomon*," *Obsidian II* 1 (Winter 1986): 151–61. Coleman argues that "critics are inaccurate when they talk about the positive, restorative effect of the Black folkloric tradition in the novel" (160) because, while it might work for Pilate and Milkman, "the situation for the Black community is just as dismal as it was before Milkman left Michigan" (160–61).

26. For a discussion of how Morrison uses fairy tales in the novel, see Jacqueline de Weever, "Toni Morrison's Use of Fairy Tale, Folk Tale and Myth in *The [sic] Song of Solomon*. de Weever refers to Corinthians as "a black princess" who has constructed an "artificial life" (140) before Porter stirs her from the passive state so endemic to fairy tale heroines.

27. See Propp, *Morphology of the Folktale*, 36.

28. The two women at Solomon's store should be added to this number because it is their intervention in the fight that prevents Milkman from being "sliced to ribbons," as the folk would say; "and he probably would have had his throat cut if two women hadn't come running in screaming, 'Saul! Saul!'" (268).

29. Grace Ann Hovet and Barbara Lounsberry argue that, "though Morrison creates some sympathy for the deserted woman, she refuses to depict Hagar as the conventional 'victim' because Hagar herself initiated her tailspin by becoming overly possessive"; see "Flying as Symbol and Legend in Toni Morrison's *The Bluest Eye, Sula,* and *Song of Solomon*," *CLA Journal* 27 (Dec. 1983): 135. While Hagar is certainly attracted to Milkman and is active rather than passive, that does not absolve Milkman of responsibility for accepting her initiated activities and for treating her as he does.

30. For a discussion of "the chorus as ritual dance, song, and commentary" in the novel, see Kathleen O'Shaughnessy, "'Life life life life': The Community as Chorus in *Song of Solomon*," in *Critical Essays on Toni Morrison*, ed. McKay, 125–33.

PATRICK BRYCE BJORK

Song of Solomon:
Reality and Mythos Within the Community

While Claudia in *The Bluest Eye* and Nel in *Sula* are too late to change what has happened in their lives, Milkman Dead, in Morrison's third novel, *Song of Solomon*, completes a heroic quest for an identity and place within the community. Morrison depicts Milkman in mythic terms. Not only does his story follow a cohesive pattern of miraculous birth, youth/alienation, quest, confrontation, and reintegration into community, but Morrison also infuses it with both Western and African-American myths which blend together the mundane with the magical and the factual with the fantastic. Morrison juxtaposes her own mythic variations with the "reality" of Milkman's conservative, middle-class family which, like himself and his community, is fractured by the absence of a historical or cultural identity. This juxtaposition is central to the novel in that Morrison uses myth to tie Milkman and his people to their historical and cultural past and, more important, to underscore their need for a black cultural and historical context.

The novel focuses on two morally and ethically antithetical positions, which are represented within the same black family. The father, Macon Dead II, who lives in and espouses the American Dream myth, promulgates the belief that the introjection of white capitalism's competitive, success-oriented motivations and actions are the only viable alternatives for the fulfillment and advancement of the black race. In short, Macon Dead (makin' dead) has

From *The Novels of Toni Morrison: The Search for Self and Place Within the Community*, pp. 83–109. © 1992 by Peter Lang Publishing.

35

buried whatever black identity or heritage he has in an effort to accumulate wealth and the semblance of white upper middle-class status; and thus, like blue eyes and Shirley Temple, Macon's myth distorts and dislocates the realities of black life.

Early in the novel he tells his son that there is only "one important thing you'll ever need to know. Own things. And let the things you own own other things. Then you'll own yourself and other people too" (55). Macon's manipulation of power and of people as objects not only inhibits him from establishing loving, sensitive relationships, but it also enables him to escape his own identity and heritage and, in turn, to not pass on any heritage to his own children save for his capitalist pronouncements and achievements. Consequently, for the Macon Dead family, the American Dream has replaced the memory of a black cultural heritage.

Macon's insensitivity has infected his entire family. His wife, Ruth, whom he treats abominably by periodically beating her and denying her love and sexual gratification, has withdrawn into a fantasy world seeking comfort in sleeping on her father's grave and nursing Milkman until he is eight years old. Macon's two daughters, First Corinthians and Magdalena called Lena, having received little love in their lives, regale themselves in the material trappings of middle-class ritual and convention. And because he knows no other way, Milkman, for a time, passively accepts his father's selfish code and, as a young adult, works for him in the real estate and rental business. In short, the atmosphere surrounding the Dead family hardly constitutes what one might call a loving and warm one but is, instead, cold and cruelly comical (Morrison's use of irony and hyperbole is worth noting here):

> Macon kept each member of his family awkward with fear. His hatred for his wife glittered and sparked in every word he spoke to her. The disappointment he felt in his daughters sifted down on them like ash, dulling their buttery complexions and choking the lilt out of what should have been girlish voices. Under the frozen heat of his glance they tripped over doorsills and dropped the salt cellar into the yolks of their poached eggs. The way he mangled their grace, wit, and self-esteem was the single excitement of their days. Without the tension and drama he ignited, they might not have known what to do with themselves. (10)

Macon and his family exemplify the patriarchal, nuclear family which traditionally has been a critical and stable feature in Western societies. However, the destructive undercurrents of manipulation and objectification within the Dead family symbolize the degeneration of Western values, particularly in light of the disjunctive social and economic realities within black American communities. As a consequence, the Macon Dead family, rigid with convention and construct, is left muted and emotionally drained.

But these images do not begin the novel. Instead, the opening scene presents a mandril from which Morrison develops her contrastive and transformational mythopoesis. When Milkman is born, he is the first black baby admitted to the town's white-only Mercy Hospital. He is born on the day after Robert Smith, a North Carolina Mutual Life Insurance agent, leaps to his death from the roof of Mercy. Vowing in a letter that he would " . . . take off from Mercy and fly away on [his] own wings," he attracts a crowd of "forty or fifty people" (3) who stand to watch even though it is the dead of winter. In the crowd are Ruth, pregnant with Milkman, and her two young daughters. The sight of Smith clad in his "blue silk wings" causes Ruth to drop her peck basket full of "red velvet rose petals": "Her half-grown daughters scramble about trying to catch them, while the mother moan[s] and [holds] the underside of her stomach" (5). In the midst of these images of flight, roses, and labor pains, Milkman's Aunt Pilate, sister to Macon and at this point in the text identified only as a woman singer, bursts into song about "Sugarman":

"O Sugarman done fly away
Sugarman done gone
Sugarman cut across the sky
Sugarman gone home. . . . (5)

She also appears as a prophetess predicting Milkman's birth, as she tells Ruth, "'a little bird'll be here with the morning'" (8). All of which compels the onlookers to think of this entire spectacle as "some form of worship" (6), and in a way it is, for what they and we are witnessing is a mythic enactment of heroic birth in addition to a prefigurement of Morrison's entire mythopoesis.

Traditionally, the mythic hero is born or enters into a barren region, a wasteland, and Morrison underscores this with symbols of inertia and disenfranchisement within the community. The Southside residents playfully call Mercy Hospital, No Mercy Hospital, and the street that it's located on, officially called Mains Avenue, has been renamed Not Doctor Street (formerly Doctor Street). It is so named because before his death, Ruth's father, Dr. Foster, had lived on the street. But the residents' act of mind over institutions has done little to change their social or economic status. Furthermore, the community is located in an unnamed upper Michigan city on Lake Superior. The setting is therefore both fixed and fluid, which compels its residents to remain in both enclosure and flight. The narrator comments that " . . . the longing to leave becomes acute, and a break from the area, therefore, is necessarily dream-bitten, but necessary nonetheless." However, since, as the narrator continues, " . . . those five Great Lakes which the St. Lawrence feeds with memories of the sea are themselves landlocked . . ." (163), the community endures this necessary duality of experience wherein the sea places physical restrictions upon them while continuing to symbolize the potential for renewal through motion.

It is fitting, then, that the novel opens with the image of flight as both destabilizing and as liberating. Mr. Smith's Icarus-like death and Milkman's predicted birth are marked by communal recognition and celebration, or as the narrator tells us, "it was nice and gay there for a while" (5); and indeed, we seem to be watching a scene of simple, albeit ironic, merriment. A child is "miraculously" born, a first-born male child marked by flight; his birth, as we later learn, is the result of a love potion given by Pilate to Ruth in order to bring Macon to Ruth's bed (who has been loveless for 13 years, another image of barrenness). When Macon learns of the pregnancy, he attempts, through various abortion techniques, to kill the unborn child because he believes that Ruth has had an incestuous relationship with her father.

During Milkman's childhood, he is sheltered and nurtured to an extreme; his mother breast-feeds him beyond infancy, and in doing so, she feels "like the miller's daughter—the one who sat at night in a straw-filled room, thrilled with the secret power Rumpelstiltskin had given her: to see golden thread stream from her very own shuttle"(13). All of these introductory images of barrenness, celebration, subterfuge, and shelter lend a kind of simple fairytale quality to the story; and further, beyond these moments, Milkman's childhood itself has a certain vagueness to it, which is also inherent in a traditional story of the mythic hero. Myth, according to Roland Barthes, "abolish[es] the complexity of human acts, it gives them the simplicity of essences . . . , it establishes a blissful clarity: things appear to mean something by themselves" (143). And indeed, with the imposition of myth, Morrison appears to have provided a clear foundation for a traditional story of heroic quest.

But there is much that is unstable in this opening scene of mythic reenactment. Barthes claims that myth " . . . transforms history into nature" (143), and to a certain degree, Milkman's historical beginnings appear to become naturalized. However, Morrison characteristically inverts and thus undercuts these "naturalized" images, and in doing so, begins to recreate her own special mythos. Milkman is born during the winter season that symbolizes death, and the spectre of his birth is greeted by Ruth's red velvet roses which also symbolize death; but more importantly, they are artificial roses and thus suggest an impoverishment to the extreme. And finally, the most obvious (and humorous) inversion in this mythic reenactment is that Milkman is born

Dead. It is a metaphor which will linger and influence much of his life, as he later says, "'You gonna do me in? My name is [Milkman], remember? I'm already Dead'" (118). Born into the community's principal family, Milkman should have nothing but silver-spoon success in his life; instead, he senses his deadness at the early age of four. When he discovers that "only birds and airplanes [can] fly" (9), he becomes bereft of all imagination. If anything, Milkman is born into and lives an entirely unnatural existence; his life is grounded from the very beginning by distortion and disaffection. The remainder of the novel encompasses Milkman's attempts to overcome his own disaffection, to learn to fly (again), and thus to transcend the unblissful inauthenticity surrounding his life.

Morrison continues her mythopoesis in the structural multiplicity that is apparent in the novel's early stages. These shifting and multiple perspectives serve to dramatize the limitations of the heroic myth as merely an existential abstraction. Surrounding Milkman are other characters who provide guidance and example and thereby confirm Milkman's centrality in the text; but often the isolation and the alienation that he experiences parallel other characters' lives. Therefore, Morrison attempts to adapt the heroic quest and its outcome to both individual and collective levels within a black historical context.

For instance, the disaffection which Milkman experiences in his adult life is, in some ways, foreshadowed by his mother. Ruth has lived a "baby doll" existence (197), she has been made weak and passive by the "affectionate elegance" (12) of her father's class-conscious upbringing, and she has been rendered invisible and inconsequential by her boorish and dominating husband. She has, in short, lived her life in service to the patriarchal order. She finds meaning and presence in her life through a watermark on the dining room table. Throughout her father's life, it was there that a bowl of "fresh flowers had stood. Every day." Now, she regards the stain as "a mooring, a checkpoint, some stable visual object that assure[s] her that the world [is] still there . . . that she [is] alive somewhere" (11).

Loveless and invisible, Ruth also clings selfishly to Milkman, using him, like the watermark, as a measure of personal stability while realizing that "her son [has] never been a person to her, a separate real person. He [has] always been a passion" (131). Milkman is "her single triumph," and her personal effrontery to a world that has given her neither love nor purpose. The used has necessarily become the user; first in her father and later in Milkman, she lives her life in the memory and passion of another's gaze.

In perhaps the most telling scene, the entire family's torpid position is made analogous to their touring car. Each Sunday, Macon takes his family for a Sunday drive and although "it [is] a less ambitious ritual for Ruth . . . , [it is] a way, nevertheless, for her to display her family." For Macon, this ritual is "much too important for [him] to enjoy" (31). Ironically, however, what appears as a dignified, stately ritual for the Dead family is seen with "a whole lot of amusement" (32) by some community members. Again, the community's playfulness serves to identify incongruity in their midst. For the Dead family, the "wide green Packard" has no practical function beyond the self-serving ritual of familial exposition:

> [Macon] hailed no one and no one hailed him. There was never a sudden braking and backing up to shout or laugh with a friend. No beer bottles or ice cream cones poked from the open windows. Nor did a baby boy stand up to pee out of them. He never let rain fall on it if he could help it and he walked to Sonny's Shop—taking the car out only on these occasions. (32)

To the community, then, "the Packard [has] no real lived life at all. So they [call] it Macon Dead's hearse" (32).

Increasingly, as Milkman matures, he feels these "burdens" (31) of the family's unsubstantial rituals. He feels a desire, a "concentration on things behind him," and senses that there is "no future to be had" (35). The cultural deadness of his family and the anger and isolation of his home provide the impetus for liberation. Milkman's second stage of growth, the period of alienation and desire for understanding, reflect the ordering principal behind the mythic pattern. He begins to acknowledge a vague yearning for wholeness in his otherwise other-directed existence. At the age of twelve, he befriends a more worldly boy, Guitar, who takes "him to the woman who [has] as much to do with his future as she [has] his past" (35).

Long since barred from the respectable Macon Dead family, Pilate, her daughter, Reba, and Reba's daughter, Hagar, emerge at an important juncture in the text, for they provide a contrary and disruptive influence in the folk image that they project to Milkman. His perceptions of Pilate, formed as they are by Macon who thinks of his sister as a "snake" (54), by townspeople who identify her as "ugly, dirty, poor, drunk," and by "sixth-grade schoolmates" who subsequently tease him about his "queer aunt" (37), become less other-directed when he first meets her.

Pilate and her family subsist in materially impoverished surroundings, making and selling bootleg wine, but Milkman sees that Pilate, while "she [is] anything but pretty" (37), is neither dirty nor drunk. She presents herself to the boys as she appears in the beginning of the novel with the presence of strength, confidence, and good humor. She is the archetypal, black folk singer and oral storyteller whose personal stories give shape to a collective consciousness.

To the two young boys, her presence is magical and mysterious, and as the odor of pine and fermenting wine sends them into "a pleasant semi-stupor" (46), Pilate entrances the boys with a partial story of her life:

> "Hadn't been for your daddy, I wouldn't be here today. I would have died in the womb. And died again in the woods. Those woods and the dark would have surely killed me. But he saved me and here I am boiling eggs. Our papa was dead, you see. They blew him five feet up into the air. He was sitting on his fence waiting for 'em and they snuck up from behind and blew him five feet into the air. So when we left Circe's big house we didn't have no place to go, so we just walked around and lived in them woods. . . . And talking about dark! You think dark is just one color, but it ain't. There're five or six kinds of black. Some silky, some woolly. Some just empty. Some like fingers. And it don't stay still. It moves and changes from one kind of black to another." (40)

Encapsulated into Pilate's untethered story is the familiar violence, degradation, and victimization that surround black life. The woods and the darkness convey the fear, loneliness, and alienation of black reality, but Pilate also testifies to the courage and self-sufficiency that she and Macon demonstrated and, even though they now travel diametrically opposing paths, they continue to demonstrate.

As Pilate continues to testify, it is Guitar and not Milkman who responds with questions about her father, her father's farm, its location, and the year of Pilate's and Macon's untimely flight. But characteristic of an oral storyteller, Pilate relates events to events and moment to moments which intersect with a pulsing poetic quality that transforms historical fact into a felt experience. When Guitar asks, "'What year?'", Pilate responds, "'The year they shot them Irish people down in the streets. Was a good year for guns and gravediggers'" (42). Pilate's poetic valences of personal history collide with Guitar's worldly desire for a sanitized, concrete version of events, and as such, Pilate's otherworldliness, her home and her lifestyle embody a funkiness far removed and yet not removed from the realities of the two boys' lives.

One aspect to Morrison's work which seems most apparent is the desire to establish and maintain a black cultural heritage in the face of the homogenizing effects of late capitalism. Each of her novels pinpoints historical moments of disruption and transformation in that heritage. Both *The Bluest Eye* and *Sula* focus primarily on the 1940's when heavy black migrations to the cities precipitated black incorporation into modern American capitalism. In *Song of Solomon*, this incorporation seems complete as the novel's central positioning of a black bourgeois family suggests. For Macon Dead, late capitalism and its socializing effects have replaced the rural, Southern past and he has therefore made it inaccessible to his children.

The pervasive influence of late capitalism is a signpost to repression and desire for the Dead family; but, in Aunt Pilate, they also share a common thread—desperately stretched thin—to Pilate's embodiment of a black heritage. This explains why on a sensual level Milkman is able to recognize the folk heritage surrounding Pilate and her home:

> ... it was the first time in his life that he remembered being completely happy.... He was sitting comfortably in the notorious wine house; he was surrounded by women who seemed to enjoy him and who laughed out loud. And he was in love. No wonder his father was afraid of them. (47)

Milkman sees a family who, unlike his own, lives their lives simply: "They ate what they had or came across or had a craving for" (29). The three women treat him with generosity, kindness, and love; and, as he thinks, "all of them [have] a guileless look about them . . ." (46). He and we have entered into what appears to be a social utopia, an alternative world of blissful clarity where difference articulates a form of liberation from the predictable and reified world of Macon Dead.

Even Macon himself, in spite of his objection to Pilate's difference, feels liberated as he one night walks past the wine house and hears the women singing. He, too, "surrender[s] to the sound . . ." and feels "himself softening under the weight of memory and music . . ." (29–30). Pilate's world is cyclical, expansive, and alluring to anyone who comes in contact with it. Instead of repressing the past, she carries it with her in the form of songs and stories and synthesizes it with the present. Her past softens and liberates others because she evokes and embodies a collective (un)consciousness which manifests itself in what the narrator calls, "a deep concern for and about human relationships" (150). Pilate's folk culture may appear antithetical to the Macon Dead family, but its liberating song pulses through their lives and through the lives of the entire community. Consciously, as Macon says the three are "'just like common street women'" (20), but intuitively, he and the community feel the significance of their collective difference.

On the surface, however, both families remain split apart by their two modes of self-awareness, and this point of divisiveness places Milkman in an alienated position of desire and vacillation. Identity for Pilate is found in a connective energy, one that evokes a living heritage through story and song. Macon teaches his son that identity can only be found in the future, in his linear vision to "own things," "own people," and therefore "own yourself." He wishes to escape the past because it has, for him, no materially functional purpose.

Displaced between these two visions, Milkman chooses not to choose. Rather than attaching himself to any belief or commitment and acting from any set of principles, Milkman only reacts, self-consciously and indifferently, to whatever transpires about him. As he grows older, he passively submits to being his father's lackey, collecting rents, keeping the books. His passive position is physically manifested in his deformed gait. Since one of his legs is shorter than the other, he limps, and he attempts to disguise his defect with "an affected walk, the strut of a very young man trying to appear more sophisticated than he [is]" (62).

Moreover, he seldom accepts responsibility for his actions and when he does, it is only to demonstrate his own self-righteousness. For instance, when he strikes his father for humiliating his mother, he does so because he believes himself to be "wide-spirited and generous enough" (69) to do so. To prove that he is not a bad man, Macon tells Milkman that he had seen Ruth naked and kissing her deceased father. Macon, in his own distorted way, wishes to justify his continued humiliation of Ruth, and ironically his continued support for his wife; as he believes, there is "'nothing to do but kill a woman like that'" (74).

But instead of making Milkman understand his behavior, Macon, in exposing the reason for his loveless marriage, inadvertently prompts a shocked Milkman into realizing that he "never . . . thought of his mother as a person, a separate individual, with a life apart from allowing or interfering with his own" (75). Milkman vaguely begins to realize that his reactions, be they positive or negative, are haphazard and uninformed; he had interfered in his parents' lives as a self-serving gesture without understanding that, as the narrator says, "it would change nothing between his parents" (68).

At this point in the narrative, Milkman sees himself as lacking coherence, "a coming together of the features into a total self" (70). Still, he wishes to shrug off the distortions in his life and family. And as the narrative moves quickly over the 31 years of Milkman's life, he concludes that "above all he want[s] to escape . . ." from all that he knows. Feeling "put upon" (120) by his family, Milkman yearns for some identity separate from what he considers his family's abnormalities.

Perhaps this is why he continues to be drawn to the wine house; he finds relief and escape from his tentative self and from his rigidly dispassionate home. But as the narrator says, he is "like a man peeping around a corner . . . trying to make up his mind whether to go forward or to turn back" (70). He is not anymore committed to Pilate's world than to his parents. He effectively uses Pilate's family in the same way his mother used him, as a way of extracting some shred of identity in the midst of his alienation:

> His visits to the wine house seemed ... an extension of the love he had come to expect from his mother ... they had accepted him without question and with all the ease in the world. They took him seriously too. Asked him questions and thought all his responses to things were important enough to laugh at or quarrel with him about. (79)

When he visits Pilate's home, Milkman does not feel burdened by what he is told or by other's expectations of him. And it is clear that he assumes a central position in the house which brings with it his own sense of self-importance. Since, at the wine house, he does not have "to think or be or do something" about any aspect of his life, his hosts unintentionally support his indifference or what the narrator calls his "lazy righteousness" (120).

To further complicate his involvement with the family, he and Hagar become sexually attracted to each other, and at the respective ages of seventeen and twenty-two, they consummate the relationship. For the first three years, Milkman is delighted by the affair especially since, whenever he appears, she is "all smiles and welcome." After fourteen years, however, the attraction has diminished for Milkman. His indifference is heightened in direct proportion to Hagar's increasingly possessive love, and both attitudes have destructive potential.

The narrator comments that "Milkman [has] stretched his carefree boyhood out for thirty-one years. Hagar [is] thirty-six-and nervous" (98). He feels that "there [is] no excitement, no galloping blood in his neck or his heart at the thought of her" (91). She looks to him for a definitive commitment. What Milkman does give her is a cold, business-like rejection letter thanking her for all the years of happiness. Obviously Milkman has not developed any kind of "deep concern for and about human relationships." He yearns instead to run away in narcissistic flight beyond his increasingly enclosed, static existence. For her part, Hagar responds with a stalking desire to kill Milkman, whose life ironically becomes further enclosed as he tries to avoid and hide from her.

But what of Hagar's fate? As we later learn, Milkman's mixture of frustration, isolation, and alienation become the impetus for his open motion toward independence and eventually to collective engagement. Any comparable sensations send Hagar "spinning into a bright blue place where the air [is] thin" (99). Both the presence and absence of Milkman have hurled her into a misdirected flight away from any self-identity or visioned responsibility to the self. Her identity has become fully subsumed in Milkman's gaze. Later in the novel, she worries, as she lays dying, that, like Pecola Breedlove, she has been unacceptable to Milkman because she does not have the "'penny-colored hair,' 'lemon-colored skin,' and 'gray-blue eyes'" (319) that he likes.

Early in the novel a pattern develops which shows that women exist for males as mere operatives. Mothers and lovers live for and linger in the presence and absence of dead fathers, Dead husbands, and indifferent male lovers. They appear, like Milkman, as passive victims, they convey understanding and guidance, and even, like Pilate, they appear as free-flyers who project a self-sustaining image. But never does their alienation, their awareness, or their apparent freedom lead to a positive engagement with the community. They remain decentered, disengaged, and are even killed off in the text. No matter how similar they appear, they lack Milkman's possibilities, they play no central role, their dreams, if they have them at all, remain unfulfilled until the male hero fulfills them. As Simone de Beauvoir says of women in her *The Second Sex*, the women in *Song of Solomon* "still dream through the dreams of men" (161). Thus, Morrison's use of multiple, parallel perspectives does not entirely resolve the male-centered mythic bias in the novel.

Of course Milkman does appear as a surrogate for others, including women. He is portrayed as one who attempts to find a self and place within a black cultural context, and in doing so, he can inspire and lead others. He can, in short, become a model for others to emulate. But in spite of parallel perspectives and collective identities in *Song of Solomon*, the traditional male hero remains the focus in the story, and with it remains the apparent active/passive stereotype of male mastery over the female, which itself is deeply rooted in traditional mythic structure. In the end, women cannot fully live and know the meaning of Milkman's quest as he finally does. As we shall see, Milkman is finally reconciled with his forefathers; conversely, the same sense of history is never made available to women.

This lack of full and equal participation in heroic models of myth and history is clearly and consciously illustrated through the character of Pilate. Like Sula's, Pilate's story indicates that she possesses the essences of the existential male hero. The first years of Pilate's life are peaceful and almost idyllic; she and her father and brother live and prosper on their farm in Pennsylvania until the children witness the murder of their father by a powerful white family in a land-grab scheme. Six days later, the two homeless orphans find refuge with Circe who works in a white family's mansion.

After two weeks of hiding and boredom, Pilate and Macon, Jr., set out for Virginia, "where Macon believe[s] they [have] people" (168). Soon afterward, she and Macon separate after Macon kills an old, white man when the frightened Macon stumbles upon him in a cave. In the cave, Macon finds three bags of gold, but Pilate, fearful of being accused of both murder and theft, insists that they leave the gold buried. The two children fight and the knife-wielding Pilate chases Macon from the cave. When Macon returns three days later, both Pilate and the gold are gone.

Now on her own, Pilate continues on her journey to Virginia, and on her way, she is first taken in by a preacher's family. At school, she develops a love for geography and is given a geography book by her teacher. She yearns to travel about and so, with only her geography book, she joins with migrant workers, and while she never finds her relations, she lives with a man on an isolated island off the coast of Virginia, and with him conceives her daughter, Reba. But Pilate refuses to marry the man and sets out again for Pennsylvania to retrieve what she thinks are the murdered old man's bones. She begins "the wandering life that she [keeps] up for the next twenty-some-odd years, and stop[s] only after Reba [has] a baby" (148). Thereafter, she seeks out and finds her brother, believing that "Hagar needed family, people, a life very different from what she and Reba could offer ..." (151). Hagar, as she grows older, prefers a more organized, more conventional lifestyle, which Pilate correctly assumes and hopes Macon can provide.

This is Pilate's life-history. She has overcome great odds and obstacles; she has been a woman alone who raises and provides for a family, and all the while, she lives the life of an archetypal "running man" whose vision of progress is encompassed in the physical actualizations of her geography book. But unlike the "running man" of history, Pilate does not fly away from responsibility; hers is a desired flight toward a communal consciousness, toward, as the narrator says, an "alien's compassion for troubled people" (150), which itself transcends the world's meanness and selfishness.

Another aspect which significantly forms her life is yet another of Morrison's magical infusions. Pilate has no navel. As a child, she encounters a root woman who tells her what a navel is for: "'It's for ... it's for people who were born natural'" (144). Throughout the novel, Pilate embodies the spiritual resources of African-American folk traditions, and as such, she appears as a kind of supernatural character, an earth mother, a voodoo priestess and conjour, a mythical storyteller. But in the everyday world, her lack of a navel marks her as unnatural, and as word spreads of it, she becomes unwelcome and/or isolated in any community. Her refusal to marry her lover is also a consequence of her lack; she is afraid that she cannot "hide her stomach from a husband forever" (147). And thus, her transmittal of a community spirit remains impeded. Her world is both large and marginal. It is large in that her vision encompasses all that is good and right and true in human affairs. It is marginal in that it includes only her immediate family and her father's ghost:

> It isolated her. Already without family, she was further isolated
> from her people, for except for the relative bliss on the island,
> every other resource was denied her: partnership in marriage,
> confessional friendship, and communal religion. Men frowned,
> women whispered and shoved their children behind them. (149)

Even so, as she hovers about the fringe, Pilate demonstrates her strength and
her desire to both persevere and preserve her vision. After being initiated
into the cruelties of the white world and into the insensitivities of her own
black world, Pilate chooses to build a world of her own:

> Although she was hampered by huge ignorances, but not in any
> way unintelligent, when she realized what her situation in the
> world was and would probably always be, she threw away every
> assumption she had learned and began at zero. First off, she cut her
> hair. That was one thing she didn't want to think about anymore.
> Then she tackled the problem of trying to decide how she wanted
> to live and what was valuable to her. (149)

The symbolism of cutting her hair and the definitive establishment of
her position should enable Pilate to both emulate and disarm the androcentric myth and should allow her the freedom and connection to fully develop
and perpetuate her own vital community. But even within her own family,
Pilate is unable to transmit her strength and vision. It is true that Pilate's
vision is rooted in rural, Southern society and such a utopian vision in its
totality is clearly in opposition to an urban, late capitalistic society. But Morrison does not unequivocally valorize the agrarian social mode as an obvious
alternative or answer to a Dead world. It, too, has its imperfections ironically because Pilate's utopian vision of love, generosity, and a "concern for
and about human relationships" are not adequately sustaining features in a
pragmatic society conditioned for acquisition and consumption. Thus, while
Hagar has been showered with love and concern all her life, she has actually
become damaged by such excessive and concentrated affection in that she has
no inner strength to withstand either a capitalist society or her unrequited
relationship with Milkman.

But ultimately, it is Pilate's vision, placed as it is in opposition and isolation, that lends an unstable and ephemeral quality and status to her family. And
above all, it demonstrates that while Pilate's marginality allows her the freedom to act as a guide figure and thus gives her the opportunity to disarm the
androcentric myth, she cannot do so because she lacks a full recognition and
understanding of what has transpired during her life, during her own "quest."

Morrison clearly indicates that in spite of their strength, courage, intuition, and knowledge, women, like Pilate or Sula, have been, throughout history, locked out of a fully integrated myth in which they are central and in which they can connect to and transmit a regenerative legacy, and therefore make themselves, and those around them, whole. The myth of heroism allows women to assist in and benefit from the quest for a self and place within the community, but it does not allow for origination; it is historically dictated in a patriarchal society, then, that Milkman play the central role in the mythic quest.

Milkman appears as a surrogate for his father's greed, and thus, after he and Guitar fail the first time to find Pilate's gold, Milkman decides to travel alone to Danville, Pennsylvania, because, as he says, "'Daddy thinks the stuff is still in the cave'" (222). But Milkman also has an ulterior motive; he believes that Pilate's gold will set him free from his "real life." As he takes his first airplane flight, he begins to make an unconscious connection to his aerial beginnings:

> This one time he wanted to go solo. In the air, away from real life, he felt free, but on the ground, when he talked to Guitar just before he left, the wings of all those other people's nightmares flapped in his face and constrained him. (222)

Milkman seeks freedom from all those whom he believes have treated him "like a garbage pail," dumping into him all of their "actions and hatreds" (120). But while Milkman wishes to deny the obvious, those characters surrounding him reveal to him and the reader just how detached and distorted Milkman has become. Both Milkman and Guitar represent two reactions and two alternatives to their distortion. While Milkman tentatively identifies with his father's middle-class ideology, Guitar embodies the displaced rural Southerner whose alienation, unlike Milkman's, is ensconced in racial hatred. Rather than pursue what will ultimately be Milkman's ameliorative flight toward tradition and ideals, Guitar chooses instead to right social wrongs with acts of vengeance against the dominant culture.

His position is a reaction to the primal trauma of his life when, as a boy, his father is cut in half in a sawmill accident and as recompense, his mother willingly accepts forty dollars from the white owner. His perceptions of his mother's moral cowardice and betrayal convince Guitar that his commitment to and love of black people must find its expression in hateful aggression. Guitar becomes obsessed with his disaffection to the degree that he actively participates in a secret society known as the "Seven Days." Theirs is a mission of retribution. Whenever black people are injured or killed, they respond by randomly killing white people.

The discovery of Guitar's involvement in the Seven Days brings the reader full circle to the text's original scene. Robert Smith was himself a member of the Days and Guitar was a witness to his flightless death. Like Smith, Guitar's vision of violence begetting violence keeps him on a flightless path until he is driven to madness by his own obsession for Pilate's gold. His ideology proves just as inadequate as Macon Dead's acculturated vision. However, like his father's corpse, Guitar is a split subject. While he espouses his single-minded doctrine, he nonetheless appears as Milkman's alter-ego, whose social perceptions seem more correctly fixed than Milkman's; and thus, coupled with his communal Southern background and his "slow smile of recognition" (49) toward Pilate's folk world, Guitar provides an antithetically connective energy in Milkman's search for self and place.

Guitar accurately identifies Milkman's disconnection, his lack of a cultural heritage, when he tells him that not only would Milkman not live in a place like Montgomery, Alabama, he is "'A man that can't live there.'" Guitar also makes Milkman recognize that he accepts only limited responsibility for his life and for the lives around him. He is "'not a serious person'" (104), Guitar tells him; he is merely an egg, Guitar says, whose shell needs to be broken.

In one other scene, Guitar makes Milkman analogous to a male peacock. When Milkman asks him why the peacock can't fly, Guitar tells him, "'Too much tail. All that jewelry weighs it down. Like vanity. Can't nobody fly with all that shit. Wanna fly, you got to give up the shit that weighs you down'" (179–80). Of course both characters are weighed down by their racial rootlessness—one displaced, the other detached. But Guitar, in spite of his deadly motivations, is able to more fully articulate and impress his alienation upon Milkman who would otherwise want, as the narrator says, " . . . to know as little as possible, to feel only enough to get through the day amiably . . ." (181).

The "real life" of Guitar and of Milkman's family are mirrors to Milkman, and in spite of his resistance, they reveal to him his true identity. When Milkman learns that Corinthians is dating an unsavory character, he condescendingly assumes he has "Corinthians' welfare at heart" (216) by telling his father about the affair. He takes for granted that he can take an approving or disapproving attitude. But his sister Lena reveals to her brother that he has no legitimate right, particularly in light of his uncaring, noncommital behavior, to assume a patriarchal role:

> "When did you get the right to decide our lives?"
> "I'll tell you where. From that hog's gut that hangs down between your legs. Well, let me tell you something, baby brother:

you will need more than that. I don't know where you will get
it or who will give it to you, but mark my words, you need more
than that." (217)

Lena identifies Milkman's disconnection from self and place. He has lived
an externalized existence; he grasps for those prescribed social codes—par-
tying, womanizing, male-domineering—which may help to mask and
assuage his insecure, unformed self. Since those surrounding him see
through his masks, Milkman seeks, through Pilate's gold, a more permanent
mask; but as he returns to his ancestors' world, he slowly begins to understand that culturally mythic connections prevail over his subjectively skewed
perceptions.

From the beginning, Milkman's story has been infused with irony, paradox, and contradiction. Part Two of the novel continues this cycle. It blissfully
begins with a synopsis of the Hansel and Gretel story supplanting ginger-
bread for Pilate's gold. But like the original tale of Milkman's magical birth, his
actual journey will never appear as a simple, harmless fairytale. Throughout the
novel, contradictions such as these reflect the divisiveness of Milkman's mind
and situation. In his search for a new life, he is consciously driven by a simple
desire for open motion, while at the same time, he is pulled away from such
simplicity by a subconscious attachment to the complexities of an unexplored
past which both his father and Pilate have partially shared with him.

When Milkman first visits with older residents of Danville, he is enticed
by their stories depicting Macon Dead, Sr., as a superhuman figure. To the
old men of the village, Macon, Sr., represents the ideal figure who, as an ex-
slave, overcame seemingly insurmountable odds in creating his flourishing,
rich farm. He was the American Adam who, unlike his son, embodied a
self-reliance that did not exploit and benefit from the misfortune of others.
Macon, Sr., was "head and shoulders above it all," the old men tell Milkman,
and his death, " . . . was the beginning of their own dying . . ." (237). Caught up
in the excitement of their stories, Milkman continues the myth and delights
his audience with stories of his father's "successes."

At this point, Milkman feels another surge of self-righteousness. He
wishes to avenge his grandfather's death by finding the gold, and he grows
"fierce with pride" (238) as he prepares for his search. The irony here is apparent; the freedom he seeks in the gold has been replaced by a sudden "heroic"
urge. But as with Lena's scathing observations, the fragmented Milkman
lacks any sort of experience to make him qualify for the role. And many of
the scenes which follow reinforce this inversion.

The townspeople direct Milkman to the Butler plantation, home of the
now deceased white people responsible for his grandfather's death. Once he

enters the dilapidated, decaying mansion, his quest assumes truly mythic proportions in that he discovers the ancient Circe still residing there, now approximately 175 years old, and waiting specifically for him. Circe stands guard to the entrance into Milkman's ancestral past. And like an Aeneas or a Ulysses, Milkman must establish direct contact with this past before he can form a path to the future. Circe tells Milkman the real names of his grandparents—Jake and Sing—and that Shalimar, Virginia is their original birthplace. Earlier we learned that Macon, Sr., had been misnamed when he was inducted into the Union army. By learning their true names and origin, Milkman has unconsciously begun his quest for self and place, for beneath their names and origins lay his connection to not only a personal heritage but to a deeper vein of black history and myth.

Circe also directs Milkman to the cave holding the gold. Milkman's appearance in the wilderness is significant in its ironic juxtapositions. Not only is Milkman out of his element, clumsy and obtuse as he stumbles about the woods, disconnected from his grandfather's natural world, but Milkman also appears as an unworthy, even unsavory character when, in the midst of archetypal images of cave and rebirth, he "smells money"; "there was nothing like it in the world" (253). Milkman finds no gold or anything else in the cave, and in the end, he is comically chased from it by its resident bats.

Even though he reemerges from the woods shaking from hunger and thirst, his clothes tattered, his watch broken in this timeless world, he returns to town foolishly convinced that the gold must still be in Virginia. Milkman's failed initiation prompts him to shed his heroic compulsions and return to his more pragmatic belief that, as he resolves, "he want[s] the gold because it [is] gold . . ." (260), and because the search for it continues his sense of freedom and open motion. But even this notion is undercut when, at the end of the scene, the narrator appropriately reminds us that Milkman is merely following in Pilate's "tracks" (261).

But if Milkman is comically ill-prepared for his personal rebirth in Danville, he is seriously ill-equipped for his encounter with the communal primitivism of Shalimar. Here Milkman enters a mystical, magical territory fraught with both dangers and delights. Because Shalimar has no bus or train depot, Milkman buys a car, and on his way through the South, he is buoyed by the "southern hospitality": " . . . the Negroes were as pleasant, wide-spirited, and self-contained as could be." But when Milkman finally happens upon Solomon's General Store his first meeting with the townsmen suggests that his notions about the South have been, like all of his perceptions, naively and compulsively formed.

In talking to them, Milkman learns that Guitar has unexpectedly arrived in Shalimar and has been looking for him. Guitar's presence fills Milkman

with an uncertain fear but, for the moment, his main concern is the hostility he senses from the townsfolk. "What was all the hostility for?" Milkman
wonders. " . . . they behaved as if they'd been insulted" (268–69). Without
realizing it himself, Milkman's very presence has offended the townsfolk. This
"city Negro," with his fancy clothes and brusque manner, appears to them as
just another arrogant white man:

> [Milkman] hadn't found them fit enough or good enough to want
> to know their names, and believed himself too good to tell them
> his. They looked at his skin and saw it was as black as theirs, but
> they knew he had the heart of the white men who came to pick
> them up in the trucks when they needed anonymous, faceless
> laborers. (269)

While Milkman's "white" appearance underscores his racial rootlessness,
the contrast between him and the townspeople also suggests that different
values are associated with black urban and rural culture. To these people, his
materially endowed superior airs are not adequate to justify his existence as a
black man; Milkman must prove himself in the traditionally physical struggle
with other men. Forced into taking a stand, Milkman beats another man in
a fist and knife fight. For the first time in his life, Milkman makes a kind of
commitment; his solo entrance into the rural South and this violent confrontation have emboldened him to take risks, to, as he thinks, "stop evading
things, sliding through, over, and around difficulties" (274).

His exposure to the rural South and Shalimar also forces him to begin
taking a more realistic view of the world around him. Throughout the South
he had met people who were "nice to him, generous, helpful." The men in
Shalimar, however, were "some of the meanest unhung niggers in the world"
(273). Perhaps, as he thinks, the people on his journey had been "just curious
and amused." In truth, Milkman "hadn't stayed in any place long enough to
find out" (279), which analogously sums up the whole of Milkman's life. The
basic humanness of Shalimar, of Pilate, and even of Guitar, their unpreten-
tious emotions, their struggles for survival, are completely alien to Milkman,
blocked out by a lifetime of material and emotional isolation. He has measured
self-esteem in gold and in the "hero worship" (273) associated with material
success. In Shalimar, however, the skills to measure self-worth involve those
raw emotions and survival skills.

Milkman has entered into an almost primeval world, a world that is fast
disappearing against the onslaught of a Dead world. It is a world that still
considers human beings to be on equal footing with one another, where "not
his money, his car, his father's reputation, his suit, or his shoes . . ." will help

him; "where all a man had was what he was born with, or had to learn to use
..." (280). These realizations are more firmly impressed upon him when he
joins the townsmen on a bobcat hunt. The hunt, in the tradition of Faulkner's
The Bear, functions on three different levels. On the literal level, the men
successfully kill, and eventually eat, a bobcat. On another level, Milkman is
almost strangled to death by Guitar, who has been following him in hopes
of retrieving the never-found gold. Finally, Milkman is hunting for a self
free from personal inhibition and social pretention. In the shrouded forest, a
backdrop to his bewildered psyche, Milkman realizes that he has permitted
the American Dream myth to devalue his senses and block out his natural
ability to be a loving, empathetic human being:

> Now it seemed to him that he was always saying or thinking that he
> didn't deserve some bad luck, or some bad treatment from others.
> He'd told Guitar that he didn't "deserve" his family's dependence,
> hatred, or whatever. That he didn't even "deserve" to hear all the
> misery and mutual accusations his parents unloaded on him. But
> why shouldn't his parents tell him their personal problems? If not
> him, then who?
>
> Apparently he thought he deserved only to be loved—from a
> distance, though—and given what he wanted. And in return he
> would be . . . what? Pleasant? Generous? Maybe all he was really
> saying was: I am not responsible for your pain; share your happi-
> ness with me but not your unhappiness. (280)

In the solitary wilderness of the woods, Milkman feels compelled to
confront his essential identity, and his epiphany is the impetus for personal
change and transcendence. But Morrison carefully avoids keeping Milkman
at merely an existential plane. Hunting as the traditional symbol for brotherhood and belonging frames and underscores Milkman's sudden awakening to
his essential connection to other people.

Furthermore, the wilderness, Milkman thinks, contains a language that
is "before language." "Language in the time when men and animals did talk
to one another . . . , when a tiger and a man could share the same tree" (281).
In this spirit of collective identity, Milkman feels "a sudden rush of affection"
and connection toward everyone he has known because, like him, he realizes
that, in being forced to live unnatural lives, they, too, have been "maimed" and
"scarred" (282). Thus, like Pilate, Guitar, and his father, they all have been
conditioned to live in isolation, alienation and denial.

Milkman now feels as if he truly understands the reasons for Guitar's
alienation and hatred. Moments later, however, Milkman's idealistic reverie is

ironically and abruptly halted when Guitar ambushes Milkman from behind and nearly succeeds in strangling him to death before being frightened away by a shotgun blast. Ambiguity appears to surround the ironic undercutting of this scene. Guitar's realistic entrance into Milkman's mythic initiation might suggest that his mind continues to be filled with romantic notions about the meaning of his quest. But when Milkman returns to the camp and tells the other hunters that he was "'scared to death,'" his fear turns to laughter; "he [finds] himself exhilarated by simply walking the earth" (284). He no longer limps, and unlike his earlier contrary impressions of the South and Shalimar, his new-found idealism appears secure, while at the same time he no longer fears himself or the unknown. His mythic initiation and transformation coupled with his fearlessly empathic appraisal of Guitar implies that Milkman is now able to mediate between both myth and reality. As his initiation signifies, it is the myth of brotherhood and belonging which ultimately springs from and illuminates reality.

When Milkman first arrived in Shalimar, he had heard the children singing the Song of Solomon, "that old blues song Pilate sang all the time: 'O Sugarman don't leave me here,' except the children [sing] 'Solomon don't leave me here'" (303). The song is the clue to Milkman's family history, but more significantly, it also becomes for him an affirmation for kinship and community. As he more carefully listens to the song again, Milkman is finally able to piece together his genealogy. Symbols of flying permeate the children's ritual while, as they sing, one child "turn[s] around like an airplane" (267). And as they sing, Milkman listens to them recount the flight from slavery of his grandfather's father, Solomon or Shalimar, back to the freedom of his African homeland. The song is both a variant of the flying African folktales and of the Icarus tale. Solomon literally flies off with his infant son, Jake, leaving behind his wife, Ryna, and some twenty other children. Susan Byrd, cousin to Jake's wife, Sing, confirms to Milkman the magical tale behind the song:

> "No, I mean flew. . . . He was flying. He flew. You know like a bird. Just stood up in the fields one day, ran up some hill, spun around a couple of times, and was lifted up in the air." (326)

But, as Susan continues, Solomon "'brushed too close to a tree and the baby slipped out of his arms'" (327), so that Jake, too, was left behind which signaled the long rupture in his family's history.

We have once again come full circle in the novel. From the beginning, all images and scenes of flight have ended either in death, disillusion, or desertion. Robert Smith, driven to madness and to an "artificial" flight, had wished to free himself from the death and distortion of the Seven Days. Milkman's failed flight for gold violates the principle of responsibility to others, and is especially destructive to Hagar, who later dies alone and inconsolate. And Solomon's flight, while freeing him to return to his homeland, results in the abandonment of family and friends. These types of absolute freedoms through flight are problematic because they involve the denial of personal and social bonds.

But within these negative images of flight lies a significant contradiction. The flights of Smith, Milkman, and Solomon are not, like Icarus', the result of *hubris* and the desire for an impossible kind of freedom. Instead, each character has "flown" to escape a particular brand of oppression and thus, Morrison has reconstructed the myth to reveal its inherent limitations within black culture and has shown the essential conflict it presents for both individual and community.

Milkman's flight has restored his sense of community because not only does the myth open out his family's history but, as he later realizes, to recover names was a way to pierce the invisibility that history had imposed on them:

> He read the road signs with interest now, wondering what lay beneath the names. The Algonquins had named the territory he lived in Great War, *michi gami*. How many dead lives and fading memories were buried in and beneath the names of the places in this country. Under the recorded names were other names, just as "Macon Dead," recorded for all time in some dusty file, hid from view the real names of people, places, and things. Names that had meaning. No wonder Pilate put hers in her ear. When you know your name, you should hang on to it, for unless it is noted down and remembered, it will die when you do. (333)

Milkman returns to the Southside to tell Pilate the good news of these rediscovered names and to correct her misconceptions about them. Pilate's mother died in childbirth and her name was never revealed to Pilate. "Sing, Sing" is not her father's request to sing, but a call to his wife. "You just can't fly on off and leave a body" is not simply a moral precept, but her father's plea to bury his bones which she unknowingly has carried with her for all these years.

But Milkman is not at first given his opportunity. Pilate breaks "a wet green bottle over his head" (335) and locks him in her cellar. Filled with exuberance, Milkman had come home with the vision of Solomon as a hero and model: "'He didn't need no airplane. He just took off; got fed up. All the way up! No more cotton! No more bales! No more orders! No more shit! He flew, baby'" (332). Milkman identifies with Solomon which fuels his own desire for personal identity and independence, for a freedom that transcends his own blighted world. However, Pilate's interposition furthers the mythic contradiction because she rightly blames Milkman for Hagar's death; like Solomon, he had flown off and left a body.

In the cellar-cave, Milkman begins to comprehend this contradiction, and by doing so, he experiences a true metamorphosis and eventual reemergence into his community. He makes the connection between his desertion of Hagar to Solomon's desertion of Ryna and the twenty-one children, as he wonders to himself, "Who looked after those twenty children? Jesus Christ, he left twenty-one children!" (336). Milkman realizes that the locus for his personal identity is inextricably linked to Pilate's principle of responsibility to others. And thus, he learns that objectification and commodification of people only serve to further his sense of distortion and alienation. When Milkman finally tells Pilate of his discoveries, the two return to Shalimar to bury her father's bones. At the burial site, Pilate is shot and killed by Guitar; the potential for Pilate to carry forth a new myth wherein Sing's legacy is traced to her descendants is forever silenced.

But paradoxically, in Pilate's death, we are left with an image of Pilate that offers the only definitive transcendence in the novel. As Milkman affirms, she is a person who "without ever leaving the ground . . . could fly" (340). Her spirit has surpassed all the other negative images of flight; she is the one character who, in spite of her physical restlessness and isolation, has been able to strike a balance and resolve the conflict between a personal and a collective consciousness. Deeply believing that "you can't fly off and leave a body," she alone and forever has lived a life of "honesty and equilibrium" (136) which had combined the best aspects of self, place, and motion.

As the novel closes, Pilate's spirit continues to soar through Milkman. As Guitar closes in on him, Milkman leaps, flying toward his "brother man," and not caring "which one of them would give up his ghost in the killing arms of his brother." In recognizing the mythic spirit of connection and commitment through Pilate's now usable past, Milkman does not fly away, he leaps in acknowledgment of personal kinship and brotherhood. He realizes that only in commitment is he free, "for now he knew what Shalimar knew: If you surrendered to the air, you could ride it" (341).

Milkman's reintegration into the community depends upon his acceptance of individual relationships which, in the end, he can only achieve through personal heroism. In choosing to "ride" toward Guitar, Milkman must take his ultimate risk which may very well end in his death, but as the novel's open-ending suggests, his flight forever sets in motion an open and necessary dialectic between a communal spirit and a factional reality.

J. BROOKS BOUSON

FROM

Quiet As It's Kept: Shame, Trauma, and Race in the Novels of Toni Morrison

Situated in a specific cultural moment, *Song of Solomon*, which was published in 1977, highlights the search for African-American roots. If in *Song of Solomon*, as in *Sula*, Morrison is intent on extending the African-American literary and cultural imagination, she also stages troubling scenes of shame and trauma in *Song of Solomon* as she explores the shame–pride issues surrounding the construction of black masculinity and reflects on the competing and contradictory political ideologies of assimilation and black nationalism. *Song of Solomon* tells the story of Milkman Dead, a member of the black bourgeoisie and a shame-ridden individual who carries with him the "shit" not only of his family's false class pride but also of inherited familial and racial shame. Before the middle-class, urban Milkman can attempt to "fly"—that is, feel healthy family and racial pride—he must learn about the interrelated shame–pride sources of black masculinity through his contact with the black underclass in his Michigan hometown and in the rural South where he learns his true name and thus solves the riddle of his African-American identity. Yet even as *Song of Solomon* seemingly celebrates Milkman's discovery of his African-American "roots" and his "authentic" black identity, it also anticipates a complaint commonly lodged against black identity politics: that the "idea of *the* black experience" covers up "the differences of class and privilege" that divide African Americans (Dean 60–61).

"Can't Nobody Fly With All That Shit: The Shame-Pride Axis and Black Masculinity in *Song of Solomon*," pp. 75–101, 226–229. © 2000 by the State University of New York.

Calling attention to the personal-familial and social-historical forces that shape the formation of African-American identities and also focusing on the social, class, and political tensions within the black community, *Song of Solomon* is addressed, in part, to middle-class African Americans, especially males, who have a kind of amnesia about their cultural history—about the shame and trauma of family histories rooted in slavery—and who, in donning the mask of bourgeois (white-identified) "pride," come to see poor blacks as stigmatized objects of contempt. Like *The Bluest Eye* and *Sula*, *Song of Solomon* deals with the troubling issue of internalized racism as it crystallizes black cultural anxiety about the class and color hierarchies within the African-American community. Morrison deliberately typecasts Milkman Dead as a privileged, middle-class African American only to strip away his mantle of false class pride by putting him in vital contact with the black folk, people like his Aunt Pilate or his poor Southern relations whom he originally sees through the lens of internalized racism as the shameful and inferior Other. If part of the novel's agenda is to show how Milkman Dead is brought to a new and healing sense of racial consciousness as a result of both his association with the black underclass and his discovery of his family's slavery and post-slavery "roots," *Song of Solomon* also investigates the link between the shame and trauma of racial oppression and black rage, primarily through the oppositional character of Guitar Bains, a member of the black underclass who is a militant black nationalist and political terrorist. And if the novel intends an "optimistic" ending by depicting Milkman's moment of flight and racial pride, it also undercuts that optimism by suggesting that his leap into the arms of the waiting Guitar is nihilistic and suicidal.

In its investigation of the formation of black masculinity, *Song of Solomon* exposes what shame theorists have referred to as the "collective secret" of pride and shame, the so-called master emotions which, although they serve as continuous monitors of the state of the social bond in the daily lives of individuals, have long been ignored in our culture (Scheff, Retzinger, Ryan 180, Scheff, *Bloody Revenge 39*). The "primary social emotions," pride and shame "have a signal function with respect to the social bond," writes Thomas Scheff. For while "pride generates and signals a secure bond," shame "generates and signals a threatened bond" (*Bloody Revenge 66, 3*).[1] Dependent on the level of respect or deference shown to individuals, pride results from being treated in a deferential or respectful way and shame from a lack of deference or disrespect (Scheff, Retzinger, Ryan 184). Interpersonal and also intrapsychic phenomena, pride and shame states, as Donald Nathanson explains in his description of the shame–pride axis, "form an axis intimately related to the modulation of self-esteem." Pride—" the happy confluence of the affect joy and the experience of personal efficacy"—is "always linked to the emotion shame in reciprocal fashion." Thus, "The search for shame is considerably aided by our understanding of its relationship to pride, both the true healthy pride which accompanies authentic success, and the false pride with which we defend our (denied) fragility" ("Shame/Pride Axis" 186, 204). The false pride that manifests itself as "insolence and haughtiness," as Scheff similarly observes, "may mask deep-seated feelings of inferiority, i.e., shame" (*Bloody Revenge* 44).

In *Song of Solomon*, Morrison illustrates that shame and pride are at once social emotions, which act as shaping forces in the construction of social and group identity, and intrapsychic phenomena. Part of Morrison's cultural project in *Song of Solomon* is to investigate the social and familial sources of black shame and pride and to distinguish between healthy and false pride. Morrison also explores the issue of class status in the social construction of black identities as she cross-questions the black bourgeoisie's version of African-American manhood. Examining the class divisions within the African-American community, *Song of Solomon* focuses attention on intraracial shaming—the contempt that some middle-class African Americans, like members of the Dead family, feel for poor and lower-class blacks. *Song of Solomon* also deals with the shame and pride issues surrounding skin color, the internalized racism that affords light skin a greater social value than dark skin. In deliberately setting out to confront the vexed issues surrounding color and class, *Song of Solomon* exposes what has been called the "dirty little secret" and "last taboo" of African-American culture, the existence of intraracial color prejudice and discrimination—the so-called color complex—which continues to be an "embarrassing and controversial subject for African Americans" (Russell 3, 2, 1).[2] According to bell hooks, "Those black folks who came of age before Black Power faced the implications of color caste either through devaluation or overvaluation." If being born light meant beginning life "with an advantage recognized by everyone," being born dark meant starting life "handicapped, with a serious disadvantage." The 1960s black liberation movement challenged this notion with its empowering "call to see black as beautiful." But in the late 1970s, around the time *Song of Solomon* was published, the "politics of racial assimilation," which had always operated as a "backlash," not only began to undermine black self-determination but also led, in the 1980s and 1990s, to the "resurgence" of the color-caste hierarchy (*Outlaw Culture* 174, 175, 178).

Song of Solomon acts out an important social mission as it deals with issues that African Americans find painful and embarrassing, such as the slavery origins of black American culture and the persistence of both intraracial color prejudice and class conflict within the African-American community. But because *Song of Solomon* is a densely textured narrative, it succeeds, in part, in concealing or minimizing the racial shame and trauma at its core by inviting critical analysis of its textual patterns and its use of folkloric and mythic sources. While *Song of Solomon* is mired in the excretory discourse of shame, it also, as is characteristic of Morrison's fiction, counteracts shame through its rich literary discourse. Critic-readers thus tend to avoid or minimize the narrative's racist and counterracist rhetoric, including its use of the shaming discourse of dirt and defilement, and discuss, instead, the importance of names and naming in the novel, or Morrison's use of the monomyth of the hero, or her adaptation of the flight motif and its link to both western and African-American mythic sources, or her invocation of black oral culture.[3] Aptly described as a work in which readers "passively . . . absorb the apparently disconnected information provided by the author" at the beginning and then manage to put together the "puzzle" by the end of the novel (Spallino 513), *Song of Solomon*, like the other works we have investigated, enacts the concealments and hesitancies characteristic of shame and trauma discourse. For as Morrison repeatedly feeds her readers, in a piecemeal fashion, tantalizing or horrific details that are gradually elaborated on and/or explained as the narrative unfolds, she partially conceals—in layer after layer of interpretable but disconnected details that must be reconnected by the reader—the painful content of what she is describing. It is also telling that the narrative evokes the comforting world of magic and folklore as it either recounts family stories about or depicts scenes of inter- or intraracial violence. By reactively and defensively associating scenes of trauma with the uncanny and dislocated world of folklore and magic, the narrative diverts reader attention away from its horrific descriptions of violence. Through its insistent mythologizing of African-American roots, *Song of Solomon* effectively transforms the disgrace, degradation, and stigma of slavery and racist oppression into racial pride and the transcendence of suffering, which are represented in the originary figure of Solomon, the heroic flying African. Yet the suicidal flights that begin and end the novel point to the pessimism, even nihilism, at the heart of the narrative. What underlies the at times wry humor of Morrison's novel are the contagious—and potentially overwhelming—affects of fear, shame-humiliation, contempt-disgust, and rage.

That critic-readers often tend to bypass *Song of Solomon*'s "tragic realism" and concentrate, instead, on its "magical romance" (see Brenkman 79–80) points to the power of Morrison's richly complex literary discourse to mask or divert attention away from the shame and trauma issues that impel the narrative. Morrison also uses dialogic, parodic discourse to partially shield readers from the troubling subject matter of her novel, and indeed Morrison has described *Song of Solomon* as her "own giggle (in Afro-American terms) of the proto-myth of the journey to manhood" ("Unspeakable Things" 29).

The opening scene of the novel, which tells of the aborted, suicidal "flight" of Mr. Smith that presages Milkman's birth, is often read as a deliberately staged dramatization of the birth of the mythic hero. As critics have observed, Milkman's birth is accompanied by the "ritualized celebration" of Pilate's singing and of virgins (i.e., Milkman's sisters) "strewing rose petals as a black Icarus dies" (A. Leslie Harris 72). Yet this opening scene, even as it evokes the hero's birth, is also tinged with shame. With his blue silk wings curved around his chest, Mr. Smith masquerades as the proud hero—the flying African. But he is also an object of ridicule and contempt as he stands on the roof of Mercy Hospital, and thus some of the Southside watchers snigger, a gold-toothed man laughs, and another calls him crazy. While the initial description of Mr. Smith evokes the shaming stereotype of the mad black man, the narrative later explains that Mr. Smith is a member of the terrorist organization, the Seven Days, and thus reveals that the cause of his "madness" is the racist violence perpetrated against African Americans.

Drawing attention away from such issues, the novel indulges in myth-making as it associates Mr. Smith's leap with Milkman's birth the next day in the all-white Mercy Hospital, which, in the covert countershaming and dialogic speech of the Southside residents, is referred to as No Mercy Hospital since it is a place that, in refusing to treat blacks, has shown "no mercy" toward their physical suffering. "Mr. Smith's blue silk wings must have left their mark, because when the little boy discovered, at four, the same thing Mr. Smith had learned earlier—that only birds and airplanes could fly—he lost all interest in himself" (9). Such authorial directives focus reader attention on the theme of "flight" in the narrative and lead to the unavoidability of critic-reader reactions to and interpretations of this "mythic" drama. Similarly, in telling of Milkman's conception and birth, Morrison deliberately evokes and plays on the mythic story of the hero's origins. Milkman, it is often remarked, "undergoes a 'miraculous' birth" since he is conceived through the magic of Pilate's love potion; he is "nobly born," for he is "descended from American aristocrats, property owners"; and he later "assumes the classic hero's journey of separation, initiation, and return" (Carmean 46). Thus Milkman's birth, his early years, and adult life—including his later journey south in search of gold, which becomes a search for the golden treasure of family origins and racial identity—are patterned after the proto-myth of the hero, as critic after critic has remarked. It is typically argued that before Milkman can "ride the air"—that is, transcend "human limitations"—he must "leave his parents' house, encounter dangers and obstacles along the way, endure a journey to the underworld (calling to mind great heroes who have made similar journeys: Aeneas, Odysseus, Tiresias, Dante, Jesus), after which he sees himself clearly and becomes intensely aware of his shortcomings." Consequently, he is able to throw off "the psychic baggage he has been bearing in his soul" and fly (de Weever 133). Yet if many critic-readers, in heroizing Milkman, repeat the narrative's focus on the pride of mythic flight, others become inadvertent players in a shame drama as they devalue Milkman. Morrison's character, for example, has been described as an "anti-classical hero," who exhibits "warped values, inadequate character formation, and self-centeredness," and it also has been argued that Morrison, although she follows the monomyth pattern in the novel, also "shrewdly" mocks Milkman, the "alleged hero" of the narrative, who is presented as an "intolerable egoist" and who does "little" to warrant the "honorific label" of hero (T. Harris, *Fiction* 85, 90, Brenner 117, 118).

That some critics repeat the novel's shaming devaluation of the middle-class Milkman while others counteract shame by focusing on Milkman's ultimate flight points to the shame–pride issues that inform Morrison's representation of Milkman's search for his African-American identity. In order to understand the secret shame that haunts Milkman, who comes to feel like "a garbage pail for the actions and hatreds of other people" (120), the narrative describes Milkman's middle-class upbringing in passages that recall the cozy, backyard world of illicit gossip that Morrison is so fond of evoking in her fiction. In its representation of members of the Dead family, Morrison's novel not only ridicules them for their class pretensions, but also actively humiliates them by insisting on their family pathology and by exposing the shameful family secrets that haunt them.

Intent on locating the familial and cultural sources of black male pride, the narrative initially rejects the false pride of Milkman's maternal grandfather, Dr. Foster, which is based on a mimicry of white supremacist—including antiblack racist—attitudes and behavior. The "most respected" black man in the city while Ruth is growing up, Dr. Foster, for whom Doctor Street is named, is "worshipped" by the black residents. But while members of the black community take pride in the doctor, he does not "give a damn" about them. An assimilated black who occupies a superior class position, the doctor views those below him as objects of contempt. That the doctor refers to lower-class blacks as "cannibals"—thus categorizing them as the degenerate, savage Other—reveals that he has internalized white racist constructions of black inferiority. To the light-skinned doctor, dark skin is a sign of a stigmatizing difference. The doctor's own unacknowledged status anxiety about being categorized as racially stigmatized becomes apparent in his response to his grandchildren. When he delivers his granddaughters, Magdalene and First Corinthians, he is interested only in their skin color, and he would have "disowned" Milkman for his darker skin, according to Macon (71).

In a classic countershaming strategy, the narrative uses Macon's angry, cynical voice to shame the middle-class, light-skinned Dr. Foster. "[T]he pompous donkey found out what it was like to have to be sick and pay another donkey to make you well," remarks Macon, who describes the dying Dr. Foster as an object of contempt and disgust (72). "Couldn't move, holes were forming in his scalp. And he just lay there in that bed where your mother still sleeps and then he died there. Helpless, fat stomach, skinny arms and legs, looking like a white rat" (73). Acting out a classic turning-of-the-tables script, the narrative portrays the proud, socially superior and contemptuous Dr. Foster as the degenerate, stigmatized Other and interprets his light skin as a mark of his pathological difference.

Just as the narrative rejects the false pride of Dr. Foster, so it rejects the arrogance of Macon Dead. A representative of the upwardly mobile, self-made black capitalist class, Macon, in his "drive for wealth" (28), assumes a white-identified role as he actively exploits poor blacks in the Southside area of town where he is a slum landlord. A character readers love to hate, Macon has been described as the "most hateful" character in the novel, as a "[c]old, objective, and calculating" man, and as an "acquisitive" individual who is "savagely" mocked by Morrison (Coleman, "Beyond the Reach" 154, Samuels and Hudson-Weems 58, Brenner 117). Macon, who is a "colored man of property" by the age of twenty-five, espouses the ethic of materialism: "Own things. And let the things you own own other things. Then you'll own yourself and other people too" (23, 55). In his opportunistic materialism and class elitism, he identifies with the hated white aggressor as he "behaves like a white man, thinks like a white man" (223). Even as the narrative describes Macon's success as a capitalist, it works to undercut his prideful arrogance. "A nigger in business is a terrible thing to see," says the grandmother of Guitar Bains when Macon threatens to evict the Bains family for failure to pay their rent (22). And another tenant of Macon's—Porter, the "wild man in the attic"—uses shaming, racist rhetoric when he angrily refers to Macon as a "baby-dicked baboon" and says to him, "You need killin, you really *need* killin" (28, 26).

A man with a "high behind and an athlete's stride" who "strutted" rather than "walked" (17), Macon attempts to enhance his racial and class status when he marries up by acquiring a trophy wife, the middle-class, light-skinned Ruth. Constructed as a figure of apparent middle-class respectability, Ruth is an ultrarefined woman whose life is shaped—and disciplined—by hegemonic ideologies of proper femininity and domesticity. A woman who was "pressed small" by her sterile, isolated, middle-class upbringing, Ruth is a "frail woman content to do tiny things" (124, 64). It is telling that Ruth, a woman ostensibly defined by her social standing and family background, becomes obsessed with the large water mark on her expensive mahogany table, which identifies the place where the bowl of fresh flowers stood on the table during her father's lifetime, flowers that, for her father, represented the touch of elegance that "distinguished his own family from the people among whom they lived" (12). To Ruth, the water mark is a visible reminder of her family pride: it is a "mooring," the "verification" of an "idea" she wants to "keep alive" (13). But the water mark also is the "single flaw on the splendid wood," and it becomes "more pronounced" with the passage of time after it is exposed (11–12). A signifier of the hidden stain on the family honor—the stain of blackness—the water mark represents the family's hidden racial shame. Ruth's obsession with her stained table, then, signals her own status anxiety—her own internalization of a deep sense of familial and racial shame.

As *Song of Solomon*, in an act of textual exposure, brings to light the family pathology that lies behind Ruth's middle-class refinement and the Dead family's bourgeois respectability, it risks being accused, like *The Bluest Eye* and *Sula*, of invoking the corrosive and shaming hegemonic constructions of the black family—in this case the middle-class, not the lower-class, family—as a "tangle of pathology." While Macon marries Ruth to bolster his own class standing, he soon comes to view her as a source of shame and an object of disgust. Early in his marriage, Macon claims that he discovers Ruth in bed with her dead father, "Naked as a yard dog, kissing him. Him dead and white and puffy and skinny, and she had his fingers in her mouth" (73). Although Macon forgets, and even fabricates, some of the details of this scene—and, indeed, Ruth later tells a markedly different version of this event—the "odiousness" remains (17), and some readers may feel vicarious shame-disgust as they are positioned as curious observers of this voyeuristic scene, which hints at Ruth's incestuous, and necrophilic, attachment to her dead father. After Macon witnesses this scene, he becomes suspicious of Ruth. While he knows that his daughters are his own children—for Dr. Foster would not have been concerned about their skin color unless they were fathered by Macon—he begins to read new meaning into the fact that Dr. Foster delivered Ruth's babies. "I'm not saying that they had contact. But there's lots of things a man can do to please a woman, even if he can't fuck. Whether or not, the fact is she was in that bed sucking his fingers, and if she'd do that when he was dead, what'd she do when he was alive?" That contempt can lead to a desire to rid oneself of the despised person is apparent in Macon's angry remark about Ruth. "Nothing to do but kill a woman like that. I swear, many's the day I regret she talked me out of killing her" (74).

Macon's feelings for Ruth lead him to shun her sexually and also to feel disgusted when, after fifteen years of regretting not having a son, he has one "in the most revolting circumstances" (16), for Milkman is conceived when Ruth uses an aphrodisiac prepared by Pilate to lure Macon back to her bed for four days. Whereas Ruth considers Milkman her "single triumph," her "one aggressive act brought to royal completion" (133), Macon sees his son as a source of shame. Although Macon never learns why members of the community call his son "Milkman," he guesses that the name, which sounds "dirty, intimate, and hot," is shameful, and he knows that the name has something to do with his wife and is "like the emotion he always felt when thinking of her, coated with disgust" (15–16). "[I]f the people were calling his son Milkman, and if she was lowering her eyelids and dabbing at the sweat on her top lip when she heard it, there was definitely some filthy connection and it did not matter at all to Macon Dead whether anyone gave him the details or not" (17).

In describing the origins of Milkman's shame-laden nickname, Morrison appeals yet again to her readers' voyeuristic interests while she risks provoking their shame-disgust by positioning them as witnesses to a taboo, oedipally tinged scene. Ruth, who needs "a balm, a gentle touch or nuzzling of some sort" to make her life bearable (13), nurses Milkman until he is old enough to stand up and talk. While Ruth takes secret pleasure in nursing her growing son, Milkman's "secretive eyes" convey his childish sense that there is something "strange and wrong" about this incestuous nursing ritual, which abruptly ends when Ruth is discovered by one of Macon's tenants, Freddie, a notorious gossip (14). Amused at the sight of the lemony-skinned Ruth with her black-skinned son at her breast, Freddie gives Ruth's son his nickname, "Milkman." What the adult Milkman recalls is "Laughter. Somebody he couldn't see, in the room laughing . . . at him and at his mother, and his mother is ashamed. She lowers her eyes and won't look at him. 'Look at me, Mama. Look at me.' But she doesn't and the laughter is loud now. Everybody is laughing" (77). Even as this scene suggests Ruth's desire to baby Milkman—to keep him dependent and treat him as her "velveteened toy" (132)—it also dramatizes a common shame scenario in its account of Milkman's childhood experience of maternal rejection, depicted here in his inability to hold his mother's gaze. Milkman's sense that everybody is laughing at him and his mother conveys not only the maternal transmission of shame but also the global nature of shame: the shame-vulnerable individual's feeling, in the moment of public exposure and ridicule, that his secret shame is visible to all.

Like *Sula*, *Song of Solomon* focuses on the maternal transmission of shame and it also is concerned with the dangers of excessive mothering. But whereas in *Sula* Morrison centers her attention on the woman-centered world of the black matriarchy, in *Song of Solomon* she is concerned—especially in her representation of Macon Dead—with issues surrounding the black patriarchy. bell hooks, in her critique of the black phallocentric view of the patriarchal role—the notion of the "'satisfying manhood'" that "carries with it the phallocentric right of men to dominate women"—remarks on the "chokehold patriarchal masculinity imposes on black men" (*Black Looks* 97, 113). *Song of Solomon* explores the black patriarchy through the figure of the "stern, greedy, unloving" Macon Dead (234). A domestic tyrant who keeps his family "awkward with fear," Macon actively shames his wife and daughters, First Corinthians and Magdalene, who is called Lena. He expresses his hatred for his wife in every word he addresses to her and communicates his disappointment in his daughters, thus "dulling their buttery complexions and choking the lilt out of what should have been girlish voices. Under the frozen heat of his glance they tripped over doorsills and dropped the salt cellar into the yolks of their poached eggs. The way he mangled their grace, wit, and self-esteem was the single excitement of their days. . . . [A]nd his wife, Ruth, began her days stunned into stillness by her husband's contempt and ended them wholly animated by it" (10–11). Macon terrorizes his wife and daughters in private, yet he also indulges in proud public displays of his family. "First he displayed us, then he splayed us," the adult Lena remarks of Macon's treatment of her and her sister. "All our lives were like that: he would parade us like virgins through Babylon, then humiliate us like whores in Babylon" (216).

Macon, who dons the mask of exhibitionistic self-importance and prideful arrogance to defend against his unacknowledged shame, teaches Milkman to fear and respect him. Revolted by the disgusting circumstances in which he has fathered a son, Macon dominates and shames the growing Milkman, "to whom he could speak only if his words held some command or criticism" (28). As an adolescent, Milkman expresses his inherited shame/false pride through his posture and style of walking. Noticing that one of his legs is shorter than the other, Milkman begins to slouch or lean or stand with his hip thrown out. His slouching gait—which depicts the classic shame posture—appears as "an affected walk, the strut of a very young man trying to appear more sophisticated than he was. It bothered him and he acquired movements and habits to disguise what to him was a burning defect. . . . The deformity was mostly in his mind" (62).

Feeling that, because of his leg, he cannot emulate his father, who has no physical imperfection and seems to grow stronger with age, Milkman attempts to fashion an identity in opposition to his father. Setting out to differ from his father as much as he dares, Milkman sports a mustache, shaves a part into his hair, uses tobacco, and gives away his money. But despite his expression of his own individual differences, Milkman, who works for his father as a rent collector, has adopted his father's bourgeois values and ethic of materialism, and he remains enmeshed in his family's pathological system. When the twenty-two-year-old Milkman witnesses what has become a familiar family scene—that of his father hitting his mother—he assaults his father, who "had come to believe, after years of creating respect and fear wherever he put his foot down, after years of being the tallest man in every gathering, that he was impregnable" (67). Milkman, who watches his father crumple before him, experiences contradictory emotions: shame, sorrow, and also the glee of pride. Although this scene is cast as a classic oedipal conflict in which the son triumphs over the father, Milkman also realizes that his action will not change anything between his parents. "Perhaps there were some new positions on the chessboard, but the game would go on" (68). Angry when his father tells him "all that shit" (76) about finding Ruth naked in bed with her dead father and shamed when his father's story leads to the recovery of his repressed memory of being nursed by his mother until he was too old, Milkman comes to feel "like a garbage pail for the actions and hatreds of other people" (120). Mired in the "shit" of family shame, he is caught up in a shame-shame feeling trap.

With oppositional intent, *Song of Solomon* exposes the family secrets of the bourgeois Dead family, uncovering the shame behind the class elitism and false pride of Milkman's parents. Morrison's narrative also deliberately contrasts the false pride of Macon Dead with the natural dignity of Macon's sister, Pilate, who belongs to the black underclass. In its representation of Pilate, the narrative invokes and reverses the pride–shame oppositions associated with class and race—those of high/low, clean/unclean, pure/polluted—as it interrogates the degrading stereotype of the black underclass woman as the low-unclean-polluted Other. Making subversive use of the black cultural stereotype that associates light-skinned women with desirable feminine traits and dark-skinned women with undesirable masculine traits, the novel unfavorably compares the lemony-skinned, fragile, and shame-ridden Ruth with the tall, black Pilate, who is a powerful and proud woman. Thus, in the deliberate contrast between Ruth and Pilate, the narrative works to undermine the color-caste hierarchy, which values light-skinned, middle-class women and devalues those who are dark skinned and lower class. And yet while Pilate is depicted as a woman of natural dignity and black folk pride, she also suffers from a stigmatized identity and becomes the site in the text of middle-class anxieties about the black underclass.

To Macon, who has internalized white constructions of black racial inferiority, Pilate is the stigmatized, racially degenerate Other: marked by the stain of racial and class shame, she is inferior, defective, dirty, dissmelling. After the birth of Milkman, Pilate visits her brother's family only to have Macon eventually tell her to leave his house and not return until she shows some respect for herself. "How far down she had slid. . . ." Macon thinks of Pilate, who has a "sickening smell" and lacks any "interest in or knowledge of decent housekeeping" (20). Pilate, who lives like "poor trash" and is "odd, murky, and worst of all, unkempt," would be a "regular source of embarrassment, if he would allow it. But he would not allow it" (172, 20). "Why can't you dress like a woman?" Macon asks her. "What's that sailor's cap doing on your head? Don't you have stockings? What are you trying to make me look like in this town?" Afraid that her racial and class shame will stigmatize him, he trembles at the thought that his white bankers will discover that he is the brother of the "raggedy bootlegger," who has both an illegitimate daughter, Reba, and granddaughter, Hagar. To Macon, Pilate, Reba, and Hagar are a "collection of lunatics" who make wine and sing in the streets "like common street women" (20). Although he would like to put his bootlegger sister in jail—that is, make use of the dominant society's method of disciplining and controlling the unruly underclass—he is afraid that she might "loudmouth him and make him seem trashy in the eyes of the law—and the banks" (24).

Anything but the common street woman Macon sees in her, Pilate, who is as tall as Macon Dead, looks like "a tall black tree" to Milkman (39): that is, she embodies the natural pride of the black rural folk. Yet while the narrative insists on Pilate's folk pride, it also presents the navelless Pilate as a stigmatized individual. Explaining the link between shame and stigma, Michael Lewis remarks that stigma "is a mark or characteristic that distinguishes a person as being deviant, flawed, limited, spoiled, or generally undesirable." Stigmatization, which is a "public, interpersonal event," prompts a sense of shame and embarrassment: the stigmatized individual is "imperfect" and has a "spoiled identity" (194). Moreover, through the process of "stigma contagion," stigma affects not only the "marked" individual but also those people who associate with the stigmatized person (200). Because Pilate lacks a navel—which others read as a sign of her pathological difference—she is stigmatized and thus shunned by others for fear of stigma contagion. On learning of her defect, "Men frowned, women whispered and shoved their children behind them." During her early life as a wanderer, Pilate takes up with several groups of migrant farmworkers only to have one group ask her to leave when they discover she lacks a navel and another to expel her by leaving her behind. As Pilate comes to realize, "although men fucked armless women, one-legged women, hunchbacks and blind women, drunken women, razor-toting women, midgets, small children, convicts, boys, sheep, dogs, goats, liver, each other, and even certain species of plants, they were terrified of fucking her—a woman with no navel" (148).

That Pilate's lack is associated with female sexuality in this passage calls to mind not only the cultural equation between female genitals and deficiency or lack but also between female sexuality and the fear of stigma contagion evident in the masculinist view of female sexuality as contaminating and defiling. The narrative also uses Pilate's lack of a navel to make a covert political statement by associating Pilate's birth trauma and maternal loss with the black struggle for survival. Macon recalls how Pilate came "struggling out of the womb" after their mother died, how she inched "headfirst out of a still, silent, and indifferent cave of flesh, dragging her own cord and her own after-birth behind her" (27, 28). In describing Pilate as self-born, *Song of Solomon* constructs her as an honored American type—the self-created individual. Yet it also focuses on Pilate's rebellious shamelessness as it uses this character to dialogically contest the black assimilationist and bourgeois ideology of self-help and self-improvement. Ignoring the pain and powerlessness of the social outcast's situation, the text, instead, insists that when the stigmatized, ostracized Pilate finally takes offense at the way others have treated her, she is liberated and empowered. On recognizing "what her situation in the world was and would probably always be," Pilate discards "every assumption she had learned" and begins "at zero." By focusing on the problem of how she wants to live and what she finds important in life, Pilate reinvents herself, becoming a woman who remains "just barely within the boundaries of the elaborately socialized world of black people." Pilate gives up "all interest in table man-ners or hygiene," yet she acquires "a deep concern for and about human rela-tionships" (149). In a deliberate strategy to counteract the shame associated with Pilate's stigmatized identity, the narrative, even as it presents Pilate as a shameless individual and a member of the black underclass, also constructs her as a healing figure and insists that she gains a kind of power and freedom as she resists the shame-binding rules of black society. Described as a "natural healer" (150) and as a person who values human—and family—connections above all else, Pilate becomes the site in the text of redemptive folk values.

In its representation of Pilate, *Song of Solomon* deliberately carries out an antishaming agenda as it invokes but also interrogates degrading stereo-types of the black underclass woman. Yet it also insists that Pilate's grand daughter, Hagar—who is "prissy" and hates "dirt and disorganization"—is "embarrassed" by her mother and grandmother (150, 151). Returning to its concern with the issues of class and shame and the color-caste hierarchy in the construction of African-American identities, the narrative describes how Milkman, although he is initially attracted to Hagar, ultimately adopts his family's middle-class values, viewing Hagar as someone who is not of "his own set" (91). Despite Milkman's prolonged affair with Hagar, people do not consider her a "real or legitimate girl friend—not someone he might marry," and indeed Milkman treats her as an object of shame: as a "quasi-secret but permanent fixture in his life" (91, 98). The same Hagar who hates dirt and disorganization is ultimately dismissed by Milkman, who "wouldn't give a pile of swan shit" for her (137).

When Milkman sends Hagar a letter ending their relationship, the "flat-out coldness" of the "thank you" in his letter stuns Hagar, who is sent "spin-ning into a bright blue place where the air was thin and it was silent all the time . . . and where everything was frozen except for an occasional burst of fire inside her chest that crackled away until she ran out into the streets to find Milkman Dead" (99). The deeply injured Hagar, who is confused and frozen by shame, feels the incipient fire of shame-rage burning within her. After Hagar sees Milkman with his arms around the shoulders of a light-skinned woman—a woman with silky copper-colored hair and gray eyes—she experiences both shame-depression and shame-rage. The lovelorn Hagar becomes "like a restless ghost, finding peace nowhere and in nothing" as she ruminates on her loss: "the mouth Milkman was not kissing, the feet that were not running toward him, the eye that no longer beheld him, the hands that were not touching him" (127). Then her lethargy dissipates and she feels intense rage as the "calculated violence of a shark" grows in her (128).

If Hagar is constructed as a traditional dysphoric romantic heroine—a woman who makes the man the center of her life and thus feels an utter sense of loss and despair when her love relation fails—she also is presented as a potentially violent underclass woman, a precursor of *Jazz*'s Violet Trace. Feeling that Milkman is her "home in this world" but unable to win his love, Hagar settles instead "for his fear," and so she begins stalking him, intent on killing him (137, 128). Because she trembles when she is in Milkman's presence, her "knife thrusts and hammer swings and ice-pick jabs" are "clumsy," and thus she is an "inept killer" (129). Milkman's contemptuous remark during Hagar's final attempt on his life when she stands paralyzed, holding a butcher knife in her raised hands—he tells her that her problems will be over if she drives the knife into her "cunt"—devastates Hagar, who has been so "taken over by her anaconda love" that she has "no self left, no fears, no wants, no intelligence that was her own" (130, 137).

"You think because he doesn't love you that you are worthless," Guitar says to Hagar. "If he throws you out, then you are garbage. . . . He can't value you more than you value yourself" (305–06). While Guitar finds Hagar a "[p]retty little black-skinned woman" (306), Hagar, recalling *The Bluest Eye*'s Pecola, sees herself as black and ugly. Viewing herself through the shaming eyes of Milkman, Hagar, who is languishing in bed, determines to "fix" herself when she looks at herself in the tiny compact mirror Pilate gives her. "No wonder. . . . Look at how I look. I look awful. No wonder he didn't want me. I look terrible. . . . Ohhh. I smell too. . . . I need a bath. A long one. . . . Oh, Lord, my head. Look at that. . . . I look like a ground hog. Where's the comb?" (308–09). Hagar attempts to refashion herself by purchasing new clothes and makeup. But her efforts at self-improvement and self-transformation are doomed to failure because the dark-skinned Hagar cannot possibly compete in Milkman's bourgeois world, which favors lighter-skinned women. Focusing attention on the homogenizing power of mass cultural images in shaping identity, the narrative describes Hagar's failed attempt to conform to cultural norms. Hagar dresses herself up "in the white-with-a-band-of-color skirt and matching bolero, the Maidenform brassiere, the Fruit of the Loom panties, the no color hose, the Playtex garter belt and the Joyce con brios," and she rubs "mango tango on her cheeks" and puts "jungle red" on her lips and "baby clear sky light" on her eyelids. But when Hagar presents herself to Pilate and Reba and sees herself reflected in their shaming gaze, she recognizes what she was unable to see in the mirror: "the wet ripped hose, the soiled white dress, the sticky, lumpy face powder, the streaked rouge, and the wild wet shoals of hair" (314). Hagar, who has always hated dirt and disorganization, recognizes her social distance from Milkman as she perceives herself as a sad spectacle: as the dirty black underclass woman. Having internalized hegemonic beauty standards, which link skin color and hair texture to class status and construct dark-skinned women as the racially inferior and stigmatized Other, Hagar feels unworthy, dirty, spoiled, undesirable. Milkman "hates" her hair, she insists, and he "loves" silky, penny-colored hair[4] and lemon-colored skin, a thin nose, and gray-blue eyes (315–16). When the shame-haunted Hagar dies, her death is as much an expression of her desire to do away with her spoiled, racially stained identity as it is of her lovesickness.

Racial and class shame also govern the love relationship between Porter and Milkman's sister, Corinthians, a "[h]igh toned and high yellow" woman. According to the standard black middle-class narrative, the college-educated Corinthians, who had been taught how to be "an enlightened mother and wife," should have been able "to contribute to the civilization—or in her case, the civilizing—of her community" and she should have been "a prize for a professional man of color." But despite her education and class privileges, she remains unmarried, for such men prefer wives unlike the "elegant" Corinthians, who is accustomed to black middle-class life and thus lacks the necessary "ambition," "hunger," and "hustle" such men look for in a wife (188). The granddaughter of the distinguished Dr. Foster, the forty-four-year-old Corinthians ends up working as the maid of a white woman, the State Poet Laureate, and she becomes romantically involved with the Southside yardman, Porter. The narrative deliberately brings together the elegant Corinthians and Porter, individuals who occupy opposing sites in the black social hierarchy, as it examines the issue of class and shame in the construction of African-American identities, and it also, in its initial description of Porter, reproduces the culturally embedded stereotype of the impulsive and potentially violent black underclass male by portraying him as the "wild man in the attic" (28). When Porter makes his initial dramatic appearance in the novel, he is a "crazy drunk" man perched in an attic window with a gun, who demands from the Southside onlookers "somebody to fuck" and who pulls out his penis and urinates in a high arc over the heads of the women onlookers, thus acting out the shaming invective, "piss on you" (24–25).[5] Porter's words to the crowd—he shouts that he loves the Southside people and would die and kill for them—are explained much later when readers learn that the "cowering, screaming, threatening, urinating" Porter is a member of the Seven Days terrorist organization, a group that plans and carries out black-on-white revenge killings (26).

Corinthians and Porter, who ride the same city bus, start talking to each other after Porter gives Corinthians a friendship greeting card. When they begin their romantic relationship, Corinthians not only is ashamed of Porter but she also hates him for the shame she feels. Initially refusing Porter's invitation to visit his room, she explains that her "strict" father does not want his daughters "to mix with . . . people": that is, with Southside underclass blacks like Porter (195). Porter's accusation that she is a "doll baby" and not a "grown-up woman" shames and angers Corinthians, who feels that she has been unfavorably compared to the "only people she knew for certain she was superior to": the fat, promiscuous, illiterate women on the bus. "They'd love to have a greeting card dropped in their lap," Corinthians says to Porter. "But oh, I forgot. You couldn't do that, could you, because they wouldn't be able to read it. . . . They wouldn't know mediocrity if it punched them right in their fat faces. They'd laugh and slap their fat thighs and take you right on into their kitchens. Right up on the breakfast table" (196). In dramatizing Corinthians's status anxiety, this scene also illustrates the co-construction of social identities, revealing how the construction of the lower-class Other—as sexually loose and uncivilized—functions to consolidate black middle-class identity.

If Corinthians's contemptuous, middle-class voice brings into the text the intraracist discourse of the black bourgeoisie, the narrative also acts out a kind of shaming revenge on Corinthians, who is subsequently reduced to clinging to the hood of Porter's car in a panic, lest he leave her behind. A man "who rented a tiny room from her father, who ate with a knife and did not even own a pair of dress shoes," Porter is the kind of man Corinthians's parents had kept her from "because such a man was known to beat his woman, betray her, shame her, and leave her." But after having sex with Porter, Corinthians feels, in place of the "vanity" of false class pride, a new sense of "self-esteem," and thus she is "grateful" to Porter (201). Sending out contradictory messages, the narrative presents Porter as a gentle lover and potential rescuer of Corinthians but also as a killer. And even as it seems intent on humanizing Porter and thus counteracting the initial shaming and racist representation of him as a "wild man in the attic," it also reminds readers that he is the "same

Henry Porter" who had "screamed, wept, waved a shotgun, and urinated over the heads of the women in the yard" (28, 199).

In a similar way, *Song of Solomon* sends out contradictory messages in its presentation of the underclass Guitar, who is initially described as the person who can "liberate" Milkman (36) and yet who ultimately tries to kill Milkman. "Wanna fly, you got to give up the shit that weighs you down," Guitar tells Milkman when they see a white peacock that can fly "no better than a chicken" because of its jewelry-like tail. "All that jewelry weighs it down. Like vanity. Can't nobody fly with all that shit," Guitar insists (179). Milkman, who is weighed down by "shit"—that is, the vanity of false class pride—is also capable of treating others like "shit" as he attempts to defend against the "shit" of inherited racial and family shame. Indeed, Lena accuses Milkman of "peeing" on his mother and sisters all of his life—that is, treating them in a contemptuous way—and he has similarly shown contempt for Hagar, a person he sees as worth less than "a pile of swan shit" (214–15, 137). Although Guitar offers Milkman potentially liberating advice when he insists, "Can't nobody fly with all that shit," the narrative also registers uneasiness about Guitar, who comes to embody black middle-class fears about the potentially destructive shame-rage of the violent black underclass male.

"If things ever got tough, you'd melt. You're not a serious person, Milkman," Guitar remarks at one point (104). Unlike Milkman, who is bored by talk of "insults, violence, and oppression" (107), Guitar becomes consumed by racial politics. Bringing in Guitar's oppositional voice, *Song of Solomon* examines the construction of conflicting black political identities, contrasting the middle-class assimilationist Milkman and the lower-class black nationalist Guitar. For someone like Guitar, to live in a racist society that persecutes and stigmatizes poor black people is to live in a state of chronic shame-rage. The site of black rage and revenge in the text, Guitar has been contrastingly described as a character that Morrison "purposefully makes . . . fascinating" because she does not want his "solution of violence to be easily dismissed" and as a "vindictive racist" who "gets Morrison's scorn" (Atlas, "Darker Side" 6, Brenner 117).

In explaining the personal and social forces that shape the construction of Guitar's political identity as a militant black nationalist and member of the Seven Days terrorist organization, the narrative presents Guitar as an individual who has been deeply scarred and traumatized by his childhood loss of his father. Guitar is unable to eat sweets, which make him vomit and think of dead people and white people, because when his father got sliced in half in a sawmill, his father's white boss gave Guitar and his brother and two sisters some sweet candy his wife had made especially for them, and also Guitar's mother bought candy for the children with part of the forty dollars the white sawmill owner gave her in lieu of an insurance settlement. In linking Guitar's aversion to candy to his aversion to white people, the narrative sends out the covert and countershaming message that white people make Guitar vomit: that is, they disgust him. A basic emotion originating in the rejection of bad-tasting, offensive food, disgust has evolved into "a wide range of emotion completely unrelated to food" and can signal the desire to "spit out with violence" or reject the other (Nathanson, *Shame and Pride* 127, 128). "Like anger and contempt, disgust can be a moral reaction to other people, implying that their actions or character have violated normative standards.... [A]s disgust becomes elaborated, it becomes a more general feeling of revulsion, even to sociomoral violations, and it begins to shade into anger" (Rozin 588).

At the emotional core of Guitar's aversive antiwhite racism is what affect theorists refer to as the "hostility triad" of disgust, contempt, and anger (see Rozin 589). With dialogic intent, the text sets out to countershame white racists, who construct African Americans as mad, savage, and degenerate people, by constructing whites as a mad, depraved people who viciously kill blacks. "There are no innocent white people," Guitar tells Milkman, "because every one of them is a potential nigger-killer, if not an actual one. You think Hitler surprised them? You think just because they went to war they thought he was a freak? Hitler's the most natural white man in the world. He killed Jews and Gypsies because he didn't have us. Can you see those Klansmen shocked by him? No, you can't" (155). Using the white racist discourse of difference and pathology to define whiteness, Guitar construes whites as an "unnatural" race: as a morally degenerate, violent, and uncivilized people who kill "for fun." "[I]f Kennedy got drunk and bored and was sitting around a potbellied stove in Mississippi, he might join a lynching party just for the hell of it. Under those circumstances his unnaturalness would surface" (156). Similarly, had Roosevelt found himself in a small Alabama town, "he'd have done it too." Constructing whites as a monolithic or generalized Other, Guitar insists that all whites, under the right circumstances, would kill blacks. Moreover, whites know that they are depraved, for their "writers and artists have been saying it for years.... They call it tragedy. In the movies they call it adventure. It's just depravity that they try to make glorious, natural. But it ain't." Invoking the shaming discourse of racial biology to define whiteness, Guitar explains that the "disease" whites have is "in their blood, in the structure of their chromosomes" (157).[6]

If Guitar's antiwhite racist discourse is meant, in part, to underscore the social constructedness of essentializing and pathologizing discourses of racial difference, the narrative also warns of the potentially lethal consequences of racist stereotypes and us–them thinking in describing Guitar's membership in the Seven Days, a terrorist organization that carries out revenge killings against whites. In a classic attack-other revenge script—a script that combines power, rage, and contempt scripts—members of the Seven Days assume a secret killing power over their white oppressors.[7] The Seven Days society, as Guitar explains, executes whites. "[W]hen a Negro child, Negro woman, or Negro man is killed by whites and nothing is done about it by *their* law and *their* courts, this society selects a similar victim at random, and they execute him or her in a similar manner if they can. If the Negro was hanged, they hang; if a Negro was burnt, they burn; raped and murdered, they rape and murder" (154–55). While the members of the Seven Days enact a compulsive repetition of shame and trauma scenarios, they also, through their secret acts of revenge, assume power over whites by taking on the role of the violent perpetrator. By identifying with the white aggressor and thus reversing the (white) perpetrator and (black) victim roles, members of the Seven Days attempt not only to discharge collective black shame-based rage onto whites but also to exorcise collective black trauma by relocating feelings of humiliation, terror, and vulnerability in white victims. Through a reversal of the balance of power, they secretly act out the desire to disempower and traumatize whites, instilling in them the feelings of utter powerlessness experienced by black victims of white violence. Thus, they stigmatize their white victims before killing them, for "human-induced" victimization is not only "humiliating" but it also sullies and tarnishes the victim who is rendered utterly helpless (Janoff-Bulman 80).

Claiming that he is reasonable when he kills whites—for he does not kill out of anger or for amusement or to gain power or money—Guitar explains that he participates in revenge killings because he loves black people and because he wants the black–white ratio to remain static. While the "earth is soggy with black people's blood" and white people cannot be cured of their depravity, the Seven Days is nevertheless "trying to make a world where one day white people will think before they lynch" (158, 160). If *Song of Solomon* at first glance appears to reinforce the stereotype of the pathological, violent black man in its description of the Seven Days, the narrative also actively reprojects the shame associated with this derogatory stereotype onto whites. It does this by revealing that Guitar and his cohorts are driven mad by the violent acts they commit and that their behavior is an imitation of the racist violence perpetrated by whites against African Americans. And even as *Song of Solomon* uses Guitar to express black rage and to enact a revenge fantasy, it also voices black middle-class concerns about Guitar's violent behavior. While Milkman is secretly attracted to Guitar's killing behavior—"Did you do it yet?" Milkman wonders. "How did it feel? Were you afraid? Did it change you? And if I do it, will it change me too?" (176)—he also calls

Guitar's behavior crazy and warns that killing can become habitual. "If you do it enough, you can do it to anybody. . . . You can off anybody you don't like. You can off me" (161), Milkman remarks to Guitar, his words preparing for the final sections of the novel which describe how Guitar hunts down Milkman, intent on killing him.

If Part I of *Song of Solomon*, in showing that Milkman is weighed down by the "shit" of inherited racial shame, ends in an emotional impasse, Part II attempts to work through Milkman's shame-shame feeling trap by describing how he comes to take pride in his family roots. Thus, according to the standard, text-directed reading of *Song of Solomon*, when Milkman goes on his journey to Danville and Shalimar in search of Pilate's buried gold, he discovers, instead, the real golden treasure of his family roots. But what such readings tend to bypass are the shame and pain associated with Milkman's discovery. In using folk tale and magic and following the pattern of the hero's purposeful quest as it describes Milkman's journey south, *Song of Solomon* also deflects attention away from the trauma and violence that have threatened to interrupt—if not disrupt and fragment—the narrative from the beginning, not only in the story of Guitar but also in the family story of the Deads. What lies behind the dark comedy of manners and grotesqueries of Morrison's interwoven and layered narratives about the Dead family is an originary trauma narrative, which tells of the family's slavery and postslavery beginnings in a world of racist oppression and violence.

Milkman first begins to learn about his family history from Pilate, a woman reputed to be a conjure woman who has "the power to step out of her skin, set a bush afire from fifty yards, and turn a man into a ripe rutabaga" (94). Even as the narrative associates Pilate with magic and female power, it also depicts her as a victim of trauma. Not only is the navelless Pilate's stigma a sign of her birth trauma and maternal loss, but Pilate also has never recovered from the traumatic loss of her father. The first time Milkman meets Pilate, she tells him the story of her father's murder, describing how he was killed in front of his two children, the sixteen-year-old Macon and the twelve-year-old Pilate. "They blew him five feet up into the air. He was sitting on his fence waiting for 'em, and they snuck up from behind and blew him five feet into the air" (40). When asked for specific information about her father's murder, Pilate responds in a vague way, remarking that she doesn't know "who" killed him or "why" and that "where" it happened was "[o]ff a fence" and "when" was "[t]he year they shot them Irish people down in the streets. Was a good year for guns and gravediggers, I know that" (42). If the description of Pilate communing with the ghost of her dead father serves to reinforce the idea that she is a conjure woman, it also suggests that she—and by extension the collective black folk she represents—is trauma-haunted.

Macon's account of his father's death repeats and elaborates on Pilate's fragmented memory of this traumatic and formative event. When Milkman asks Macon how he was treated by his father when he was a boy, Macon suddenly recalls the "numbness that had settled on him when he saw the man he loved and admired fall off the fence" and how "something wild ran through him when he watched the body twitching in the dirt" (50–51). An emancipated slave, Macon's father spent sixteen years making his farm, Lincoln's Heaven, profitable only to have it forcibly taken from him by whites, who tricked the illiterate farmer into signing over his property to them when he made his mark on a deed to the property. "White people did love their dogs," Macon recalls in a passage that focuses on the shame of being treated as less valuable than an animal. "Kill a nigger and comb their hair at the same time. But I've seen grown white men cry about their dogs" (52). Preserving Pilate's voice as one relaying healing folk wisdom and community values, the narrative uses Macon's elaboration of Pilate's story to bring into focus what her account omits: the shame and rage suffered by victims of white supremacist persecution and violence.

When Milkman begins his journey in search of Pilate's gold, he seemingly undergoes a corrective emotional experience as he escapes from his "real life," where he is constrained by "other people's nightmares" and where everybody wants his "living life" (220, 222). At Reverend Cooper's house in Danville, Pennsylvania, Milkman discovers a newfound family and racial pride in having "*people*," that is, family links (229). There he is visited by a series of old men who speak with "awe and affection" of his grandfather and remember "both Macon Deads as extraordinary men." To them, Milkman's father and grandfather embody black male pride. They recall Milkman's father, their contemporary, as a strong and energetic boy who "outran, out-plowed, out-shot, outpicked, outrode them all" (234). And Milkman's grandfather, "the tall, magnificent Macon Dead," was "the farmer they wanted to be, the clever irrigator, the peach-tree grower, the hog slaughterer, the wild-turkey roaster, the man who could plow forty in no time flat and sang like an angel while he did it." His farm, Lincoln's Heaven, "spoke to them like a sermon. 'You see?' the farm said to them. 'See? See what you can do? Never mind you can't tell one letter from another, never mind you born a slave, never mind you lose your name, never mind your daddy dead, never mind nothing. Here, this here, is what a man can do if he puts his mind to it and his back in it. Stop sniveling,' it said. 'Stop picking around the edges of the world'" (235). Attempting to revive their dying dream—"[b]ut they shot the top of his head off and ate his fine Georgia peaches" (235)—Milkman begins to tell the old men stories about his father. "He bragged a little and they came alive. How many houses his father owned (they grinned); the new car every two years (they laughed);

and when he told them how his father tried to buy the Erie Lackawanna (it sounded better that way), they hooted with joy. That's him! That's Old Macon Dead's boy, all right!" (236).

"I knew one day you would come back," the witchlike Circe says to Milkman, mistaking him for his father when he finds his way to the ruined mansion of the Butlers, the white people who murdered his grandfather (240). The woman who once worked for the Butlers and who hid Milkman's father and Pilate from the Butlers after the murder of their father, Circe is an embodiment of black folk memory and survival. A study in contrasts, Circe has dainty habits but wild, dirty hair and torn filthy clothes, and she has a wizened face and toothless mouth yet the cultivated voice of a twenty-year-old. In a deliberate parody of the traditional white representation of the loyal black servant, Morrison describes how Circe, who has outlived the Butlers, has, remained in the decaying Butler mansion taking care of their dogs. "You loved those white folks that much?" Milkman asks Circe (246) only to learn that what truly motivates her is the desire for revenge, the wish to turn the tables by returning white contempt with black countercontempt.

Contempt, which combines the affect of anger with dissmell, under-lies white prejudice against blacks, as shame theorists have observed. The "facial scene in contempt is the sneer, which is a learned transformation of dissmell," Gershen Kaufman writes, drawing on the observations of Silvan Tomkins. "By combining anger with dissmell, contempt functions as a signal and motive to others . . . of either negative evaluation or feelings of rejection. The face pulls away in dissmell from the offending, 'bad-smelling' other. . . . The contemptuous individual "feels elevated" and looks down on others, who are "deemed inferior, beneath one's dignity" (*Psychology of Shame* 40, 41). But contempt also breeds contempt and can lead, as it does in the case of Circe, to a desire to retaliate.

In a displaced drama, Circe acts out a revenge script that signals her long-thwarted wish to humiliate her former, and now dead, humiliators by overseeing the transformation of their mansion—a symbol of white pride and greed—into a dirty, dissmelling place. "Everything in this world they lived for will crumble and rot," Circe tells Milkman (247). Once a beauti-ful mansion, the Butler home is now "[d]ark, ruined, evil" and permeated with a "hairy animal smell, ripe, rife, suffocating" (238, 239). Acting out her long-suppressed shame-rage against Mrs. Butler—a woman who committed suicide so she would not have to live the way Circe did—Circe turns the dogs loose in the bedroom of her dead employer. "Her walls didn't have wallpaper. No. Silk brocade that took some Belgian women six years to make. She loved it—oh, how much she loved it. Took thirty Weimaraners one day to rip it off the walls. If I thought the stink wouldn't strangle you, I'd show it to you,"

Circe says to Milkman (247–48). Acting as an agent of black revenge, Circe, as Reverend Cooper tells Milkman, has evened up things. For Circe symbolically dirties—that is, shames—the once powerful and superior white family, representatives of the prejudiced white culture that has historically shamed blacks by treating them as dirty and dissmelling objects of contempt.

When Milkman's search for Pilate's gold at Hunters Cave proves futile, he goes to Shalimar, Virginia, believing that Pilate took the gold there. Because Milkman was "the object of hero worship" in Danville, he is unprepared for his reception in Shalimar where he is "damned near killed" (270) when he unwittingly insults the men he encounters by treating them as inferiors, thus reminding them of their allotted place in American society. "He hadn't found them fit enough or good enough to want to know their names, and believed himself too good to tell them his. They looked at his skin and saw it was as black as theirs, but they knew he had the heart of the white men who came to pick them up in the trucks when they needed anonymous, faceless laborers" (266). Feeling their own manhood insulted—for Milkman's middle-class monied manner reminds them that they don't have any crops of their own to harvest and that they depend on women and children for their food—they insult Milkman's manhood, engaging in a version of the ritualized insult game, the dozens. When one of the men asks if it is true that Northerners wear their pants tight because their "pricks" are "[w]ee, wee little," Milkman replies:

> "I wouldn't know. . . . I never spent much time smacking my lips over another man's dick." Everybody smiled, including Milkman. It was about to begin.
> "What about his ass hole? Ever smack your lips over that?"
> "Once," said Milkman. "When a little young nigger made me mad and I had to jam a Coke bottle up his ass."
> "What'd you use a bottle for? Your cock wouldn't fill it?"
> "It did. After I took the Coke bottle out. Filled his mouth too."
> "Prefer mouth, do you?"
> "If it's big enough, and ugly enough, and belongs to a ignorant motherfucker who is about to get the livin shit whipped out of him." (267)

Described as a "cruel game" in which words are "weapons aimed at the destruction of another man's honor and pride" and in which "opponents try to bring each other to the point of initiating physical combat," the dozens game uses taunts—including "accusations of cowardice, homosexuality, or stupidity"—to humiliate the opponent. Because this verbal game often takes place before a group, losing can be "devastating," for the "loser may be seen as ineffectual, or even worse, effeminate" (Majors and Billson 97, 93, 92, 97).[8] In its staging of the dozens game, *Song of Solomon* dramatizes the link between shaming insults and violence by showing how the "name-calling toilet contest" between Milkman and the Shalimar men (269) leads to a fight between a knife-wielding local man and Milkman, who defends himself with a broken bottle. Afterward an enraged Milkman thinks that if "he'd had a weapon, he would have slaughtered everybody in sight," and, echoing the class elitism and internalized racism of his father and grandfather, he contemptuously dismisses the men, viewing them as "black Neanderthals" and "savages" (269, 270, 276).

Milkman assumes, when the older men invite him to go on a night hunt, that they plan to "test him, match and beat him" (269). Finding himself in the woods at night with a "mean bunch of black folk," Milkman feels he has not done anything to "deserve their contempt." In a conscious attempt to rehabilitate Milkman's character, the narrative describes his sudden questioning of his middle-class—and narcissistic—sense of entitlement. "He didn't deserve. . . . It sounded old. *Deserve*. Old and tired and beaten to death. Deserve. Now it seemed to him that he was always saying or thinking that he didn't deserve some bad luck, or some bad treatment from others. He'd told Guitar that he didn't 'deserve' his family's dependence, hatred, or whatever. That he didn't even 'deserve' to hear all the misery and mutual accusations his parents unloaded on him. Nor did he 'deserve' Hagar's vengeance" (276). As Milkman recognizes that he has selfishly refused to be responsible for the pain of others or to share their unhappiness, he feels "his self—the cocoon that was 'personality'"—give way. Alone in the dark in the woods where there is nothing to aid him—"not his money, his car, his father's reputation, his suit, or his shoes"—Milkman is stripped of his false class pride (277).

And yet, ironically enough, just as Milkman feels a "sudden rush of affection" for other people and believes he really understands his friend, Guitar, who has been "maimed" and "scarred" by his past (278), Guitar attempts to kill Milkman, and almost succeeds. "Your Day has come," Guitar tells Milkman as he fastens a wire around Milkman's throat (279) only to be scared off by the close sound of the baying dogs, who have treed a bobcat. Later, during the ritualized skinning of the bobcat, Milkman recalls Guitar's words: "*Everybody wants a black man's life. . . . Not his dead life; I mean his living life. . . . It's the condition our condition is in*" (281–82). That Guitar is associated with the predatory bobcat—for Guitar is described as a "natural-born hunter," as someone who has catlike movements and who can see like a cat with his "phosphorous" eyes (85, 118)—points to the narrative's embeddedness in hegemonic discourse. In describing Guitar as an instinctual, animallike killer, the narrative evokes the race- and class-coded stereotype of the lower-class black male as a potentially dangerous predator. Adding to the complexity of this scene, the bobcat (hunter) also signifies the traumatized black male (the hunted), who is preyed on by white society or by lynch mobs who want the life of a black man or who, like Milkman, is the victim of black-on-black violence. Indeed, during the skinning of the bobcat, just before Milkman pulls out the animal's heart, he recalls Guitar's earlier explanation that he engages in revenge killings because he loves black people, words that come back to haunt Milkman after his friend has attempted to kill him: "*It is about love. What else but love? Can't I love what I criticize?*" (282; see 223).

If, as it is sometimes claimed, the bobcat hunt is consciously patterned after an Africanized, tribal hunting ritual in which the initiate, Milkman, comes into his black manhood—and, indeed, Milkman is suggestively rewarded with the heart of the bobcat—the narrative also deliberately undercuts Milkman's moment of manly pride by interjecting into this scene a peacock, which was established earlier in the text as a signifier of false male pride (283; see 179). The narrative also sends out mixed messages in its description of Milkman's discovery of his true family name as he decodes the children's song—the song of Solomon—which is the original version of Pilate's blues song. Milkman is initially elated when he learns that his grandfather, Macon Dead, was Jake, the son of the flying African—Solomon—who left his wife and twenty-one children and flew back to Africa. "That motherfucker could fly! Could fly! . . . He could fly his own self! . . . He just took off; got fed up. *All the way up!* . . . No more shit! He flew, baby" (328). But to fly away is also, the narrative insists, to place individual needs above the family, and, by extension, the community. "Who'd he leave behind?" Sweet asks Milkman. "Everybody! He left everybody down on the ground and he sailed on off like a black eagle. 'O-o-o-o-o-o Solomon done fly, Solomon done gone / Solomon cut across the sky, Solomon gone home!'" (328–29). The "Song of Solomon" is, at once, a song of male pride and shame, for as Morrison herself has remarked, "The fathers may soar, they may triumph, they may leave, but the children know who they are; they remember, *half in glory and half in accusation*" (Watkins 46, emphasis added). Thus flying—the proud and glorious moment of escape from the "shit" of racial shame—is also associated with the blaming, shaming accusations of those left behind. In a similar way, as Milkman takes pride in his family name, the narrative also reminds readers of the painful, shameful racist legacy of African-American names, names that people got "from yearnings, gestures, flaws, events, mistakes, weaknesses. Names that bore witness. Macon Dead . . . Pilate, Reba, Hagar, Magdalene, First Corinthians, Milkman, Guitar . . . Cock-a-Doodle-Doo, Cool Breeze, Muddy Waters, Pinetop,

Jelly Roll, Fats, Leadbelly, Bo Diddley . . . Shine, Staggerlee, Jim the Devil, Fuck-Up and *Dat* Nigger" (330).

The text's hesitancies and ambivalences—which originate in its painful emotional content—are given final expression in the closing scenes. "Perhaps that's what all human relationships boiled down to: Would you save my life? or would you take it?" Milkman thinks when he realizes that a "deranged" Guitar is after him (331, 330). In an uncanny repetition of family trauma, the trauma-haunted Pilate is killed by Guitar after she buries her father's remains on Solomon's Leap. Pilate's final words are healing. "I wish I'd a knowed more people. I would of loved 'em all," she tells Milkman. "If I'd a knowed more, I would a loved more" (336). Constructed as an ancestor figure in this scene— as an embodiment of folk wisdom and natural pride—Pilate can fly without leaving the ground. And yet the killing of Pilate—the character designated by the narrative as a natural healer—suggests the text's inability to heal the deep emotional wounds that result from collective black shame and trauma.

"'You want my life? . . . You need it? Here.' Without wiping away the tears, taking a deep breath, or even bending his knees—he leaped. As fleet and bright as a lodestar he wheeled toward Guitar and it did not matter which one of them would give up his ghost in the killing arms of his brother. For now he knew what Shalimar knew: If you surrendered to the air, you could *ride* it" (337). Despite the positive rhetoric of the closure, which depicts Milkman's heroic flight and his manly confrontation with the murderous Guitar, Milkman's leap can also be read as a suicidal and nihilistic gesture: an enactment of Milkman's wish to disappear and thus escape the "shit" of his chronic shame. Moreover, the fact that Milkman's search for his African-American roots ends in a traumatic assault sends out the covert message that the middle-class African-American male cannot truly understand his racial heritage without experiencing, firsthand, what trauma specialists have referred to as the "black hole" of trauma (van der Kolk, "Foreword" ix). But the narrative, as we can see in the critical conversation surrounding the closure, also generates a powerful—and text-directed—wish to see Milkman rescued and to turn shame into pride. By deliberately withholding information—the reader does not know if Milkman will live or die—the closure poses a crisis of interpretation and compels reader involvement in concluding what remains inconclusive and in completing the emotional work the text began in its exploration of black male shame and pride.

Presenting a cognitive puzzle at the end, Morrison compels readers to think and she also involves them emotionally in the text's shame–pride drama. Some critics, in insisting on Milkman's failure at the end, read an implicit shame drama in the closure. According to this view, Milkman's flight is "destined to be either suicidal or murderous," and "however changed by his experiences," he "plunges, in darkness, to the earth" (Bowman 13). While Morrison's prose is celebratory, writes another critic, behind the "seemingly upbeat ending of her novel lies Morrison's disdain for Milkman," and when he leaps "into Guitar's arms and certain death," his action is irresponsible, for he avoids "doing something meaningful in life, preferring the sumptuous illusion that he will ride the air" (Brenner 119). But although the narrative seems unable to transform, in any permanent way, shame into pride, most critic-readers follow the text's directives and interpret the closure as a heroic gesture and thus an affirmation of black pride and achievement. Such commentators assert that Milkman's final gesture "affirms his relation to Solomon and Pilate" and as a "'lodestar' setting his own course, he meets them in their mythic and elemental flight," or they argue that Milkman, in his final flight, is able to "transcend death" and "embrace the life of humanity" (Carmean 61, O'Shaughnessy 125). Since Milkman "has achieved … connectedness" to his African-American community, "it does not matter whether Milkman survives his encounter with Guitar," writes one commentator (Duvall, "Doe Hunting" 111). And yet another asserts, "The novel does not end with a cliff-hanger; the final battle is both a confrontation and a confirmation, marking Milkman's emergence as a champion who understands and will defend his world," and whether or not Milkman dies, his "joyful acceptance of the burden of his past transforms his leap toward Guitar into a triumphant flight" (A. Leslie Harris 71, 76).

That most critic-readers enact an antishaming gesture as they turn shame into pride suggests that *Song of Solomon* generates in some readers the wish to rescue the character and also to avoid the painful content of the novel by reading it primarily as an ultimately triumphant "heroic" quest. Because shame is a contagious emotion and, indeed, people are ashamed of shame, critic-readers may feel at once riveted to the text, which appeals to readers' voyeuristic interests, but also want to avert their gaze—that is, avoid or bypass the shameful content of the novel. The novel itself, while shaming the bourgeois Dead family, also bypasses shame by de-emphasizing the shameful legacy of slavery that haunts African Americans in its suggestion that the real gold Milkman seeks is the *golden* legacy of his racial heritage. Indeed, the myth of the Flying African encapsulates the fantasy-wish to escape or bypass the "shit" of racial oppression and shame and also the desire to convert shame into pride.

There may be something golden in the survival of the slaves and of family stories about one's black family roots in slavery, but slavery also constitutes a shameful and largely secret legacy in the African-American cultural memory. In *Song of Solomon*, Morrison focuses on intraracial shaming, the color-caste hierarchy, and black-on-black violence as she depicts the effects

of shame and trauma on the lives of African Americans and on the construction of African-American cultural and political identities. While Morrison,
in *Song of Solomon*, is also invested in extending the black cultural imagination and memory by looking back to African-American "roots" in slavery,
she will carry out the emotional and cultural work of fully confronting the
catastrophic and painful issue of slavery later, in *Beloved*. There she will bear
witness to the horrors of slavery and racist oppression, which "dirtied" the
selves of the slaves, as she attempts to aesthetically confront and begin to
heal the deep and abiding wounds inflicted on black Americans in our race-
divided American culture.

NOTES

1. Because group inclusion "is necessary for human survival, showing and
detecting shame have survival value," according to Scheff. People need to feel connected, and shame "automatically signals a threat to the safety of [the] *social self*"
(*Bloody Revenge* 51). The emotions of shame and pride, which "have a unique status
relative to social relationships," are not infrequent but, instead, are "an almost continuous part of human existence not only in crises but also in the slightest of social
contacts" (*Bloody Revenge* 3, 51).

2. In *The Color Complex: The Politics of Skin Color Among African Americans*
(1992), Kathy Russell, Midge Wilson, and Ronald Hall provide a detailed history
of color prejudice in the United States and they also discuss its persistence into the
1990s. They point out that "the desire for lighter skin is nearly universal. Throughout Central and South America, Asia, and even Africa, society is prejudiced against
those with dark skin, especially young dark women. Various theories for this have
been advanced, but in a race-stratified society like America the consequences have
long been clear. Before the Civil War, the degree of pigmentation could mean the
difference between living free and enslavement, and since then variations in skin
color and features have divided the educated from the ignorant, the well-off from
the poor, the 'attractive' from the 'plain'" (41).

Charles Parrish, in a 1940s study of skin-color stereotyping in African-
American teenagers, discovered that junior high students employed "as many as 145
different terms to describe skin color, including 'half-white,' 'yaller,' 'high yellow,'
'fair,' 'bright,' 'light,' 'red-bone,' 'light brown,' 'medium brown,' 'brown,' 'brownskin,'
'dark brown,' 'chocolate,' 'dark,' 'black,' 'ink spot,' 'blue black,' and 'tar baby.' Each
term was associated with a particular personality type: in general, light to medium
skin tones were linked to intelligence and refinement, while dark skin tones suggested toughness, meanness, and physical strength." Even though Parrish's study is
some fifty years old, "similar attitudes about skin color prevail among today's Black
youth. Many believe that light skin is feminine and dark skin is masculine, and very
light skinned boys and very dark skinned girls often suffer from being at odds with
this cultural stereotype" (66).

3. For some essays focusing on names and naming in the novel see Lucinda
MacKethan, Paula Rabinowitz, and Ruth Rosenberg, "And the Children." For some
representative discussions of Morrison's use of the monomyth of the hero see Patrick
Bjork, Gerry Brenner, Charles De Arman, Jacqueline de Weever, A. Leslie Harris,

Trudier Harris, *Fiction*, Dorothy Lee, Marilyn Mobley, *Folk Roots*, Wilfrid Samuels. Discussions of the novel's flight motif and its use of the folktale of the flying Africans (see, e.g., Susan Blake) are standard in the conversation surrounding the novel. For some recent discussions of the novel's representation of black oral culture and communal voices see Joyce Middleton and Marilyn Mobley, "Call and Response."

4. "The politics of hair parallels the politics of skin color" among African-American women, write the authors of *The Color Complex*, Kathy Russell, Midge Wilson, and Ronald Hall. "Among Black women," they explain, "straight hair and European hairstyles not only have been considered more feminine but have sent a message about one's standing in the social hierarchy. 'Good hair' has long been associated with the light-skinned middle class, 'bad hair' with Blacks who are less fortunate." Although the Afro hairstyle was popular in the 1960s, "the old attitudes about hair quickly resurfaced" after the sixties ended. "The tradition of calling hair that was straight and wavy 'good' and hair that was tightly curled and nappy 'bad' had never really gone away." And in the post-1960s world, "hair remains a politically charged subject. To some, how an African American chooses to style his or her hair says everything there is to be said about that individual's Black consciousness, socioeconomic class, and probable lifestyle, particularly when the individual is a woman" (82). See also Noliwe Rooks's *Hair Raising: Beauty, Culture, and African American Women*.

5. Remarking on the link between excretory epithets and shame, Donald Nathanson explains that shame expressions—such as, "piss on you," "pisser," "shit," "you little shit"—capture the moment of embarrassment when the shamed individual feels "infantile, weak, and dirty, unable to control . . . bodily functions." Although shame "is much more than just excretion," excretory epithets "are about shame" ("Shame/Pride Axis" 198).

6. As Utelinde Wedertz-Furtado points out, it is significant that Guitar remarks that the Seven Days organization originated after the blinding of a black veteran of World War I (see *Song of Solomon* 155). By linking 1920s black militancy to that of the 1960s, "Morrison suggests the cyclical rising of black militant groups after non-violent means have failed to guarantee justice and civil rights" (227). Ralph Story links the Seven Days to black secret societies of the nineteenth century, such as the Knights of Liberty, an organization that was formed in 1846 to free slaves (152). Guitar's advocacy of violence also recalls the militant rhetoric of the 1920s inspired by the black nationalism of Marcus Garvey. For example, one of Garvey's "chief lieutenants," Hubert Harrison, asserted, "If white men are to kill unoffending Negroes, Negroes must kill white men in defense of their lives and property." In the 1960s, black nationalist Malcolm X remarked, "Revolutions are never fought by turning the other cheek. . . . Revolutions are based upon bloodshed." And Vincent Harding, a radical voice in the 1960s Black Power movement, commented, "If we must fight, let it be on the streets where we have been humiliated. If we must burn down houses, let them be the homes and stores of our exploiters. If we must kill, let it be the fat, pious white Christians who guard their lawns and their daughters while engineering slow death for us. If we must die, let it be for a real cause, a cause of black men's freedom as black men define it" (Berry and Blassingame 410, 417, 419–20).

In the essay "The Psychopathic Racial Personality," the rhetoric of Garveyite Bobby Wright echoes Guitar's words about the depravity of whites. "[I]n their relationship with the Black race, Europeans (Whites) are psychopaths and their behavior reflects an underlying biologically transmitted proclivity with roots deep in their evolutionary history" (2). Since there is no evidence that Whites and Blacks can live together in peace—"without Whites attempting to oppress and exterminate the Blacks"—and since "Blacks are at war with psychopaths, *violence is the only way*" (13).

7. In his description of the "defending scripts" used to protect against shame, Gershen Kaufman explains that rage—"[w]hether in the form of generalized hostility, fomenting bitterness, chronic hatred, or explosive eruptions"—functions to protect the self against exposure and thus defends against shame. Like rage scripts, contempt scripts protect the self, for "[t]o the degree that others are looked down upon, found lacking or seen as lesser or inferior beings, a once-wounded self becomes more securely insulated against further shame" (*Psychology of Shame* 100). Moreover, power scripts, which aim at gaining power over others, also protect the self against shame. "When power scripts combine with rage and/or contempt scripts, the seeking of revenge is a likely outcome. . . . Now the humiliated one, at long last, will humiliate the other" (*The Psychology of Shame* 101).

8. In the dozens game, write Richard Majors and Janet Billson in *Cool Pose*, the players typically attack their opponents' families, especially mothers, in rhyme, and as the exchange becomes "progressively nasty and pornographic, virtually every family member and every sexual act is woven into the verbal assault" (93). In the verbal game, "humiliations are squeezed into rhyming couplets that testify to the player's ability to keep cool under mounting pressure" (92). For the African-American adolescent male, the dozens game "might be defined as a rite of passage because of the way it tests his control, character, and courage. In the final analysis, if he can handle the insults peers direct at his mother in the dozens, then it is likely he can take whatever insults society might hurl at him" (96).

JOHN N. DUVALL

Song of Solomon, *Narrative Identity,* *and the Faulknerian Intertext*

$\mathbf{A}$s the title of this chapter suggests, I believe that Morrison's intertextual engagement with canonical white modernist writing tells us something about her ongoing construction of authorial identity in her first four novels. Although I have speculated on Morrison's relation to Virginia Woolf in the previous chapter, I have waited until this moment to consider more fully the implications of what it means to read an African-American writer in the context of white writing. My reason for doing so is largely pragmatic. Since completing her master's thesis in 1955, Morrison has had much more to say about William Faulkner's fiction than about Woolf's; the very quantity of Morrison's commentary on Faulkner, therefore, provides the source material for developing an understanding of her relation to high modernism.

In fact it was at the 1985 Faulkner and Yoknapatawpha Conference in Oxford, Mississippi, that Morrison once again elaborated a self-representation regarding her relation to her published fiction, the story in which she continues to be the writer who was almost a writer. Although in 1983 she claimed she knew she was a writer after completing *Sula*, in 1985 Morrison gives a different account of when her sense of herself as a writer emerged:

> And it was only with my third book, *Song of Solomon*, that I finally said [. . .] "this is what I do." I had written three books. It was only

From *The Identifying Fictions of Toni Morrison: Modernist Authenticity and Postmodern Blackness*, pp. 71–98, 159–162. © 2000 by John N. Duvall.

after I finished *Song of Solomon* that I thought, "maybe this is what I do *only*." Because before that I always said that I was an editor *who* also wrote books or a teacher *who* also wrote. I never said I was a writer. ("Faulkner" 301)

But even without a consideration of the way her third novel gives access to a portion of her aesthetic autobiography, one can still acknowledge that *Song of Solomon* intensely foregrounds the processes of identity formation in the novel's central character, Milkman Dead. It does so, unlike her first two novels, on decidedly male grounds. From the novel's one-word dedication (Daddy), Morrison draws upon a transfigured representation of her own family history, emphasizing male genealogy. The novel's very title derives from what Morrison herself has called the "genuinely autobiographical," as I discussed in chapter 1, since her maternal grandfather was John Solomon Willis.[1] The portrait of "Lincoln's Heaven," the farm that had belonged to Milkman's grandfather in Pennsylvania, is in fact drawn from stories Morrison knew about her own grandfather's farm, eighty-eight acres given to Morrison's great-grandmother during Reconstruction. "The land got legally entangled," Morrison tells Colette Dowling, "because of some debts my grandfather, who inherited it, owed—or, rather, didn't know he owed. It was like the old man in *Song of Solomon*. Those people didn't really understand what was happening. All they knew is that at one point they didn't own the land anymore and had to work for the person who did" (54). Like Morrison's family, the Dead family migrates to the Midwest in order to escape racism and violence.

The locale of the novel's opening initially suggests a distance from Morrison's Lorain, Ohio, set as it is in Michigan. For years I have assumed that the setting of part I was Detroit, though that does not seem to square with the geography of the state. On closer examination, it appears that it is a Michigan of the imagination, not one locatable on any map. The novel's first sentence creates a problem when Robert Smith announces his intention to fly "to the other side of Lake Superior" (3). This implies that his point of departure is on the opposite side of the lake, yet the only part of Michigan touching Superior is the Upper Peninsula, a place where very few African Americans live. While it does seem significant that Smith wishes to fly to Canada, that site of freedom for African Americans escaping slavery, it probably is a pointless exercise attempting to name the precise Michigan locale (could it be working-class Marion or Port Huron?). What this ambiguous geographical reference points to is that, fictively speaking, Morrison hasn't left home yet. Morrison seems to confirm the irrelevance of specific locale in a comment she makes to Jane Bakerman at the time of *Song of Solomon*'s publication: "I think I call [the setting] Michigan; they sort of travel around a little bit. But all of mine start here in the Midwest!" (39). Milkman's Michigan, Morrison's comment suggests, is but a minor displacement from the novelist's Ohio and her own working-class, Great Lakes town of Lorain. Yet although Morrison metaphorically stays at home, leaving home is precisely what Milkman Dead thinks he wants.

In this regard, *Song of Solomon* participates in and arguably completes Morrison's fictive meditation on those aspects of authorship that are linked to the cultural masculine. Soaphead Church opens the space of writerly self-examination; Shadrack pushes this reflexive examination into the realm of communal ritual. But Morrison's third novel is a departure from the first two in its focus on a male character, Milkman Dead, a name that had served as the working title for *Song of Solomon*. In bringing African-American male identity to the foreground, Anthony/Toni has performed a daring experiment with gender that her act of self-naming suggests: *Song of Solomon* is a portrait of the African-American woman novelist as a young *man*. Beginning on Morrison's date of birth, the novel takes us through the first thirty-two years of Milkman's life. What is striking is how this time frame corresponds to the fictional Milkman's real-life double, Toni Morrison. Milkman's story stops at the moment of a completed project of self-discovery, authenticity, and connection to his ancestors. Like another novel published in 1977, Leslie Marmon Silko's *Ceremony*, *Song of Solomon* tells of a movement from alienation to authenticity. In Morrison's life, the time of the novel's ending (1963) corresponds to a time of upheaval—a marriage that had soured, an impending divorce, and an almost therapeutic turn to fiction as she joins a writer's group. In short, Milkman is represented as having achieved an authentic identity at the very moment when Morrison begins her search for identity through her writing, and he undergoes the same self-examination crucial to other Morrison characters, such as Soaphead Church, Sula, Pilate, and subsequently Jadine Childs in *Tar Baby*.

In a novel that focuses on matters of African-American masculine identity, it is worth speculating on such identity as it may relate to Morrison's sense of authorial identity. If Morrison engages Ralph Ellison intertextually in *The Bluest Eye*, a similar project of reclamation occurs in *Song of Solomon*. Only now it is Faulkner, whose major texts examine the forces that shape the identity of Southern white men, who is the focus of Morrison's gaze.

The Faulknerian intertext, however, is not as overtly signaled as the biblical intertext of *Song of Solomon*. Morrison's act of naming her third novel at first suggests the kind of mythic intertext that James Joyce invokes in *Ulysses*. But the biblical intertext of Morrison's title does not supply the kind of narrative context that *The Odyssey* provides Joyce. In this regard, Morrison's act of titling her third novel may be more akin to E. L. Doctorow's titling his fictive reexamination of the Rosenberg executions *The Book of Daniel*—that is, an evocative rendering of the narrator's stance toward the story related. The biblical poem of Solomon does suggest certain ways of thinking about Morrison's novel: both Solomon's song and the song Milkman discovers that sings his family's African genealogy detail sexual suffering. The dialogue between the lovers in the biblical text speaks to Milkman's relationship with Hagar, just as Morrison's meditation on American culture's reification of color makes the woman's assertion, "I am very dark, but comely" (Song Sol. 1.5), resonate in a culturally fresh way. At the same time, the verse also points to the way that skin color can signify in the African-American community. But in *Song of Solomon*, the explicit intertext of Morrison's act of titling deflects attention away from her reading and recasting of Faulkner, a project that continues even into Morrison's later fiction, which is more invested in recovering African-American history. To approach Morrison with Faulkner as one context is to hear a critical dialogue that can be taken as an African-American reclamation of canonical modernism.

In a novel as obsessed with names and naming as *Song of Solomon*, including the potential of names to subvert white authority, one passage particularly suggests one way to begin thinking about Morrison and Faulkner. Macon Dead, who bears his father's name (itself the product of a mistake on a post–Civil War form), walks by his sister's house: "Surely, he thought, he and his sister had some ancestor, some lithe young man with onyx skin and legs as straight as cane stalks, who had a name that was real. A name given to him at birth with love and seriousness" (17).

Macon's desire for an authentic name is shared by a character in Faulkner's *Go Down, Moses*:

> not *Lucius Quintus @c @c @c*, but *Lucas Quintus*, not refusing to be called Lucius, because he simply eliminated that word from the name; not denying, declining the name itself, because he used three quarters of it; but simply taking the name and changing, altering it, making it no longer the white man's but his own, by himself composed, himself self progenitive and nominate, by himself ancestored [. . .]. (269)

Faulkner's Lucas Beauchamp, the descendant of a white plantation owner's incestuous miscegenation and perhaps Faulkner's most complex rendering of African-American masculinity, speaks to the possibilities of self-fashioning. Like Morrison, Faulkner changed his name, adding the "u" to his patronymic as a symbolic act of self-fathering. Morrison's reference to John Solomon Willis, her maternal grandfather, is interesting, inasmuch as she appropriates his middle name. It is, as I pointed out previously, the middle name of her maternal grand*mother* Ardelia Willis, that Morrison transforms into the masculine "Anthony" to provide the ostensible genesis for "Toni." This curious need to construct identity through the name links Billy Falkner/ William Faulkner to Chloe/Toni and serves as a metonymy for a larger relationship between the two Nobel prize-winning authors.

Any discussion of Morrison's work in relation to modernism (or post-modernism) in general or to Faulkner in particular is likely to be met with misunderstanding. To speak of a Faulknerian intertext in Morrison's fiction runs the risk not only that some readers will see this as an attempt to question her genius, but also of calling up images of racial and sexual abuse in the American past.[2] Does not the very positing of such a relationship imply that, without a white Southern male's seminal texts, those of an African-American woman would never have come to fruition? But arguing for an intertextual relationship between Morrison and Faulkner does not require granting Faulkner's the status of master text. In fact, my purpose is not a discussion of Faulkner's influence on Morrison but rather to suggest how reading Morrison reshapes the way one reads Faulkner.[3]

The point of examining the relation between Morrison and Faulkner certainly should not be to measure Morrison on the yardstick of a Faulkner but rather to understand how her texts reclaim those of the modernists.[4] The broader notions of intertextuality, emphasizing the infinitely resonating signification of language, mean that one can validly read not only Faulkner's influence on Morrison, but also Morrison's influence on Faulkner—how her fiction and literary criticism may cause one to rethink Faulkner in a fundamental way. This is a point Aldon L. Nielsen has made in his work on race and intertextuality:

> We read Melville within the text of Ralph Ellison's *Invisible Man*, but we must also read Melville differently because of Ellison's text. We must read the transcendence of Ralph Waldo Emerson alongside our reading of the blackness of Huck Finn. We must attempt to understand what the Middle Passage means in black consciousness, and how it means differently in the texts of Harriet Beecher Stowe, and how her texts figure differently when read by black writers. (24)

Nielsen's insistence that the texts of black and white writers must be read against each other develops both from his critique of the way liberal pluralism maintains a sub rosa racial essentialism and from his understanding that race is an unstable social construction:

The races, and their signifiers, exist only in relation to all other points in our systems of racial signifying. Just as the terms *black* and *white* serve, not, as observation will always confirm, to denote clearly demarcated differences in skin pigmentation, but to organize the meanings of human lives beneath constructed racial rubrics, so do language practices recognized as racially motivated among native speakers serve to carve up territories of racial connotation rather than to reflect preexistent cultural facts. (7)

In this chapter, my intertextual reading hopes to extend Nielsen's project to the specificity of Toni Morrison and William Faulkner. Both Faulkner's and Morrison's representations of racial identity emerge in the liminal space between blackness and whiteness and the communal urge (both black and white) to deny the brute material fact of the mixture of the races.

African-American literary theory and criticism, however, frequently make problematic the issue of race and intertextuality through a politically understandable urge to focus solely on African-American texts, a part of the aesthetic past that historically has not received equal status or attention. Taking their cue from Morrison herself, some argue that the most appropriate frame for assessing her literary work is an African-American folk and oral tradition.[5] In his work on the theory of African-American literature, Henry Louis Gates, Jr., does acknowledge that African-American writers revise texts by white writers with "a sense of difference based on the black vernacular" (*Signifying* xxii). His project, however, is to understand the "web of filiation" created when black writers reinvent the tropes of other black writers (*Signifying* xxii). This is precisely the work Michael Awkward takes up in *Inspiriting Influences*, an illuminating study of African-American women writer's use of the black aesthetic past.

In her book on Morrison, Denise Heinze follows Gates's and Awkward's position on what texts should be read as the intertext of African-American fiction. Using W. E. B. Du Bois's famous discussion of black American "identity" in *The Souls of Black Folk* as an always divided "double-consciousness," Heinze notes that double-consciousness may intersect with Bakhtin's double-voicedness, the Russian theorist's trope for intertextuality. Still, for Heinze, the issue is quite clear: "Morrison's double-consciousness cannot ultimately be explained in terms of her relationship to the dominant culture" (10). She turns to Awkward's reading of *The Bluest Eye* to support this claim; for Awkward, Morrison's novel needs to be understood in relation to other African-American texts that represent Du Bois's notion of double-consciousness, particularly Hurston's *Their Eyes Were Watching God*. Despite Morrison's claim not to have read Hurston until after the publication of *The Bluest Eye*,

Heinze concurs with Awkward's thesis that Morrison's novels function as refigurations of the African-American aesthetic past (Heinze 10–11). Awkward's linking of Morrison and Hurston does not need to depend on Morrison's reading of Hurston, since such a reading strategy is already legitimated by theories of intertextuality, whether Eurocentric (Bakhtin's double-voicedness, Kristeva's mosaic of quotations, Barthes' authorless text) or Afrocentric (Gates's Signifyin[g]).

While not wishing to gainsay the value of Heinze's approach, I would nevertheless suggest that the converse of her claim also has a legitimacy: *the double-consciousness of Toni Morrison's work cannot ultimately be understood without some consideration of its relation to the dominant culture.* More overtly than any relation to Hurston's work, Toni Morrison's fiction resonates with that of William Faulkner, a writer whose canonical status clearly marks him as a part of the dominant culture. Before considering some of these fictional resonances, however, I would like to examine a different sort of evidence. Morrison herself in a number of forums has commented upon Faulkner's fiction. Morrison's remarks about the relation of her work to Faulkner's show a decided ambivalence. His influence is at times affirmed, at times denied, at times simultaneously affirmed and denied. That she has read Faulkner closely and carefully is undeniable, so the question of Morrison's relation to Faulkner in some sense turns on what it means that a writer is always inescapably also a reader. In 1955, as a master's student at Cornell, Morrison completed her thesis, "Virginia Woolf's and William Faulkner's Treatment of the Alienated." Her sixteen-page chapter on Faulkner focuses primarily on Thomas Sutpen and Quentin Compson. In *Absalom, Absalom!* and *The Sound and the Fury*, Morrison sees "elements of Greek tragedy," such as "the fall of a once great house" and "old family guilts inherited by an heir"; moreover, "the fact that incest plays such an important part ... is evidence that Faulkner patterns these histories after the Greeks" ("Virginia" 24). What these comments point to, I believe, is that any piece of writing (even the academic prose of a master's thesis) is always unavoidably a form of intellectual autobiography, no matter how little the autobiographical impulse forms part of the writer's intentions. We might say, for example, that Morrison's previous work on the classics as an undergraduate at Howard University prepared her to make the kinds of claims she does in her master's thesis about Faulkner. So that when one sees incest and family history as elements of Morrison's fictional matter in, say, *The Bluest Eye* or *Song of Solomon*, one need not attribute this presence to Faulkner per se nor even to Greek tragedy. The relation between Morrison's texts and those of the aesthetic past, therefore, is not determined but overdetermined. What this means from a reader's perspective is that numerous cultural texts examine incest and that this whole matrix of prior representations becomes available for a critical examination of what and how incest might mean in Morrison's work.

In the first published interview in which Morrison mentions Faulkner, she bristles at Thomas LeClair's suggestion that some readers—white readers—will not understand a certain scene in *Sula*; says Morrison:

> There is a level of appreciation that might be available only to people who understand the context of the language. The analogy that occurs to me is jazz: it is open on the one hand and both complicated and inaccessible on the other. I never asked Tolstoy to write for me, a little colored girl in Lorain, Ohio. I never asked Joyce not to mention Catholicism or the world of Dublin. Never. And I don't know why I should be asked to explain your life to you. We have splendid writers to do that, but I am not one of them. It is that business of being universal, a word hopelessly stripped of meaning for me. Faulkner wrote what I suppose could be called regional literature and had it published all over the world. It is good—and universal—because it is specifically about a particular world. That's what I wish to do. (LeClair 124)

Her mild approval of Faulkner's fiction—its goodness depends on its representation of particularity—nevertheless signals her desire to put distance between herself and Faulkner, as well as other canonical novelists, and to position herself specifically as an African-American woman author writing the specificity of African-American experience. At the same time, the particular authors Morrison mentions (Tolstoy, Joyce, and Faulkner) reveal the scope of her ambition as a writer.

Morrison reiterates her difference more forcefully in an interview with Nellie McKay in 1983:

> Our—black women's—job is a particularly complex one [. . .]. We have no systematic mode of criticism that has yet evolved from us, but it will. I am not *like* James Joyce; I am not *like* Thomas Hardy; I am not *like* Faulkner. I am not *like* in that sense. I do not have objections to being compared to such extraordinarily gifted and facile writers, but it does leave me sort of hanging there when I know that my effort is to be *like* something that has probably only been fully expressed perhaps in music, or in some other culture-gen that survives almost in isolation because the community manages to hold on to it. (152)

In distinguishing herself from Faulkner, Hardy, and Joyce, Morrison stresses the particularity of African-American experience, from its aurality to its investment in the supernatural (152–53).

Both the LeClair and the McKay interviews, however, serve as a prelude to Morrison's much fuller treatments of the ways Faulkner may have influenced her. Morrison's remarks framing her reading from her then work-in-progress *Beloved* at the 1985 Faulkner and Yoknapatawpha Conference serve as one of the clearest instances of her ambivalence toward Faulkner. Prior to her reading she said, "there was for me not only an academic interest in Faulkner, but in a very, very personal way, in a very personal way as a reader, William Faulkner had an enormous effect on me, an enormous effect" ("Faulkner" 296).[6] But after her reading, in answer to the first question put to her regarding the effect Faulkner had on her literary career, Morrison responds:

> Well, I'm not sure that he had any effect on my work. I am typical, I think, of all writers who are convinced that they are wholly original and that if they recognized an influence they would abandon it as quickly as possible. [...] My reasons, I think, for being interested and deeply moved by all his subjects had something to do with my desire to find out something about this country and that artistic articulation of its past that was not available in history, which is what art and fiction can do but sometimes history refuses to do. [...] And there was something else about Faulkner which I can only call "gaze." He had a gaze that was different. It appeared, at that time, to be similar to a look, even a sort of staring, a refusal-to-look-away approach in his writing that I found admirable. At that time, in the '50s or the '60s, it never crossed my mind to write books. But then I did it, and I was very surprised myself that I was doing it, and I knew that I was doing it for some reasons that are not writerly ones. I don't really find strong connections between my work and Faulkner's. ("Faulkner" 296–97)

Morrison's attempt here to make Faulkner a "was"—to relegate his influence to her pre-writerly past—seems (especially in light of her subsequent comments about him) as unreliable as Faulkner's frequent claim to those who did not know better that he had never read Joyce, a claim undercut by others who heard Faulkner recite long passages of Joyce's work from memory (Blotner 287).

Still, in *Playing in the Dark*, Morrison's discussion of racial figuration in canonical literature by white authors—Cather, Poe, Twain, and

Hemingway—appears to give some credence to her claim that Faulkner has receded from her consciousness. His work is mentioned twice in passing, with only a brief elaboration in the conclusion of her discussion of *The Narrative of Arthur Gordon Pym* and *Huckleberry Finn*:

> We are reminded of other images at the end of literary journeys into the forbidden space of blackness. Does Faulkner's *Absalom, Absalom!*, after its protracted search for the telling African blood, leave us with just such an image of snow and the eradication of race? Not quite. Shreve sees himself as the inheritor of the blood of African kings; the snow apparently is the wasteland of unmeaning, unfathomable whiteness. (58)

This general omission of Faulkner's texts in *Playing in the Dark*, however, does not mean that Faulkner has fallen away from her field of vision; indeed at another level Faulkner reappears in Morrison's critical text through her reading of Faulkner criticism.[7] Her development of "the common linguistic strategies employed in fiction to engage the serious consequences of blacks" draws liberally on James A. Snead's book on Faulkner, *Figures of Division* (*Playing* 66–69).

If Faulkner belongs only to Morrison's past, then what does one make of her comments regarding her experiences teaching *Absalom, Absalom!* from a 1993 interview in *The Paris Review*?

> Faulkner in *Absalom, Absalom!* spends the entire book tracing race, and you can't find it. No one can see it, even the character who is black can't see it. I did this lecture for my students that took me forever, which was tracking all the moments of withheld, partial or disinformation, when a racial fact or clue *sort* of comes out but doesn't quite arrive. I just wanted to chart it. I listed its appearance, disguise and disappearance on every page, I mean every phrase! […] Do you know how hard it is to withhold that kind of information but hinting, pointing all of the time? And then to reveal it in order to say that it is *not* the point anyway? It is technically just astonishing. As a reader you have been forced to hunt for a drop of black blood that means everything and nothing. The insanity of racism. So the structure is the argument. […] No one has done anything quite like that ever. So, when I critique, what I am saying is, I don't care if Faulkner was a racist or not; I don't personally care, but I am fascinated by what it means to write like this. (Schappell 101)

Clearly, Morrison still reads Faulkner. And if she still turns to Faulkner's texts, how is she to contain that "very personal" and "enormous effect" ("Faulkner" 296)? Does Faulkner exist for her as a reader, as a teacher, as a critic, but not as writer? This writerly desire to deny influence leads Morrison to a compartmentalizing of self and identity that belies her portrayals of characters who overcome such fragmentation.

Indeed, Morrison's denial of Faulkner's influence on her as a writer contradicts one of the central enabling claims of her critical project in *Playing in the Dark*. She contends that she developed the ability to see moments of racial figuration that literary critics cannot only after she stopped "reading as a reader and began to read as a writer" (*Playing* 15). It is this fundamental difference, she believes, that allows her, as "a writer reading," to understand that "the subject of the dream is the dreamer"; her insistence on a special understanding of "how language arrives" for a writer produces insightful speculations regarding how Cather may have struggled over her representation of Till in *Sapphira and the Slave Girl* or what writerly conflict Hemingway might have experienced by silencing an African-American character in *To Have and Have Not* (*Playing* 17). If one removes the burden of authorial consciousness from these two moments, Morrison's insights still stand, perhaps more clearly, as instances of the way racial ideology functions both in Cather's and Hemingway's texts and more broadly in their particular cultural moment. My point is, simply, that when Morrison claims, as she does in *The Paris Review* interview, that her classroom critique of Faulkner proceeds from being "fascinated by what it means to write like" Faulkner, she is reading the same way she reads Cather and Hemingway—as a writer reading. It may be a useful and enabling fiction for Morrison to see her novels as unmarked by Faulkner. Nevertheless, the rhetorical separation between reader and writer that Morrison wishes to maintain in her critical discourse largely collapses.

As a step toward seeing Morrison as a writer reading Faulkner, I wish to consider her *Song of Solomon* as a rewriting of Faulkner's *Go Down, Moses*. The critical dialogue in which *Song of Solomon* engages *Go Down, Moses* suggests that she reclaims Faulkner in ways that question the male-centered world of the hunt and that refuse the gambit of tragedy.

*   *   *

In her master's thesis, Morrison's characterization of Thomas Sutpen's and Quentin Compson's alienated relation to history also accurately describes Isaac McCaslin's alienation from his past as he comes of age in a defeated South and discovers in the ledgers the horror of his grandfather's incest and miscegenation ("Alienation" 24). Her own character, Milkman Dead, in *Song of Solomon*, similarly comes of age alienated from his family's history, almost as a result, one might say, of patriarchs such as Lucius Quintus Carothers McCaslin, whose forced mixture of the races in Mississippi results in the special status accorded lighter-skinned African Americans in Milkman Dead's Michigan. In other words, Ike's family problem, as he confronts the racism of the white community, is too much history; Milkman's difficulty in seeing the racism within the African-American community (at least in part I) is not enough history. But while *Go Down, Moses* is another tragedy (inasmuch as Roth Edmonds repeats his great-great-great grandfather's incestuous miscegenation, the act that motivated Isaac's repudiation in the first place), *Song of Solomon*, although similarly structured by intergenerational repetitions, finds Milkman ultimately breaking free of certain destructive cycles of the Dead family and Western patriarchal social organization.[8]

A number of other parallels invite a consideration of these two narratives together. In both novels, the male protagonists apparently come to some transcendent moment while hunting, for hunting is something more than the literal stalking of animals; the hunted animals in both are totemic substitutes for characters. Both novels blur boundaries between the natural and supernatural worlds. But perhaps most important, the creation of the adult subjectivity of Isaac McCaslin in *Go Down, Moses* and Milkman Dead in *Song of Solomon* serves as the site of conflict and competition. Certainly those who struggle to create Isaac's and Milkman's subjectivities bear certain parallels. Macon Dead, for example, approximates McCaslin Edmonds, while Guitar and Pilate split the function of Sam Fathers.[9]

In *Go Down, Moses*, McCaslin Edmonds speaks the paternal voice of the Old South, inviting Isaac to take his rightful place in L. Q. C. McCaslin's patriarchal design. Similarly, Macon hopes to create in Milkman a son who will approve of the middle-class values Macon has adopted. Undoubtedly, Macon's perspective on life is best summarized in his words to his twelve-year-old son upon finding that Milkman has disobeyed him by visiting Pilate:

> After school come to my office; work a couple of hours there and learn what's real. Pilate can't teach you a thing you can use in this world. Maybe the next, but not this one. Let me tell you right now the one important thing you'll ever need to know: Own things. And let the things you own own other things. Then you'll own yourself and other people too. (55)

What of course is chilling in Macon's pedagogical moment, teaching his son the path toward self-possession, is that the father, himself the son of a former slave, advocates owning others as a component of self-possession.

Macon's teachings are subverted, however, from two directions—by his sister Pilate and by Milkman's friend Guitar—and their presence together seems to constitute a play on Faulkner's Sam Fathers, the former slave who ultimately teaches Ike McCaslin an alternative to owning things. Both Pilate and Guitar act as Milkman's guides to ostensibly different world pictures—Pilate, the part-Native American advocate of the rights of ghosts, and Guitar, the materialist who wishes to awaken Milkman to African Americans' real conditions of existence. Although Macon, the bourgeois fetishizer of material, seems to recognize the threat Pilate poses to his desire to shape his son, the unacknowledged threat that resides in Guitar's friendship with Milkman forms the basis of much of the novel's plot.

Guitar Baines, removed from the well-heeled world of Not Doctor Street, acts as Milkman's guide to the wilderness of Southside, where the African-American underclass lives. The novel's opening underscores the importance Guitar will have as Milkman's guide and mentor. When Milkman's mother, Ruth, goes into labor, Guitar is sent around to the emergency room to fetch help (7). Later, at age seventeen, Guitar befriends the twelve-year-old Milkman and from that moment, Guitar is always there for his young friend. That the older boy befriends a younger one is unusual, but the friendship is odder still when we recall that approximately seven years earlier Macon turned Guitar's family out on the street for not paying their rent.

Why, then, does Guitar want to claim Milkman? As a member of the Seven Days, a secret society that hunts down and kills whites for the murders of African Americans that go unnoticed by white justice, Guitar is forbidden to marry and will never have a son. Milkman represents the possibility of creating an ideological heir, just as Sam Fathers sees Ike as the hope for a spiritual heir. (Sam, the son of a light-skinned slave woman and a Chickasaw chief, has a genealogy similar to what Milkman discovers about racial mixing in the Dead Family. Faulkner's novel, however, emphasizes male genealogy, so that despite Sam's racial mix, he clearly identifies himself through his father as "Indian.") The childless and dispossessed Sam Fathers effects a refiliation by subverting the teachings of McCaslin, offering instead both practical and mystical knowledge of the wilderness. In effect, Sam has managed to make an heir of a member of the dominant class that dispossessed the Chickasaws; as a consequence of Ike's appropriating Faulkner's conception of a Native-American world picture, the young man repudiates his white past and patrimony. Guitar's coup would be just as great as Sam's were he to succeed. Milkman's status as a member of the African-American middle class makes him an attractive conquest to Guitar. What finer ideological offspring could Guitar wish for than the son of the man who dispossessed the Baines family? What is at stake, then, in Macon's and Guitar's struggle to claim Milkman is

whether Milkman will grow up to be "white" or a "black"; that is, will Milkman accept the values of the African-American middle class, which models itself on white middle-class American culture, or will Milkman cast his
lot with the African-American community? Here again, Morrison seems to
equate black authenticity with black poverty, for the only African-American
communities in the *Song of Solomon* are economically distressed.

One particular moment when Guitar tries to comfort his friend
occurs after Milkman strikes Macon for hitting Ruth, Milkman's mother.
Guitar's sympathy takes the form of a brief narrative based on his hunting
experience:

> Anyway I stayed on the trail until I saw some bushes. The light
> was good and all of a sudden I saw a rump between the branches.
> I dropped it with the first shot and finished it with the next. Now,
> I want to tell you I was feeling good. I saw myself showing my
> uncles what I'd caught. But when I got up to it—and I was going
> real slow because I thought I might have to shoot it again—I saw
> it was a doe. [...] I felt ... bad. You know what I mean? I killed a
> doe. A doe, man. [...]
>
> So I know how you felt when you saw your father hit your
> mother. It's like that doe. A man shouldn't do that. You couldn't
> help what you felt. (85)

Guitar's story would certainly be understood by Ike McCaslin, who knows
that the hunter must not kill does because they, more than bucks, insure that
there will be deer to kill in the future. But in "Delta Autumn," doe hunting takes on a number of meanings. For one of the men, it is a way to tease
Roth Edmonds about the young African-American woman with whom
Edmonds has had an affair. Does, however, take on a different significance
for Ike (who does not yet know of Roth's affair) in the context of America's
imminent involvement in World War II: "It's a good time to mention does [
...]. Does and fawns both. The only fighting anywhere that ever had anything of God's blessing on it has been when men fought to protect does and
fawns" (323). But from the protection of women and children, the metaphor
returns by the story's end to the specificity of the young African-American
woman. After learning that his kinsman Roth Edmonds has repeated the
very act—incestuous miscegenation—that caused him, Ike, to repudiate his
patrimony, he intuits that the deer Roth has killed is a doe.

In both *Go Down, Moses* and *Song of Solomon*, then, killing a doe
metaphorically suggests hurting an African-American woman. Yet in
Guitar's realization that Milkman doesn't grasp the metaphor ("Chances

were Milkman didn't even know what a doe was" [86]), there seems a kind of wry intertextual gloss that calls into question the efficacy of the metaphor, a metaphor that suggests that the female's safety depends upon the honor of good male hunters. In particular, Guitar's metaphor sheds a different light on his membership in the Seven Days and his work of hunting and killing white people.

I wish to approach an understanding of Guitar's involvement in the Seven Days somewhat obliquely, holding in suspension the doe hunting metaphor and drawing temporarily on a different metaphor—that of urinating. On one of the Dead family's weekly Sunday drives when Milkman is a little boy, he asks his father to stop so that he can relieve himself. Milkman's sister Lena accompanies the boy. She returns in tears because Milkman has peed on her (34–35). By itself the moment is not significant. But at the end of part I, Lena, more than twenty-five years later, recalls the moment for Milkman and turns it into a metaphor for the thoughtless way he has treated the women of the family, since "there are all kinds of ways to pee on people" (214):

> You've been laughing at us all your life. Corinthians. Mama. Me. Using us, ordering us, and judging us. . . . You don't know a single thing about either one of us—we made roses; that's all you knew—but now you know what's best for the very woman who wiped the dribble from your chin because you were too young to know how to spit. Our girlhood was spent like a found nickel on you. When you slept, we were quiet; when you were hungry, we cooked; when you wanted to play, we entertained you; and when you got grown enough to know the difference between a woman and a two-toned Ford, everything in this house stopped for you. You have yet to wash your own underwear, spread a bed, wipe the ring from your tub, or move a fleck of your dirt from one place to another. And to this day, you have never asked one of us if we were tired, or sad, or wanted a cup of coffee. You've never picked up anything heavier than your own feet, or solved a problem harder than fourth-grade arithmetic. Where do you get the *right* to decide our lives? (215)

When Milkman fails to answer the question, Lena continues: "I'll tell you where. From that hog's gut that hangs down between your legs" (215). Something more than Milkman's literal phallus, however, grants him authority within the family, and Lena recognizes this too. Again we are pointed back to the moment Milkman strikes his father. Lena concludes: "You are exactly like him. [. . .] You think because you hit him once that we all believe you were protecting [our mother]. Taking her side. It's a lie.

You were taking over, letting us know you had the right to tell her and all of us what to do" (215–16). The reproduction of the father-function and the preservation of patriarchal privilege reside in Milkman's striking Macon. Milkman claims his privilege as an adult male to control and select the sexuality of "his" women.[10] Lena's anger boils over in this moment, after all, because Milkman has determined that it is inappropriate for his sister Corinthians to see Porter. Although Milkman might have a legitimate reason for his objection to Porter (namely, his involvement with the Seven Days), Milkman goes about breaking off his sister's relationship in a heavy-handed way, telling Macon, and thus, once again, aligning himself with the authority of the father.

Milkman is not the only male who pees on women. In fact the three men—Milkman, Macon, and Porter—in conflict over Corinthians are joined by moments of urination. When Macon discovers the gold of the old white man he presumably has killed in the cave, he "like a burglar out on his first job, stood up to pee" (170). Here too Macon is linked to the peacock ("luxury fanned out before him like the tail-spread of a peacock" [170]), a recurring figure that in this context suggests a pun lurking in the bird's name.[11] Macon's urinating signals the shift about to take place in his relationship with his sister Pilate. His insistence that the gold will allow them to recoup the loss of their farm in the aftermath of their father's murder meets her equally strong belief that it would be wrong to take the gold of the man Macon has just killed. This moment, in which brother and sister come to blows, creates a permanent break between the two.

Porter's act of urinating is by far the most spectacular of the three. Standing in the window of his attic apartment (an apartment Macon owns), the drunken Porter threatens suicide. His drunken shouts turn from a demand that the crowd of women "Send me up somebody to fuck!" (25) to his assertion that "I love ya! I love ya all" (26). Between the former and the latter, Porter "leaned his shotgun on the window sill, pulled out his penis and in a high arc, peed over the heads of the women, making them scream and run in a panic that the shotgun had not been able to create" (25). Porter's mixed messages—one of self-interest, the other suggesting altruism—take on special significance when we recall that his attempted suicide results from his work as a member of the Seven Days. His ambivalent utterances, spoken in drunkenness, reveal the ideological fraternity of Porter, Macon, Milkman, and Guitar; despite differences of class and political perspective, each acts on the assumption of male privilege that is grounded in the possession of women. Moreover, Porter's assertion to the women below that "I love ya" casts an odd light on Guitar's insistence that his killing of whites is motivated purely by love of African-American people. To link Milkman and Guitar in ideological brotherhood might seem particularly objectionable given Milkman's lack of social or race consciousness and Guitar's deep awareness of the injustices suffered by the African-American underclass. Nevertheless, the way these males position themselves in relation to the female points to a profoundly similar world picture.

In order to elucidate my meaning, we need to ask, "What precisely is the Seven Days, and does the group's stated mission correspond to its praxis?" As Guitar explains to Milkman, the Seven Days enacts an Old Testament, eye-for-an-eye form of justice:

> when a Negro child, Negro woman, or Negro man is killed by whites and nothing is done about it by *their* law and *their* courts, this society selects a similar victim at random, and they execute him or her in a similar manner if they can. If the Negro was hanged, they hang; if a Negro was burnt, they burn; raped and murdered, they rape and murder. (154–55)

Although Guitar stresses the indifference of the members of the group, it is clear that the Seven Days began as a particular response to a particularly personal kind of sexual violence against African-American men: "It got started in 1920, when that private from Georgia was killed after his balls were cut off and after that veteran was blinded when he came home from France in World War I" (155). What Guitar leaves unsaid is crucial. The one man was castrated and the other blinded because white American males perceived a threat to their possession of white women. The returning veterans had experienced a radically less segregated world in France, a world in which white women would have been available to them sexually. (One of the members of the Seven Days, Empire State, in fact married a white woman in France and becomes mute when he discovers her in bed with another black man.) The white males responsible for the violence against African-American men were sending a particular message—one form of miscegenation, African-American men and white women, would not be tolerated.

Tellingly, the kinds of crimes the Days avenge include a number that involve sexual possession, such as the rape of an African-American woman by a white man or the lynching of an African-American man for his interest in a white woman. One day at Tommy's barbershop, the men of the Days passionately discuss the news regarding the murder of Emmett Till, a black teenager from Chicago who was murdered in Mississippi by three white men for whistling at a white woman; the three men were acquitted by an all-white jury.[12] Morrison's inclusion of the historical figure Till gives weight to the discussion the members of the Seven Days have regarding the plight of African-American men; the history of violence against black men is no fiction. Guitar notes, "Ain't no law for no colored man except the one sends him to the chair" (82).

In the Seven Days' focus on African-American men, African-American women (and hence African-American people as a whole) tend to get lost. One of the more extended passages in which we hear the teachings of Guitar Baines occurs in chapter 10. Milkman complains that everyone in his family wants something from him, to which Guitar responds:

> Look. It's the condition our condition is in. Everybody wants the life of a black man. Everybody. White men want us dead or quiet—which is the same thing as dead. White women, same thing. They want us, you know, "universal," human, no "race consciousness." Tame, except in bed. [. . .] But outside the bed they want us to be individuals. You tell them, "But they lynched my papa," and they say, "Yeah, but you're better than the lynchers are, so forget it." And black women, they want your whole self. Love they call it, and understanding. "Why don't you *understand* me?" What they mean is, Don't love anything on earth except me. (222)

In Guitar's view, the African-American man is the supreme marginal figure, silenced not only by whites, but undermined and unmanned even by African-American women. Milkman here objects to Guitar's major premise—that his killing is motivated by the love of African-American people—pointing out that "except for skin color, I can't tell the difference between what the white women want from us and what the colored women want. You say they all want our life, our living life. So if a colored woman is raped and killed, why do the Days rape and kill a white woman? Why worry about the colored woman at all?" (223).

Guitar's angry response to this question cuts to the heart of the matter in much the same way as Porter's drunken shouts do, revealing a level of meaning unavailable to the speaker: Guitar's "nostrils flared a little: 'Because she's *mine*'" (223). As the chief spokesman for the Seven Days, Guitar here makes it abundantly clear that all the Days, not just Porter, pee on women, particularly African-American women. In his response we see the issue of race bracketed momentarily and instead discover what is really at issue—male possession of women. Thus the Seven Days' "heroic" stance on saving the African-American race parallels Milkman's "defense" of his mother. Both are about males staking claim to woman-as-property, so that we might say that the rule of Milkman in the family or of the Days in society is one and the same—perpetuation of patriarchal authority, pea/e-cock power.

The Seven Days epitomizes patriarchal organization. The group is all male and does not permit its members to marry or to form permanent attachments with women. The very name suggests the originating authority of the monotheistic God the Father of the West who created the heavens and earth in six days and rested on the seventh.[13] But there is no rest for the Seven Days (Guitar's day is the Christian Sabbath) in its unarticulated effort to establish masculinity as violent mastery and manhood as the right to say what one's women do. African-American male violence does not simply imitate white male violence, the former *self-consciously* imitates the latter. Thus, the unrecognized mission of the Seven Days seems to be the following: if white male violence works to keep African-American men from white women, then African-American men need to organize to insure continued property rights in African-American women.

Guitar's emphatic reason for "protecting" African-American women ("Because she's *mine*") resonates with another moment in *Go Down, Moses*. In part 5 of "The Bear," a year and a half after the death of Sam Fathers, Lion, and Ben, Ike goes one last time to the hunting camp before the timber company to which Major DeSpain has sold the timber rights begins to denude the area. On his way to meet Boon under a sweet gum tree in a clearing, Ike encounters a huge rattlesnake, over six feet long, that he addresses as Sam in "The Old People" had addressed the spirit of the big buck six years earlier: "'Chief,' he said: 'Grandfather'" (314). This address prepares us for what we suppose will be another transcendent moment where Ike communes with his ideological parent, Sam Fathers. However, the part-Chickasaw he next sees is the inept hunter Boon, sitting under the gum tree with his disassembled rifle, while in the tree forty or fifty squirrels are trapped with no chance of escape. Boon shouts at the approaching figure that he does not recognize as Ike: "Get out of here! Dont touch them! Dont touch a one of them! They're mine!" (315). Boon, speaking a message antithetical to the wisdom of Sam Fathers, has been co-opted by the values of the timber company to which he owes his job as town marshal and can see in the absurd plenty in the gum tree only something to be hoarded.

In turn, then, the sweet gum tree under which Boon sits in *Go Down, Moses* takes us to the sweet gum in chapter 11 of *Song of Solomon* where Milkman sits, exhausted from hunting with the men of Shalimar, Virginia. As Milkman rests, he begins to question the self-centered attitude he carries with him. In this moment, Milkman very nearly becomes the ideological heir to Guitar in much the same way that Ike becomes the spiritual heir to Sam Fathers—via the male communion of the hunt. Listening to the hunters signal their dogs, Milkman feels that he understands hunting and, by knowing what hunting is, that he understands Guitar:

> Down either side of his thighs he felt the sweet gum's surface roots cradling him like the rough but maternal hands of a grandfather. Feeling both tense and relaxed, he sank his fingers into the grass. He tried to listen with his fingertips, to hear what, if anything, the earth had to say, and it told him quickly that someone was standing behind him and he had just enough time to raise one hand to his neck and catch the wire that fastened around his throat. (279)

This epiphany shatters with Guitar's attempt on Milkman's life. But something larger ruptures in this moment and its aftermath. On the verge of accepting Guitar's worldview in which "does" need the protection of good male hunters, Milkman is nearly killed by his mentor. Milkman escapes to find that the hunters have treed a bobcat with its "glistening night eyes" (280). From the outset, Guitar is described as "a cat-eyed boy" (7), so that the bobcat's death and subsequent butchering at King Walker's gas station take on a special significance.

As the hunters butcher the bobcat, the scene alternates between the graphic details of the way the cat is dismembered and Milkman's memories, which are italicized, of pieces of the teachings of Guitar Baines.[14] Each cut rends another hole in the fabric of Guitar's patriarchal world picture:

> Luther reached into the paunch and lifted the entrails. He dug under the rib cage to the diaphragm and carefully cut around it until it was free.
>
> *"It is about love. What else but love? Can't I love what I criticize?"*
>
> Then he grabbed the windpipe and the gullet, eased them back, and severed them with one stroke of his little knife.
>
> *"It is about love. What else?"*
>
> They turned to Milkman. "You want the heart?" they asked him. Quickly, before any thought could paralyze him, Milkman plunged both hands into the rib cage. "Don't get the lungs, now. Get the heart."
>
> *"What else?"*
>
> He found it and pulled. The heart fell away from the chest as easily as yolk slips out of its shell.
>
> *"What else? What else? What else?"* (282)

As the hunters finish their work, Milkman asks them what they plan to do with the bobcat. The hunters' two-word response ("Eat him") returns us to an earlier key moment in Milkman and Guitar's friendship, when they prepare to steal Pilate's "gold," the bag that actually contains the remains of Jake, Milkman's paternal grandfather. Milkman and Guitar, passing a Buick dealership, see a white peacock, which Milkman notes for its strutting and inept flying. Guitar suggests catching it and to his friend's puzzled question ("What we gonna do if we catch him?"), he replies: "Eat him!" (179). Here Milkman asks Guitar why the peacock "can't fly no better than a chicken" and Guitar responds:

> "Too much tail. All that jewelry weighs it down. Like vanity. Can't nobody fly with all that shit. Wanna fly, you got to give up the shit that weighs you down."
>
> The peacock jumped onto the hood of the Buick and once more spread its tail, sending the flashy Buick into oblivion. (179)

Macon, as I noted earlier is linked to the peacock, but in this passage we begin to see Milkman as the peacock, for Milkman from the time he is fourteen also struts (62). That the bird stands on the Buick seems suggestive, since Macon purchases a new Buick every two years; thus, the peacock on the car indicates the way Macon's wealth props up Milkman. Guitar's description of the peacock's failure to fly well certainly is apropos of the Milkman who flies off to Danville, Pennsylvania, to find the gold, since Milkman carries with him all the markers of comfortable middle-class life, notably, his Cutty Sark, a gold Longines watch, and his Florsheim shoes. And, after offending the men at Solomon's store in Shalimar by his showy display of wealth and inquiries about their women, Milkman is linked both metonymically and metaphorically to another cock, "a black rooster [that] strutted by, its blood-red comb draped forward like a wicked brow" (265).

Song of Solomon's drama of the peacock and the bobcat raises questions about the nature of the male world of the hunt—a world *Go Down, Moses* celebrates—through a complex series of self-reflexive turns: while hunting for gold, which only slowly reveals itself as a hunt for his heritage, Milkman goes on a coon hunt during which he becomes the "coon" who is hunted. Milkman's hunt is play and sport. He doesn't really need the gold. But Guitar and the men of Shalimar play for keeps; their hunting is deadly serious: the poor men of Shalimar need the meat they kill and Guitar's killing is, he believes, for a higher cause. In King Walker's gas station, Milkman finally sees through the falseness of Guitar's teachings, a new state objectified by the final image of the dead bobcat's head: "The tongue lay in its mouth as harmless as a sandwich" (283). No more will Guitar's words and language on race influence Milkman's thinking. Guitar's claim to kill for love ("It is about love. What else?") stands exposed; it's not about love but something else indeed—male power and possession. Milkman does not jettison entirely his relationship with Guitar, for he takes up the hunters' offer to get the heart—that which was nurturing and sustaining in his friendship with Guitar. The entrails of that cat Guitar, both his racism and nostalgia about hunting, are part of the shit that has weighed Milkman down and will not let him fly. But after the attack of his cat-eyed friend and the subsequent death and dismemberment of the bobcat, Milkman loses the limp that looks like a strut and ceases to be both the vain peacock and the cock who pees on women.

Milkman's encounter with the prostitute Sweet neatly objectifies his transformation, since her occupation would normally position her as a commodity, her sexuality bought, not shared; she is the kind of woman men routinely treat with no consideration. And yet Milkman interacts with her in a way that directly addresses the catalogue of shortcomings Lena had pointed out to him at the end of part I and serves almost as reparation for the thoughtless way he had used his cousin Hagar:

> He soaped and rubbed her until her skin squeaked and glistened like onyx. She put salve on his face. He washed her hair. She sprinkled talcum on his feet. He straddled her behind and massaged her back. She put witch hazel on his swollen neck. He made up the bed. She gave him gumbo to eat. He washed the dishes. She washed his clothes and hung them out to dry. He scoured her tub. She ironed his shirt and pants. He gave her fifty dollars. She kissed his mouth. He touched her face. She said please come back. He said I'll see you tonight. (285)

But what exactly allows Milkman now to engage in reciprocal relations with women, and if he can achieve some distance on the male hunt metaphor, why can't Ike? Neither his mother nor his wife provide Ike an alternative to the metaphor of the hunt. Yet almost simultaneous with Milkman's rejecting the excesses of Guitar's thinking, we see Milkman's unconscious movement toward the other mentor of his youth, Pilate, inasmuch as he imagines the bobcat's heart pulling out of its chest cavity "as easily as yolk slips out of its shell" (283). This image takes us back to the first meeting between Milkman and Pilate during which she makes for him the perfect soft-boiled egg. And so over his breakfast eggs the next morning he specifically asks his new friends in Shalimar if they have ever heard of Pilate Dead.

In moving toward the perspective of Pilate, Milkman aligns himself with the one character in the novel who has achieved a special purchase on patriarchal forms of social organization. Because she has no navel, she is prevented from joining a community in the prescribed fashion, as a woman claimed in marriage by a man; to have sex with a man is to reveal she has no navel and thus to be shunned for her difference. After her split with Macon, she is taken in by a preacher's family and begins her new life as a female Huck Finn. (The preacher's house, she tells Ruth, was "a nice place except they made me wear shoes" [141].) She quickly discovers the problems associated with her sexuality. Pilate becomes the object of the preacher's advances, which causes the preacher's wife to send her packing. Twice cast out from groups of migrant farm workers, Pilate finds things no better in towns: "All her encounters with Negroes who had established themselves in businesses or trades in those small Midwestern towns had been unpleasant. Their wives did not like the trembling unhampered breasts under her dress, and told her so" (144). And in such towns Pilate finds that the only economic opportunity available to an unmarried African-American women is working either as a laundress or as a prostitute.

Continually rejected, Pilate reevaluates life in a way that places her in the tradition of Emersonian self-reliance, making her a kind of cross between Henry David Thoreau and Hester Prynne. Performing Thoreau's call to reassessment, Pilate "threw away every assumption she had learned and began at zero" (149) in order to ask herself fundamental questions about how to live in the world. And like Hester, who places her hair under her cap, Pilate cuts her hair signaling a repression of her sexuality, since that is what has caused her the most trouble. Again like Hester, Pilate sets up housekeeping on the margins of the community. While Hester only dreams of a time when women's and men's roles will be reformulated, Pilate establishes a woman-centered alternative community that consistently operates without regard for middle-class conventions or the expectations of men.[15] Her house, as critics have noted, is the site of funkiness where people can eat, act, and be authentically, and contrasts with the middle-class repressions of the Dead household. But although Pilate represents an alternative to the ideology of masculine possession, her alternative family's repudiation of middle-class conventions (which constantly serves as a reminder that Macon Dead's values are inauthentic) links her representation of authentic blackness to black poverty every bit as much as Guitar Baines's politics that locate authenticity in the impoverished community of South Side.

Still, just as Faulkner attempts to represent an alternative to white masculinity in Native American spirituality through Sam Fathers, who communes with his spirit ancestors, Morrison uses Pilate to underscore the possibilities of non-Western spirituality. In doing so, the novelist begins to link the aesthetic to the ethical. As I noted in the previous chapter, there is a significant parallel in Sula's and Pilate's moments of self-reflection on the nature of their lives, yet Pilate creates a more useable identity out of that moment of philosophical reduction. Like Sula, Pilate figures a part of the artist's relation to the community. Both are eccentric and, though nominally a part of their communities, are also apart from them. Although one of the characters best loved by readers of Morrison's fiction, Pilate herself, while respected and sometimes feared, is not beloved by the community. When Hagar comes in late to get her hair done, neither beautician wants to do her hair, but as Marcelline rationalizes, it's best not to turn Hagar down because Pilate "wouldn't like it" (312). If people turn to Pilate, it is because she has conjure powers and potions, can defeat apparently physically stronger men, and can also make fools of the police.

In addition to her spiritual powers, she also has an expressive form—the song she sings at Milkman's birth that is the secret genealogy of the Solomon family. But although figuring elements of artistic identity, she is not the artist whole and complete; she may be the keeper of the oral text and its medium, but she does not know its meaning. Nevertheless, by expressing both the spiritual and the aesthetic, Pilate makes a turn that Sula cannot. Sula's limitation is that her artistic gaze cannot encompass the moral and the ethical; her sexuality is her only textuality. But Pilate insists on the realm of morality, perhaps best indicated by the bag of bones she keeps with her to remind herself of her implication in what she believes to be the death of the white man whom Macon struck in the cave. The bones, of course, turn out to be actually those of her father, but that does nothing to diminish the genuineness of her belief that one must claim responsibility for one's acts.

If his ancestors are important to Faulkner's Sam Fathers, who addresses their spirits in the form of the animals of the forest, the departed dead are equally important to Pilate. In fact, there is a ghostly visitor to Pilate's wine house, that—had they known of it—would have been taken by the people of South Side as a far surer sign of Pilate's unnaturalness than that stigmatized by the missing navel. For Pilate speaks with her dead father, Jake/Macon, who comes to her wearing "a white shirt, a blue collar, and a brown peaked cap" (150). Pilate's relation with the spirit world is an index of the alternative spirituality she represents, and—along with her matrilineal household—creates a link between American and West African culture, a link that Morrison develops more fully in *Beloved* through Baby Suggs's religion of the maternal body. Throughout part I and a significant portion of part II of *Song of Solomon*, Milkman consistently fails to recognize the possibility of ghosts. Freddie's claim that his mother died of ghosts only elicits Milkman's laughter. Later he will not credit his own senses when the ghost of his paternal grandfather witnesses Milkman's and Guitar's attempt to steal Pilate's "gold"—actually the bones of the grandfather. Indeed, even when face to face with a possible ghost, Milkman does not believe. Having arrived in Danville, Pennsylvania, and trying to discover where Circe lives, Milkman asks direction of a man whose description matches Jake's above: "One of them was a Negro. A tall man, elderly, with a brown peaked cap and an old-fashioned collar" (227)—Oleh, Chief, Grandfather indeed![16]

Milkman's encounter with Circe is even more decidedly ghostly, marked by a particular recurring smell that announces the onset of possible supernatural moments in *Song of Solomon*: "a sweet spicy perfume. Like ginger root—pleasant, clean, seductive" (239).[17] The odor of ginger masks what had seconds earlier been an overwhelming stench of decay. From this dreamlike encounter with a woman who, as Milkman notes, "*had* to be dead" (241), he gets decisive clues both to the reality of ghosts and to uncovering his family's history—the names of his paternal grandfather and grandmother, Jake and Sing. (Milkman knows that Pilate claims her father appears to her speaking a single word—sing—which she takes as a command to sing.)

Like Ike McCaslin, who as a youth is granted his desired glimpse of Old Ben, the mythic bear, only after relinquishing his watch and compass, Milkman solves the riddle of his family's past in the song the children of Shalimar sing only after losing his watch, the final marker of his allegiance to his father's middle-class world. The parallel between Isaac and Milkman points to Milkman's developing artistic consciousness. The dense and difficult part 4 of "The Bear" reveals that Ike's quest is not simply for knowledge of the woods. Sitting in the commissary of his father's farm, he examines the ledgers of the old plantation and learns to read between the lines of the cryptic dialogue between father and uncle; connecting the fragments, he interprets the hidden secret of McCaslin genealogy—old McCaslin's incestuous rape of his black daughter. Clearly a defining moment for Isaac, he repudiates a particular enactment of Southern white identity as inauthentic and embraces instead that of his Native-American/African-American mentor, Sam Fathers. Just as Faulkner uses his character Ike, the one who produces an active interpretation of a coded text, to allegorize the eccentricity of artistic consciousness, Morrison also uses Milkman's act of interpretation to suggest his path toward artistic production. In terms of artistic identity, by reading correctly the meaning of the children's song of Solomon, Milkman becomes the other half of the equation, completing Pilate's reproduction of the text by supplying its latent meaning. In the novel's allegorizing of authorship, it seems that one does not get to be Pilate unless one has also been Milkman. In 1963 Morrison, like her fictive double Milkman, is poised to make a turn toward family history and genealogy in her personal quest to begin writing herself through *The Bluest Eye*. As we have seen in Morrison's texts from her first novel through *Playing in the Dark*, the space between thoughtful interpretive reading and writing is never very great, whether we think of that dream interpreter turned writer, Soaphead Church, or Toni Morrison herself who reads as a writer.

The Milkman, then, who returns to Michigan is a changed man. Spiritually renewed, he believes in ghosts.[18] More importantly, he acknowledges his implication in Hagar's death.[19] Like Pilate, who keeps the sack of bones because she maintains that one is responsible for one's dead, Milkman will now possess a box of Hagar's hair, a sign that in addition to being the heir to Pilate's relation to the aesthetic, he will also continue to link ethics to a developing artistic consciousness.

In almost a mirror reflection to the way Milkman becomes the spiritual heir to Pilate, Pilate's granddaughter Hagar is seduced by the worldview of Macon Dead. Chapter 13, which interrupts and delays Milkman's triumphant return, chronicles what happens to Hagar after Milkman leaves her still standing in Guitar's apartment after her failure to kill Milkman. And while Milkman moves slowly away from his father's and Guitar's teachings, Hagar loses her hold on the alternative formation represented by Pilate's house. Indirectly, one might argue, Hagar's death may be traced to Macon Dead inasmuch as she becomes crazy as a result of loving Macon's son, who is raised to reproduce Macon's middle-class values. (Milkman in name is, of course, quite literally another Macon Dead.) Milkman's rejection of Hagar precisely because she does not fit his middle-class design causes her to desire to be like the women Milkman desires—light-complexioned and possessing all the totemic markers of middle-class feminine beauty. So at the very time that Milkman on his journey through Pennsylvania and Virginia progressively loses all the signs of middle-class gentility (his Cutty Sark, Florsheim shoes, and Longines watch), Hagar gathers to herself its feminine counterparts (an Evan-Picone skirt, Con Brios, and Van Raalte gloves). It would, however, be inappropriate to label Macon as the sole or final author of Hagar's desire, for he merely embodies the larger metaphysical system that informs men that they have priority over women and that tells African Americans that white is good and black is bad.

If all he learned was that his great-grandfather reputedly could fly, then Milkman's joy at the novel's ending would be trivial. *Song of Solomon*, Morrison's first novel to foreground the activity of men, however, raises a tough question—one that cannot be answered fully by one novel: is it possible for African-American men to reconceive their masculinity in a nonpatriarchal fashion, that is, in a way that does not reduce African-American women to objects of possession? The example of Milkman Dead suggests that the possibility is open for such a reconception. Ike McCaslin fails to provide the key to a nonpatriarchal society because his renunciation—his refusal to profit from a system of male power that perpetuates racial injustice—is just that, simple negation and refusal, a withdrawal from life. He generates no alternative vision of how to live in the world, and the transmission of patriarchal authority is in no way disrupted by Ike's refusal to be its embodiment; his passivity leads to Roth Edmonds's tragic reenactment of the incestuous miscegenation that so horrified Ike when he read the McCaslin ledgers.

But Milkman has his Pilate/pilot, a woman who opens paths more sustaining than Sam Fathers's hunting trails, even though those trails lead him once again to African-American poverty as the only site of authentic black identity. Nevertheless, she teaches him how to treat women as fully human and that flying is a state of being rather than a physical act: "Now he knew why he loved her so. Without ever leaving the ground, she could fly" (336). As she lies dying in Milkman's arms, she tells him: "I wish I'd a knowed more people. I would of loved 'em all. If I'd a knowed more, I would a loved more" (336). The kind of flying Milkman ultimately understands and values is Pilate's flying, the ability to transcend self and self-love. And surely Pilate's claim serves as an intratextual critique pointing out the inauthenticity of Guitar's claim (one echoed by Porter and Robert Smith) that the Seven Days' killing is done for love. What weighed Milkman down for so much of *Song of Solomon* is male ego (much as Hagar is destroyed by her desire to be the desire of male ego), forged in the structures of a patriarchal society.

The novel's conclusion is noteworthy for its ambiguity that has occasioned a variety of critical response.[20] Does Milkman actually fly? Does he live or die following his struggle with Guitar? Finally, I believe, it does not matter whether Milkman survives. He has achieved the very connection to an African-American community that Guitar all along has criticized his friend for lacking. Guitar may believe himself to be the one acting from higher principles, yet Milkman, who even in this moment sees Guitar as his brother, now achieves the transcendence he wrongly felt he had won under the sweet gum tree. Guitar's adherence to the vision of masculinity as violent mastery may win the day, but Milkman's transformation suggests that masculinity can be conceived in tropes other than those of deadly possession.

But perhaps another reason why the novel's denouement is so ambiguous is that Morrison could not easily imagine Milkman after the moment of his sense of authentic identity as completed project. Could Milkman find permanent happiness in Shalimar? Should he take the spirit of Shalimar back to Michigan? Would he repudiate the economic advantage represented by his father's property? Clearly the funk has erupted in Milkman but the question remains: Can the funk rise economically? Despite his sense of triumph at having found the site of authenticity in rural black poverty, it is hardly a triumph in which Morrison could fully participate or with which she could identify, especially in the aftermath of publishing her best-selling third novel. And that is because Morrison herself does not choose black poverty as the location of her cultural identity. Put another way, in a heated exchange between Milkman and Guitar, Guitar attacks his younger friend for hanging out with the black middle class. Milkman responds, unconsciously echoing his father, "What's wrong with Negroes owning beach houses?" (103). In 1977 and in terms of the logic of *Song of Solomon*, Morrison's answer is fairly straightforward: quite a bit is wrong with such ownership because it inhibits the possibility of authenticity. Yet in a 1998 profile of the author, Morrison's attitude toward possession seems markedly different:

> Even without the upcoming tour [to promote *Paradise*], Morrison's life seems hectic. She rents an apartment near Princeton University in New Jersey [. . .]; another apartment in lower Manhattan; and a stone house in Rockland County, N.Y. Plus, she is having rebuilt the house she owned on the Hudson River just north of New York City, which burned to the ground on Christmas Day 1993. Three residences? Or four, counting the house in progress? "I was a child of the Depression," she shrugs and laughs. "I have bad dreams about eviction." (Gray 68)

How might one account for this changed attitude from the time Morrison was composing *Song of Solomon* in the mid-1970s to this more recent and relaxed position?

Her third novel was the main selection of The Book of the Month Club, the first African-American novel so designated since Richard Wright's *Native Son*. Additionally, *Song of Solomon* won awards from both the National Critic's Circle and the American Academy and Institute of Arts and Letters. Morrison's success as an author, over and above her work as an editor (a position she left following the publication of her third novel), meant that she finally was earning an income that placed her very comfortably in the middle class by any purely economic measure. Perhaps, then, the lived contradiction between her fictive resolutions—which had consistently made black poverty the only place in which an African American could hope to attain an authentic identity—and her certain recognition of her own sharply rising income led her to rethink her early fiction's identifications. Clearly she must have realized that having money does not necessarily mean that an African American is "white" or a sellout. What she would need was a way to reimagine blackness that allowed for the individual to develop economically as well as spiritually.

The chapter that follows explores *Tar Baby*, the novel that Morrison wrote after *Song of Solomon* and that begins the author's attempt to rethink blackness and its relation to class. Like her previous novel's title, *Tar Baby* overtly signals one of her intertexts, this time the African-American folk tale. And just as in *Song of Solomon*, Morrison rewrites a modernist, but now it is neither Ellison, nor Woolf, nor Faulkner. In *Tar Baby*, Morrison rewrites Morrison. This rewriting critically engages—in ways as striking as her use of *Invisible Man* and *Go Down, Moses*—the triumphant achievement of completed authenticity (Milkman) and the valorization of the black agrarian community (Shalimar). In rewriting her modernist novel, as well as her fictively imagined self, Morrison points the way to an understanding of her later novels as the product of postmodern blackness. Morrison's exploration of African-American identity through a transfigured meditation on her male genealogy in *Song of Solomon* becomes in *Tar Baby* a coded meditation on descent through the female side of her family. Morrison's intensely reflexive fourth novel crucially participates in her fictive project of reclaiming both modernist technique and personal identity. Near the end of *Song of Solomon*, Milkman's voice echoes across the valley as he calls to Guitar, a moment suggesting the hinge that joins the doubled worlds of these two novels: *tar, tar, tar—Tar Baby*.

NOTES

1. As Samuels and Hudson-Weems point out, in *Song of Solomon* "Morrison had obviously drawn from her personal history; the story of Solomon Willis, her grandfather, is the source of this work." (8).

2. Barbara Christian suggests that white critics who contextualize Morrison with Woolf and Faulkner do so out of an unacknowledged racism. For Christian, such critics' motivation is to demean Morrison's African-American heritage (19–20). According to Christian, what empowers her to go on and speak about the relationship of Morrison to white modernism is that Christian is "an African American woman critic" (20) and therefore better understands the importance of African-American identity to Morrison. Christian's argument is an example of the identity politics that I discussed in chapter 1 and that I return to in this chapter.

3. Although Harold Bloom's version of intertextuality, *The Anxiety of Influence*, may seem implicit in some of my thinking, I wish to distance my work from Bloom's oedipalization of anxiety. Bloom's sense of poetic misprision, however, does seem to have some utility, so that one might say the strong novelist (such as Morrison) will inevitably misread her own work's relation to the aesthetic past. Bloom's point in this regard may be suggestive in the inevitably racialized context of thinking about Morrison and Faulkner: if overidentifying with one's aesthetic precursors is a metaphorical form of slavery, then reading one's difference is creatively liberating.

4. David Cowart has explored stylistic and thematic similarities between Morrison and Faulkner. Cowart judges Morrison's fiction a success inasmuch as

she performs "meaningful variations on (Joyce's and Faulkner's] themes—freedom, identity, history" (89).

5. For example, in her interview with Nellie McKay, Morrison claims:

> Black people have a story, and that story has to be heard. There was an articulate literature before there was print. There were griots. They memorized it. People heard it. It is important that there is sound in my books—that you can hear it, that I can hear it . . .
>   That oral quality is deliberate. (152)

Trudier Harris's "study of the influence of oral traditions upon" (1) Morrison's fiction is the fullest treatment to date on this topic.

6. Morrison was asked again in 1994 about her student reading of American literature and responded, "As for Faulkner, I read him with enormous pleasure. He seemed to me the only writer who took black people seriously. Which is not to say he was, or was not, a bigot" (Dreifus 73).

7. Patrick O'Donnell suggests that "one of the reasons Morrison has little to say about Faulkner in *Playing in the Dark* is that, perhaps, she has already said a great deal about him in her fiction" (225).

8. Harue Minakawa briefly notes a connection between *Song of Solomon* and *Go Down, Moses*: "Milkman goes through a process similar to what Ike McCaslin goes through in 'The Bear.' Hunting strips one to the essentials" (52–53). Although not specifically addressed in Morrison's thesis, *Go Down, Moses* is in her bibliography, as are all of Faulkner's novels published prior to 1955. More recently, Lucinda MacKethan, drawing on my earlier work on Morrison and Faulkner, develops a reading of *Song of Solomon* and "The Bear" that compliments my own.

9. Two articles particularly note the subversion of Macon's teachings. Robert James Butler, who sees the novel growing "out of this dialectic between the possibilities of space and the securities of place" (63), focuses on Guitar's influence on Milkman. Valerie Smith, arguing that the novel opposes linear time (exemplified by Macon Dead) and cyclical time (as Pilate lives it) foregrounds Pilate's shaping hand (726).

10. Juliet Mitchell summarizes the Lacanian view: "The phallus is not identical with the actual penis, for it is what it signifies that is important. [. . .] The phallus [. . .] indicates the desire of the mother (the desire for the phallus) into which the child is born. [. . .] The primary dyadic relationship between mother and child . . . enters immediately into the possibility of a dialectical relationship between three terms: mother, child, and phallus. So already, even so to speak *before*, [the child] wants to be the phallus for the mother [. . .]. In submitting to the completely unreal possibility of castration the little boy acknowledges the situation and learns that one day he, too, will accede to the father's function. He pays thereby his symbolic debt to the father he has murdered in his rivalrous thoughts. So the phallus is intimately connected both with the symbolic father and the law" (396–97).

11. Earlier Macon's walk is described as a strut, again linking him to the peacock (17).

12. Emmett Till's murder has been the occasion of other African-American writers to think in the space between history and fiction. Morrison herself has written a play, *Dreaming Emmett* (1985). Ishmael Reed even more metafictionally titles his novel *Reckless Eyeballing* (1988) which in turn is the title of the play that the

novel's main character, Ian Ball, has written about Till; the novel chronicles Ball's efforts to have his play produced.

13. That the members of the Seven Days invoke the authority of monotheistic Christianity to name their organization recalls Julia Kristeva's point in *About Chinese Women* that "monotheistic unity is sustained by a radical separation of the sexes: indeed, this separation is its prerequisite. For without this gap between the sexes . . . it would be impossible, in the symbolic sphere, to isolate the principle of One Law—One, Purifying, Transcendent Guarantor of the ideal interests of the community" (19). The Seven Days, by passing judgment and telling its victims "Your day has come," aligns itself with transcendent authority and attempts to be the guarantor of the ideal interests of the African-American community, all the while reducing African-American women to property.

14. Charles Scruggs briefly comments on this scene, suggesting that when Milkman removes the bobcat's heart he "realizes that Guitar was trying to tell him how he could save his own life, that he could save it only if he bridged the gap between himself and others, between himself and the past" (322). Far from teaching Milkman how to save himself, Guitar's teachings reinscribe a significant aspect of the Dead father's ideology of possession. Weinstein much more closely reads this scene, though in a largely unironized way so that Guitar's claim that the killing of whites is done out of love for African Americans is less problematic than I see it. The very title of Weinstein's book, *What Else But Love?*, in fact is the question Guitar asks.

15. Susan Willis suggests that Morrison's "three-woman utopian households" (41) contrast with Faulkner's failure to conceive of the radical possibility represented by Judith, Clytie, and Rosa living together without men at Sutpen's house. The three-woman household in *Absalom*, however, is primarily concerned that they not be raped by the desperate and defeated men returning to a ravaged land. Willis of course writes prior to *Beloved*, but her sense of utopian households becomes problematic if we think of Sethe, Denver, and Beloved. Sethe's emotional and sexual longings cannot be exhausted in female bonding and in fact her very life is threatened by her obsessional attachment to Beloved.

16. That Milkman comes to a belief in ghosts as a result of his movement toward Pilate reminds us that Isaac McCaslin is similarly introduced to a world beyond the material by his mentor in "The Old People" when Sam Fathers shows the boy the spirit of the dead buck.

17. See for example the description of the ginger-smelling air prior to Guitar's and Milkman's unacknowledged encounter with the ghost of Jake (186).

18. Milkman's belief in ghosts is another sign that he has moved beyond his father's middle-class values, values that derive from the white ruling class. Morrison tells a pointed story on this matter: "Once a woman asked me 'Do you believe in ghosts?' I said, 'Yes. Do you believe in germs?' It's part of our cultural heritage" (Watkins 50).

19. Gerry Brenner's claim that the Milkman who returns to Pilate "assigns himself no culpability" (18) for Hagar's death depends on an odd interpolation of the word "it" in the line "What difference did it make?" (336). Let's look at what precedes this sentence:

> Hagar was dead. The cords of his neck tightened. How? In Guitar's room, did she . . . ?

What difference did it make? He had hurt her, left her, and now she was dead—he was certain of it." (336).

Brenner reads the sentence as follows: "What difference did [Hagar's death] make?" The context, however, suggests a more plausible reading. Milkman starts to ask himself if Hagar killed herself as he had suggested she do in Guitar's room, but then he realizes that how she died is irrelevant: "What difference did it make [how Hagar died]?" Milkman recognizes that his treatment of her implicates him in her death no matter what the particular circumstances surrounding that death are.

20. The moment is hardly the suicidal gesture that some critics have made it out to be (Brenner 18; Butler 72). Guitar's rifle has Milkman pinned down. There are not many options for life-affirming action open to Milkman, but he does act with a knowledge of his life-long friend and stands up. Guitar's sense of fair play—there are rules good hunters follow, after all—and his love for his friend lead him to lay aside his rifle.

Although I do not wish to grant special privilege to the author's reconstruction of this scene, Morrison's comments on the novel's ending seem germane. In an interview with Pepsi Charles, Morrison calls *Song of Solomon* an "absolute triumph" since "a man learns the only important lesson there is to learn. And he wins himself, he wins himself. And the quality of his life improves immeasurably. Whether its length improves or lengthens is irrelevant" (50).

DANA MEDORO

Justice and Citizenship in Toni Morrison's Song of Solomon

They called me "the angriest Negro in America." I wouldn't deny that
charge. I spoke exactly as I felt. I believe in anger. [. . .] I'm not for wanton
violence, I'm for justice.
                              —Malcolm X, *The Autobiography of Malcolm X*

Deconstruction keeps open the "beyond" of currently unimaginable transformative possibilities precisely in the name of Justice.
                              —Drucilla Cornell, *The Philosophy of the Limit*

Published in 1977, Toni Morrison's *Song of Solomon* remains haunted by
the debates and struggles of the previous two decades. Her characters seem
to represent or embody different positions from the civil rights movement
of the 1950s and 1960s, conjuring in both oblique and explicit ways the
words of its prominent spokesmen: W.E.B. Du Bois, Martin Luther King,
Jr., Booker T. Washington, and Malcolm X. While the novel is often read as
an account of the trauma wrought by racial injustice, it is, at the same time,
an attempt to express an idea of justice loyal to this experience.[1] This paper
focuses on the figures of Guitar and Pilate, contending that each articulates
and develops a concept of justice in *Song of Solomon*, and that each informs—
or exerts pressure on—the other's configuration of justice. Although the
text does not ultimately sustain Guitar's eye-for-an-eye directive, as the

From *Canadian Review of American Studies* 32, no. 1 (2002): 1–15. © 2002 by the University
of Toronto Press.

scholarship on the novel concurs, neither does it entirely dismiss or discredit it. Guitar has his say in two separate, lengthy dialogues; he also speaks on behalf of consequence in the enaction of justice: "'The earth is soggy with black people's blood,'" he says about his involvement in the deadly Seven Days. "'And before us Indian blood. [. . .] I had to do something'" (*Song* 154). Pilate, I will argue, gestures toward a promise of justice, an ever-arriving ideal outside or beyond the necessity of force or retribution. In Morrison's words: "She is something we wish existed on a wider scale" (*Conversations* 140). If Pilate stands for an ethical ideal, with an attendant ontological reconfiguration, Guitar stands for the reality of its absence in African American lives, announcing the force of law that often accompanies an ethical portal in an unjust world.

With the violent death of a father in their pasts, Pilate and Guitar also sketch divergent responses to severed kinship ties or bloodlines. Their losses are indicated in the novel's dedication, simply "Daddy," which functions as a kind of intimate appeal or entreaty, a consecration of a bond. From the beginning, this bond at once generates and raises questions about the novel's genealogical quest. It also grounds a rudimentary precept: that while white America's political self-image may rest on a myth of being "happily bereft of ancestry in the garden of the New World" (to quote R.W.B. Lewis), black America's does not (*American Adam* 5). In *Song of Solomon* the American Eden is in turn a slave plantation, a battlefield, and the turf of the Ku Klux Klan. For African Americans it is often a dangerous place where orphan-hood is not a metaphor for innocence or liberation. In a sense, Morrison puts this metaphor on trial, asking as she does in *Playing in the Dark*: "What are Americans always so insistently innocent of?" (*Playing* 45).

The novel's historical allusions establish a world in which African Americans pay a heavy price for the Faulknerian might-have-been of America's innocence. Structured by flashbacks and progressions through antebellum and post-reconstruction America, *Song of Solomon* marks its temporal periods with the devastating loss of fathers and ancestors, including Ruth's and Guitar's as well as Macon's and Pilate's.[2] It is not until Milkman asks about his grandfather's killers that he begins to understand why everyone around him seems haunted or unhinged:

> "Did anybody ever catch the men who did it—who killed him?" Reverend Cooper raised his eyebrows. "Catch?" he asked, his face full of wonder. "Didn't have to catch 'em. They never went nowhere." "I mean did they have a trial; were they arrested?" "Arrested for what? Killing a nigger? Where did you say you was from?" (231–232)

The death of an ancestor is thus experienced not only as the unredressed loss of an individual figure but also of a collective sense of belonging to the land as legitimate citizens rather than as slaves or ex-slaves. For every African American who steps forward and is cut down, countless others relinquish considering the attempt. As Milkman gradually discovers, the significance of the first Macon Dead's farm lies with the fact that it spoke to other men "like a sermon":

> "You see?" the farmer said to them. "See? See what you can do? Never mind you can't tell one letter from another, never mind you born a slave, never mind your daddy dead, never mind nothing. [...] Stop picking around the edges of the world. Take advantage, and if you can't take advantage, take disadvantage. We live here. On this planet, in this nation, in this country right here. [...] But they shot the top of his head off and ate his fine Georgia peaches. And even as boys these men began to die and were dying still." (235)

These words resonate from the novel as echoes of the Civil Rights Movement, of its often sermon-like appeals for justice and its urgent calls for citizenship. They correspond, in a way, to the words of Martin Luther King (also shot to death) on the refusal to wait in the sidelines for equity or acceptance:

> When you are forever fighting a degenerating sense of "nobodiness"—then you will understand why we find it difficult to wait. There comes a time when the cup of endurance runs over, and men are no longer willing to be plunged into the abyss of despair. I hope, sirs, you can understand our legitimate and unavoidable impatience. (qtd. in *Race* 72)

Song of Solomon repeatedly establishes the exigency of justice for African Americans, compelling formidable questions about the definition and implementation of this concept or ideal. Does justice, for instance, necessarily involve retribution, law, obligation and consequence? Or, does it rest on something else altogether—and, if so, how does one begin to define and exercise it? Does it require Guitar's Malcolm X-like desire for restitution, or Pilate's belief in being haunted? Does it somehow require both of these?

Shifting Milkman's quest from gold to the name of his grandfather, the novel's plot indicates that a willingness to trace and secure some knowledge of the past constitutes a starting point for justice. This is not necessarily a straightforward task, of course, but a constant returning to the ground of history—or, to use another metaphor from the novel, to the dead letter office toward which historical memory swiftly moves. The reference to the dead letters in the opening pages of the novel captures a significant legal term or concept: a dead letter is the term for a law that is written but not enforced or animated (like the US constitution in African American life). So, to return to history—to a legal document, for instance—involves acknowledging or interpreting what falls on the outside of it. Thus, the novel includes clever manoeuvres around policies, indicating a vitality not captured in or reduced by official documentation and procedure. A particularly significant example occurs in the opening pages with the anecdote of Not Doctor Street and No Mercy Hospital:

> Town maps registered the street as Mains Avenue, but the only colored doctor in the city had lived and died on that street, and when he moved there in 1896 his patients took to calling the street, which none of them lived in or near, Doctor Street. Later, when other Negroes moved there, and when the postal service became a popular means of transferring messages among them, envelopes from Louisiana, Virginia, Alabama, and Georgia began to arrive addressed to people at house numbers on Doctor Street. The post office workers returned these envelopes or passed them on to the Dead Letter Office. Some of the city legislators [...] saw to it that "Doctor Street" was never used in any official capacity. And since they knew that only Southside residents kept it up, they had notices posted [...] saying that the avenue [...] had always been and would always been known as Mains Avenue and Not Doctor Street. It was a genuinely clarifying public notice because it gave Southside residents a way to keep their memories alive and please the city legislators as well. They called it Not Doctor Street, and were inclined to call the charity hospital at its northern end No Mercy Hospital. (4)

However, at the same time that this passage applauds the manipulation of legal policies, it also indicates the extent to which American law persistently shuts down black freedom, progressively subdivides legislation to sustain the inequity and segregation depicted in the novel.

With direct references to dates and names, *Song of Solomon* offers us glimpses of the judicial history of the US, from the establishment of the Freedmen's Bureau in the nineteenth century to the segregated hospitals and cemeteries of the twentieth. It opens with a suicide note dated 1931, and thus calls attention to a time when organizations like the NAACP were underway and hard at work against discriminatory laws. Allusions to racial uplift groups, factory ID cards and Jim Crow laws follow the suicide note and immediately establish a framework for subsequent events: we are asked to keep in mind that the poverty and the struggles of the characters here are linked both to slavery and to the legislation surrounding it. In 1931, they are only two generations away from the Black Codes, Reconstruction, and the heyday of the Klan. If this point is not clear, or to make a related observation about historical amnesia, Morrison has Milkman ask: "'Your father was a slave?'" (53); to which his father incredulously answers, "'What kind of foolish question is that? Course he was. Who hadn't been in 1869?'" (53).

Morrison writes about a period in which the US was still tangling itself in knots in order to sidestep the Constitution and undermine African American rights. In *The Civil Rights Record: Black Americans and the Law, 1849–1970*, Richard Bardolph thus recounts the first four decades of the twentieth century:

> Despite the very real changes that were recasting the black community in the quarter century after 1910, the relationships between the races had shown little change by 1938. While a few prophets of the scientific assault upon racism were beginning to be heard, the national mind had hardly begun by that year to divest itself of the old creeds upon which the structure of discrimination was grounded. The [African American's] status as second-class citizen, as hewer of wood and drawer of water, was still deeply embedded in law and custom. Black Americans were still tightly trapped in urban and rural slums. The black worker's income in 1938 still fell short of being half that of white workers. Jim Crow trains, buses, and street cars were still the common lot of millions. (169)

The legal strides made in the post-bellum era to ratify black citizenship remained suspended between paper and active policy. In other words, the fourteenth and fifteenth Constitutional Amendments were essentially dead letters until the 1960s. Moreover, the Ku Klux Klan organized itself in direct response to these amendments and, through enacted and inferred violence, systematically thwarted them. One of the chants of Klan initiation was "the negro has no rights," and Klan terrorists repeatedly blocked black people from voting, jury service, and office holding (*Civil Rights* 52). They also organized lynch mobs. In response to such terrorism, all factions of the Civil Rights Movement, including allied communist and labour parties, demanded legal and federal protection for African Americans from brutality, intimidation, and lynching. Although for decades the NAACP fought in court for these laws, the federal government persistently stayed out of the states' detours around the Constitution. Due to formidable resistance from Southern states, efforts to secure congressional action against lynching repeatedly met with defeat. As Bardolph so movingly puts it, "For the years 1910 to 1938, there is nothing to report in the way of federal legislation to protect [African Americans] from injury and outrage, and to accelerate their progress toward full enjoyment of their civil rights" (188).

Throughout *Song of Solomon*, references to lynching and to the fear of being lynched consistently emerge, recalling the fact that black men and women, well into the twentieth century, found themselves with few legal protections from violence and murder. Pilate, for instance, relies on this truth of African American life when she spins the yarn to the sheriff that the bones in her sack belong to the body of her lynched husband. And Guitar's involvement in the Seven Days is, as he announces, "about trying to make a world where white people will think before they lynch'" (160). His reference to the "picture of those white mothers holding up their babies so that they could get a good look at some black man burning on a tree'" (157) is historically accurate, as is the news about Emmett Till's torture and murder for allegedly whistling at a white woman. The announcement of Till's death in the novel initiates, moreover, a debate about accommodation, retaliation and the law, and it ends with Guitar's statement, "Ain't no law for the colored man except the one sends him to the chair'" (82). Guitar's justification of the Seven Days and his frantic questions about the law strike a chord because the novel clearly frames them with the history of slavery, lynching, and segregation. "Where's the money," he asks, 'the state, the country to finance our justice? Do we have a court? [. . .] If there was anything like or near justice or courts when a cracker kills a negro, there wouldn't have to be no Seven Days'" (160).

According to Milkman, Guitar "sounds like that red-headed negro named X'" (160), and to an extent, Malcolm X's presence lurks behind Guitar's characterization, giving resonance and legitimacy to the position that perhaps only the threat of counter-violence produces swift concessions from the white power structure. With Guitar, we have an adamant, anti-accommodation position from the Civil Rights Era. As Malcolm X once remarked,

> I don't go for non-violence if it also means a delayed solution. To me a delayed solution is a non-solution. Or I'll say it another way. If it must take violence to get the black man his human rights in this country, I'm for violence. (*Autobiography* 367)

Through similar statements, Guitar speaks for the necessity of justice to inhere in some principle of restitution or repercussion. His outrage sheds light on the pressure for citizenship and the law: while these concepts may be anchored in a flawed structure (of white patriarchy) they carry certain preliminary obligations and protection from harm. They also bury the legal definitions of African Americans as property.[3]

Guitar's words summon a history of white violence, including not only lynching but also the dangerous work relegated to black labourers. This latter aspect transpires in the memory of his father's death at the saw mill, a memory that seems to drive Guitar's eye-for-an-eye concept of justice as well as his desire to force protections around black lives.[4] Guitar's father's severed body forms a haunting image, a grisly literaiization, even, of W.E.B. Du Bois's notion of being "torn asunder into a double consciousness":

> He remembered anew how his mother smiled when the white man handed her the four ten dollar bills [instead of life insurance]. Her husband was sliced in half and boxed backward. He'd heard the mill men tell how the two halves, not even fitted together, were placed cut side down, skin side up in the coffin. Facing each other. [. . .] And he had worried then, as a child, that when his father was wakened on Judgment Day his first sight would not be the glory or the magnificent head of God—or even the rainbow. It would be his own other eye. (224)

In the absence of a system of justice for African Americans, Guitar and the Seven Days create their own. Otherwise, the conditions surrounding his father's death prevail, as do the opportunities for even an FDR to join a lynching party.

> "You could've taken him and his wheelchair down to Alabama," [Guitar asserts] "and given him some tobacco, a checkerboard, some whiskey, and a rope and he'd have done it too. What I'm saying is, under certain conditions they would *all* do it." (157)

The text makes it increasing clear, though, that the Seven Days fundamentally resembles or mirrors the Klan, and that the dubious issue of blood purity informs their struggle. The retributive killing, Guitar explains, secures the death of several generations and keeps the ratio of black-to-white blood static. Here, Guitar's characterization departs from Malcolm X's ghostly presence. Unlike X, Guitar has no vision of justice beyond vengeance, no sense of a system beyond a balanced coffin. Thus entrenched in the system he hates, he joins Milkman in the quest for gold. For Guitar, this quest promises the purchase of weapons, the instruments of terminated genealogies.

According to Pilate, "'you can't get rid of nobody by killing them'" anyway (208). While this declaration at first seems naive or otherworldly, it initiates Pilate's perspective on justice[5] and permits a tension to develop between Pilate's position and Guitar's. Her words about love, her way of life, and her rejection of material things, also point to the social vision articulated by Du Bois, and shared by both King and Malcolm X just before their murders: that the goal for equal justice under the law was a first step toward transforming America's capitalist structure. For Du Bois, the prerogative of private capital over black lives formed the basis of the nation's racism and violence; only the repudiation of capitalism could initiate a just society. Increasingly influenced by this position, Malcolm X followed suit with announcements like, "you show me a capitalist, I'll show you a bloodsucker" (qtd. in "Pilgrimage" 392). The Civil Rights Movement was, moreover, primarily a black workers' movement, supported and fortified across the country by communist organizations, black membership in unions, and socialist groups like the League of Revolutionary Black Workers and the Black Panthers. And, because of its anti-capitalist direction, the Civil Rights Movement experienced considerable setbacks from red scares and purges.[6]

With Pilate we have a key to this history and a vision of citizenship and justice beyond the structures in place. Her characterization, repeatedly framed by a language of expenditure, distribution and relinquishment, is set in opposition to that of the text's arch-capitalist and Booker-T figure, Macon Dead. Stripped down of earthly possessions, only she is able to hear their murdered father from beyond the grave. She deciphers his refrain "'you just can't fly on off and leave a body,'" not as a reference to himself, but to the man Macon may have murdered in the cave (208). For Pilate, it's a call for justice that includes her because she witnessed the event. "'If you take a life, then you own it,'" she explains.

> "You responsible for it. [. . .] So I had to go back for it [the body].
> I've had it every since. Papa told me to, and he was right, you know.
> You can't take a life and walk off and leave it. Life is life. Precious.
> And the dead you kill is yours. They stay with you anyway, in your
> mind." (208)

She calls the bag of bones her inheritance, and like her dead father's refrain, it becomes an object of interpretation in the novel. Her father's words, "'sing, sing,'" also generate different readings. While they recall the name of Pilate's mother, they also form a command and link Pilate's singing to her past—even her slave past, where singing often functioned as a way for slaves to get around the laws that prevented them from talking to each other. Pilate's father's ghost speaks from another realm and time, and his words are not entirely clear or readable. They are distorted by the unjust circumstances of his death and they call for the living's willingness to heed and interpret them.

In *The Philosophy of the Limit*, a study of deconstruction and justice, Drucilla Cornell similarly and persuasively illustrates that justice involves at once a call to interpretation and a barrier to full accessibility. Justice rests on one's humility, she says, before the otherness of the Other and on the transformation of the subject according to an ethics of responsibility. The call to responsibility must constitute the subject in such a way that being is reconceived as "being in contact" (*Philosophy* 98). According to Cornell, the postulate of autonomous subjectivity is not only an illusion, but also unethical. Doing away with morality in the opening pages of her study—because it establishes a "right way to behave versus an ethical or good way"—Cornell focuses on the kind of person "one must become in order to develop a nonviolative relationship to the other" (13). Following Adorno and, primarily, Derrida, she begins with an emphasis on interrelationship, expansiveness, tenderness; she then moves into an illumination of what she terms the "ethics of deconstruction" and into an answer to the question: "What can Good be figured as?" (95).

Taking a stand against the criticism of deconstruction as a kind of toothless inactivity, she argues that it is rather a philosophy that demands we think differently about the beyond and about the possibility of a truly different future; in so doing, it invites us to approach the threshold of that which is excluded, perceived as threatening, not part of us. Neither does deconstruction deny facts of the systems in which we live; it beckons us, though, to their limits and to the possibility of their transformation. Turning to Derrida's discussion of community in *Of Grammatology*, for instance, she reiterates that speech necessarily implies writing, and that community, as an organization by which people recognize one another, implies both. If writing unites kinship systems in the attempt to ward off human violence, it also identifies norms, circumscriptions, classifications which "carry within them their own violence" (51). "The very power to name" is for Derrida,

> the originary violence of language which consists in inscribing within a difference, in classifying. [. . .] To think the unique within the system, to inscribe it there, such is the gesture of arche-writing: arche-violence. (51)

We must acknowledge this Derridean double-gesture: the possibility, in other words, of a nonethical opening of ethics (108). As Derrida puts it, "there is not ethics without the presence of the other, but also, and consequently, without absence . . . difference, writing (108). Cornell clarifies this idea with the case of South Africa's apartheid, showing that the nullification of apartheid involves the silencing of whites and thus a kind of violence to their difference. But, it is a necessary violence, an imperative we are called to (as she puts it) "by any version of the Good worthy of its name" (114). We cannot think simply in terms of justice versus injustice, nor in terms of the certainty of a present Good (117). Rather, justice must be held apart from a present system, must function as a limit to which we are drawn and for which we are answerable.

Justice performs then as a disruption of the present and as endless pressure on the law. It is the *perhaps* that always questions the *is*, not as *telos*, but as the "not yet that remains other than the present, arriving from both the past and the future" (136). Using a kind of diaspora metaphor, Cornell remarks that the Good, an impossible presence, can be fragmented across the laws, so that laws function as principles guiding ethical behaviour rather than simply as determinants distributing violence and power. If Justice and the Good are thus always incomplete, then the laws remain open to interpretation and reinterpretation—and rights can always be undermined if they fail in "the locus of responsibility" (151).

The past too, as historical memory, exposes the limits of justice. Justice is the ought and the ought-to-have-been that renders precedence uncertain (154). Present law and the ideal of justice are not the same things. Taking as an example United States legal history, Cornell asserts that there are two myths in the justification of US law: that of the Founding Fathers and of the "full readability of the Constitution" (158). Such prerogatives cannot continue to be rendered as transparent truth; they must be rearticulated as indefinite interpretations, as inconclusive directions toward the promise to Justice.

We are required, in the name of what is Good, to start with difference, not with identity, and with interpretation and transformation, not with precedence and calculation (122). Justice as the Good reconstitutes the subject as a promise to the other. It requires that rights can never by guaranteed as absolutely right or fully present. As Cornell reminds us, death always prevails against the myth of full presence. This is a disrupted ontology, a conjoining of being and non-being that "does not [. . .] begin with the "I" that strives to establish his rights" (135). For the law to be just, it has to sustain the conditions for its own contradiction and destruction. And it is interpretation that separates law from justice—releasing both from myths of atemporal morality and permitting an opening for responsibility and for what she calls the dream of the "subject of dialogue" (177).

In *Song of Solomon* the enactment of Pilate's concept of responsibility involves the claims of interpretation or conversation over violence and retribution. But, like Cornell's investigation, Morrison's novel does not entirely throw out the function of enforcement or force in justice. The scene in which Pilate wields the knife against the man who beats her daughter emblematizes this point. Coming up from behind. him, Pilate aims the knife at his heart and has "'a little talk'" with him. Pilate then describes her position, asks the villain what he thinks she should do, and then obtains a promise from him. "'I won't never put a hand on her,' he says, 'I promise'" (95). After insuring that it's a "'real promise,'" Pilate withdraws the knife. Here, the knife seems to symbolize or sustain the possibility of consequence that laws enact and for which Guitar speaks; the promise Pilate secures introduces the ideal of justice that extends beyond retaliation or restitution. And the whole scene rests on one person listening to another. Pilate discerns the necessity or ethics of listening from her father's ghost. Like interpretation, listening involves being in contact and being open to the call of responsibility.

This "being in contact" involves questions of ontology and citizenship in *Song of Solomon*, questions and possibilities that form around Pilate's absent navel. Frightening as it is to most characters in the text, her absent navel signifies a new way of being and of being just in the world: beyond blood lines and blood kinship, and towards an articulated, performed relationship with others. This new relationship with others is made urgent, moreover, through the text's delineations of violent injustice in America. Here, I bring Kimberly Benston's brilliant argument about community into the question of citizenship in *Song of Solomon*, and work from her point that Pilate "embraces the other through performance" ("Re-Weaving" 99). Benston asserts that Morrison's black community rests on improvisation, on a communal protagonist, and not on the genealogical and oedipal authority registered in the novel's guest motif. I shift the focus to the novel's vision of citizenship, and claim that its investigation of genealogy in turn recasts a politics of blood identity.

Born after her mother's death and in communication with her father's ghost, Pilate is pulled, to borrow a phrase from Derrida's *Specters of Marx*, "in two directions of absence" (*Specters* 25). She thus occupies an ontological space where memory and hope dislocate present time, and where, as both Derrida and Cornell assert, life can be lived justly. While she does not entirely repudiate kinship ties—she lives near Macon, she converses with her dead father—Pilate places these ties in the realm of speech and writing, and outside of the mystical bonds of blood. She does not have a navel, but she carries around a spool of black thread. She dismisses, moreover, the different definitions of brother and cousin, stating, "what the difference in the way you act toward 'em? Don't you have to act the same way to both?'" (44). Although Pilate lives in "'the Blood Bank, because blood flowed so freely there,'" she leaves her door symbolically unlocked; her daughter Reba donates blood to the local hospital "as often as they would let her" (32, 95). And, at the end of the novel, blood seeps from Pilate's body as she expresses her wish to have "'knowed more people. [...] if I'd a knowed more, I would a loved more'" (226).

Blood and blood lines are, or have been, significant aristocratic and capitalist humbugs in United States history, the ancient concept of *jus sanguinis* (the law according to blood) persisting into the twentieth century and informing concepts of citizenship. Its purity and authority persistently wielded against African Americans in their struggle for belonging, blood is at the root of white supremacy. It was written into the laws of the land and, through intricate fractions and categories of blood quantum, secured a colour line across US rights and protections. The hidden menace of black blood, and not necessarily skin colour, was the main substance of segregation; theories of mongrelization and intense fears of miscegenation both produced and emerged out of it. As Senator Theodore Bilbo explained in his 1947 treatise *Take Your Choice: Separation or Mongrelization*, it would be better to

> see civilization blotted out with the atomic bomb than to see it slowly but surely destroyed in the maelstrom of miscegenation, interbreeding, intermarriage and mongrelization. [...] By the absolute denial of social equality to the Negro, the barriers between the races are firm and strong. But if [it] should be broken down, then the mingling of the tides of life would surely begin and the Southern white race, the Southern Caucasian, be irretrievably doomed. (55)

Publications like the senator's continued through the 1960s, all focussing on the pollution of white American blood.

In order to enact Jim Crow laws, the states had to define the so-called Negro, and the definitions changed according to different laws. Thus, as late as 1959, individuals with any "negro blood whatsoever" in Arizona were forbidden to marry whites; those with one-sixteenth negro blood or more could not intermarry in Florida, and those with one-eighth or more could not cohabitate. In the state constitution of Georgia, intermarriage was forbidden between whites and anyone with "ascertainable" traces of either Negro, African, West Indian, Asiatic Indian, Mongolian, Japanese, or Chinese blood in their veins. As one Georgia senator proclaimed, "in the South we have pure bloodlines and we intend to keep it that way" (qtd. in *Jim Crow Guide* 61). In the mid-twentieth century, most states prohibited intermarriage and classified black people as those possessing any trace of African blood whatsoever, which led, of course, to more legislation in the matter of blood donations and transfusions.

In an incredibly tongue-in-cheek and well-researched exposé of American racism, titled the *Jim Crow Guide to the USA* (first published in 1959),

Stetson Kennedy addresses statutory definitions of race. He explains, for instance, that:

> Most American laws defining race are not to be compared with those once enforced by Nazi Germany, the latter being relatively more liberal. In the view of the Nazis, persons having less than one-fourth Jewish blood could qualify as Aryans, whereas many of the American laws specify that persons having one-eighth, one-sixteenth, or "any ascertainable" Negro blood are Negroes in the eyes of the law and subject to all restrictions governing the conduct of Negroes. (47)

This focus on blood, this other "red scare," undergirded a politics of racial identity and promoted the capitalist structure. As Du Bois repeatedly pointed out, white labourers joined white landholders against black labourers, insuring their own economic oppression in the process. Blood was linked to the privileges of white society; it created a diversion from issues of poverty and injustice across the races, and the Civil Rights leaders knew it.

In *Song of Solomon*, blood kinship is disconnected from a vision of justice and citizenship. Blood is not the ink that inscribes identity and belonging. While it symbolizes certain bonds, it has nothing to do with their articulation and enaction. Pilate both asserts and does not assert lines of blood. When she explains her anger to the man who beats Reba, for instance, she asks, "'you know how mamas are, don't you? You got a mama, ain't you?'" (94). In the act of articulation and out of a desire to avert violence, she calls up the significance of a blood bond. It is uttered, even manipulated, to make a connection that is not based on blood. She also does not differentiate between those to whom responsibility is and is not owed. She keeps a bag of a dead stranger's bones with her, contending that "'The dead you kill is yours'" (208). These words rung out across the American soil, soggy with black people's blood. *Song of Solomon* is a novel about the power of articulation over blood relations—the articulation or call that announces citizenship and animates justice. It is echoed later in *Beloved*'s epigraph: "I will call them my people which were not my people. And her Beloved which was not beloved."

Notes

1. See, for example, Jill Matus's *Toni Morrison*, a study of trauma in Morrison's work. Briefly noting its "precise historical texture," Matus places *Song of Solomon*'s thematics of bereavement in the broad context of "life in racist America" (73, 80).

2. In her excellent chapter on *Song of Solomon*, Matus argues that this is a novel about the "father's trauma and the genealogy of the paternal line."

3. In his essay "Bearing Witness: Toni Morrison's *Song of Solomon* and *Beloved*" Rob Holton, who points out Morrison's recurring legal metaphors, similarly asserts that "at issue in the actions of the Seven Days [. . .] is not only a sense of revenge, but also the empowerment (however inadequate) of marginalized witnesses whose historical testimony must finally be taken seriously" (81).

4. The violent death of a father also binds Guitar's characterization to Malcolm X. The circumstance surrounding Malcolm's father's murder by white attackers are unclear, but it is known that he was thrown across streetcar tracks and that his body was almost completely severed. In *Song of Solomon*, the scene is altered and Guitars father's body is severed in half at the saw mill. While it is not the same thing as a lynch mob, the dangerous work results in a similar kind of death and secures the point that protections are not in place around the lives of African Americans.

5. To clarify this point: where Pilate represents and pulls toward something ideal and just, Guitar (despite his corruption) pulls in the opposite direction, toward confronting the horrible reality of injustice. I don't think Pilate's position entirely cancels out Guitar's.

6. See Manning Marable's *Race, Reform, and Rebellion: The Second Reconstruction in Black America, 1945–1990* and Melvin Leiman's *The Political Economy of Racism: A History*.

Works Cited

Bardolph, Richard. *The Civil Rights Record: Black Americans and the Law, 1849–1970*. New York: Thomas Crowell, 1970.

Benston, Kimberly. "Re-Weaving the 'Ulysses Scene': Enchantment, Post-Oedipal Identity, and the Buried Text of Blackness in Toni Morrison's *Song of Solomon*". In *Comparative American Identities: Race, Sex and Nationality in the Modern Text*. Ed. Hortense Spillers. New York: Routledge, 1991.

Bilbo, Theodore G. *Take Your Choice: Separation or Mongrelization*. Poplarville, Mississippi, 1947.

Cornell, Drucilla. *The Philosophy of the Limit*. New York: Routledge, 1992.

Derrida, Jacques. *Specters of Marx*. Trans. Peggy Kamuf. New York: Routledge, 1994.

Holton, Robert. "Bearing Witness: Toni Morrison's *Song of Solomon* and *Beloved*." *English Studies in Canada* 20.1. (March 1994): 80–95.

Kennedy, Stetson. *Jim Crow Guide to the USA*. Westport: Greenwood, 1959.

Leiman, Melvin. *The Political Economy of Racism*. London: Pluto, 1993.

Lewis, R.W.B. *The American Adam*. Chicago: Chicago UP, 1955.

Malcolm X and Alex Haley. *Autobiography of Malcolm X*. New York: Grove P, 1966.

Marable, Manning. *Race, Reform, and Rebellion*. Jackson: UP of Mississippi, 1991.

Matus, Jill. *Toni Morrison*. Manchester: Manchester UP, 1998.

Metcalf, George. "The Pilgrimage of Malcolm X." *Portrait of America*. Vol. II. Ed. Stephen B. Oates. Boston: Houghton Mifflin, 1987.

Morrison, Toni. *Beloved*. New York: Plume, 1988.

———. *Conversations with Toni Morrison*. Ed. Danille Taylor-Guthrie. Jackson: UP of Mississippi, 1994.

———. *Playing in the Dark*. New York: Plume, 1992.

———. *Song of Solomon*. New York: Plume, 1987.

Smith, William Benjamin. *The Color Line*. New York, 1905.

WES BERRY

Toni Morrison's Revisionary "Nature Writing": Song of Solomon *and the Blasted Pastoral*

African American contributions to the genre of nature writing have been few.[1] As Elizabeth Dodd points out in the recent *PMLA* forum on literatures of the environment, "African Americans seem largely absent from this burgeoning literary, cultural, and critical movement." Exceptions include Alice Walker, whose collection *Living by the Word* contains several essays dealing with ecological issues, and Eddy Harris, whose travel narrative *Mississippi Solo* offers some of what one expects from the genre: attention to the details of landscape, excursions into spaces distanced from human population centers, and philosophical reflections about the relationships between humans and other-than-human nature.[2] Furthermore, Toni Morrison expands the possibilities of African American environmental writing by exploring through a black male protagonist the healing potential of southern woodlands; she accordingly forces a reevaluation of African American attitudes toward "wilderness" and "wildlife." Her novel *Song of Solomon* examines the complicated interactions of an African American protagonist with southern fields and woodlands, as do texts by Zora Neale Hurston, Richard Wright, Eddy Harris, and others. The significant difference is that Morrison's portrayal of a black man returning to the South, learning his family history and experiencing a newfound sense of rootedness in the place, relates an affirmative relationship of African Americans with

From *South to a New Place: Region, Literature, Culture*, edited by Suzanne W. Jones and Sharon Monteith, pp. 147–164. © 2002 by Louisiana State University Press.

133

landscape in a language recalling narratives of regeneration through wilderness in the American nature-writing tradition.

Many of the standard texts we consider to be "nature writing" are informed by what critic John Tallmadge calls the "excursion": "a simple neighborhood walk during which the curious naturalist merely records observations." Tallmadge cites Gilbert White's *Natural History of Selbourne* as an early text structured by this framework. Other practitioners of the mode include William Wordsworth, "for whom nature provided lessons in the conduct of life and the motions of the mind," Ralph Waldo Emerson, Henry Thoreau, Edward Abbey, John Muir, Aldo Leopold, Annie Dillard, Terry Tempest Williams, and other Anglo-American writers. Eddy Harris's memoir of his Mississippi River quest is structured by such an excursion, going beyond the "neighborhood walk" by venturing within a riparian landscape packed with natural history, myth, more-than-human life, and unique human settlements. Most African American writing that gives intensive treatment to the nonhuman environment does so within the context of human communities. Jean Toomer's *Cane* paints detailed scenes of the Georgia landscape, but Toomer seldom writes about landscape for landscape's sake, chronicling instead how the nonhuman environment and human actions share a mutual influence. Zora Neale Hurston's *Their Eyes Were Watching God* likewise deals with how human communities interact with southern landscapes, her primary topography being the "Glades" of Florida. Other examples include Dori Sanders's *Her Own Place*, chronicling the life of hard-working African American farmers in South Carolina, and Gloria Naylor's *Mama Day*, a novel set in an island community between South Carolina and Georgia. These texts satisfy one of the tenets for an environmentally oriented work that Lawrence Buell outlines in his book *The Environmental Imagination*: "The nonhuman environment is present not merely as a framing device but as a presence that begins to suggest that human history is implicated in natural history." "Nature" is more than a mere backdrop; it is a force shaping and being shaped by human action. Accordingly, African American writing about the more-than-human environment is seldom separated from cultural and historical contexts.[3]

In canonical nature writing, wilderness is often a destination, a playground where a person can be freed for a while from the mathematical progression of modern civilization. In the words of environmental historian William Cronon, wilderness generally "represents a flight from history": "Seen as the original garden, it is a place outside of time, from which human beings had to be ejected before the fallen world of history could properly begin.... Seen as the bold landscape of frontier heroism, it is the place of youth and childhood, into which men escape by abandoning their pasts and entering a world of freedom where the constraints of civilization fade into memory. . . . No matter what the angle from which we regard it, wilderness offers us the illusion that we can escape the cares and troubles of the world in which our past has ensnared us." Richard Slotkin concurs: "The characteristic American gesture in the face of adversity is . . . immersion in the native element, the wilderness, as the solution to all problems, the balm to all wounds of the soul, the restorative for failing fortunes." This motif of an individual recuperating from adversity and loss through immersion in "wild" or "natural" landscapes recurs often in contemporary Anglo-American writing. In nonfiction and autobiography about southern places, this pattern is manifest in *The Horn Island Logs of Walter Inglis Anderson*, in which the narrator, who has suffered from mental disease, undergoes a recuperative experience by immersing himself in the elements of an island off the Gulf Coast; and in *Crossing Wildcat Ridge: A Memoir of Nature and Healing*, Philip Lee Williams shares how North Georgia woodlands—trees, birds, insects, water, and other non-human life—advance his recuperation from open-heart surgery and depression. Environmental philosopher Barry Lopez writes: "That wilderness can revitalize someone who has spent too long in the highly manipulative, perversely efficient atmosphere of modern life is a widely shared notion." These southern texts by Anglo writers testify to this belief.[4]

In novels and memoirs by minority writers, however, "wilderness" is bound up with cultural memory to an extent that it is seldom just a place to escape to. In *Mississippi Solo*, Harris makes clear that his canoe voyage on the Mississippi River is more than a jaunt through the countryside to explore its natural history. He is also concerned with the human history of the river, including the settlements dotting its banks. Other texts written by African Americans represent the complexities that individuals may confront in realizing "healing potential" in landscapes fraught with historic violence. In Richard Wright's *Uncle Tom's Children*, for instance, chirping night crickets (a pleasant music for some who live in rural households where windows are left open on summer nights) become for minority protagonist Big Boy a surprising sound: at once a part of a pastoral imagery of butterflies, bees, sweet-scented honeysuckle, and twittering sparrows, but also a sound intermixed with the shouts of a lynching mob. Additionally, Harris's *South of Haunted Dreams* offers an account of "fronting" southern landscapes that, from the perspective of black history, pose both physical and psychological challenges. This travel narrative operates under the rubric of masculine exploration, with Harris, the solo quester, traveling into exotic southern landscapes that he imagines as potentially threatening, a type of *Heart of Darkness* on a BMW motorcycle. Harris brings along with him his cultural memory, which shapes how he experiences the physical environment.[5]

Likewise, in Hurston's *Their Eyes Were Watching God* and Toni Morrison's *Beloved*, undomesticated spaces are a mixed blessing. In Hurston's novel, when the matriarch of a plantation threatens to whip Nanny and sell her child, Nanny flees into a swamp. She recalls her fright to Janie: "Ah knowed de place was full uh moccasins and other bitin' snakes, but Ah was more skeered uh whut was behind me. . . . Ah don't see how come mah milk didn't kill mah chile, wid me so skeered and worried all de time. De noise uh de owls skeered me; de limbs of dem cypress trees took to crawlin' and movin round after dark, and two three times Ah heered panthers prowlin' round." Nanny perceives this swamp with complicated emotions; it terrifies her but also offers her sanctuary—from the wrath of the "Mistis." Morrison's *Beloved*, furthermore, explores how Paul D. constructs an imaginary barrier between himself and rural southern landscapes—both "wild" and domesticated—as a means of coping, of staying sane in places where he lacks the freedom to own a piece of land. He escapes from slave bondage several times and travels in Georgia, Alabama, North Carolina, Kentucky, Delaware, "and in all those escapes he could not help being astonished by the beauty of this land that was not his. He hid in its breast, fingered its earth for food, clung to its banks to lap water and tried not to love it. On nights when the sky was personal, weak with the weight of its own stars, he made himself not love it. Its graveyards and low-lying rivers. Or just a house—solitary under a chinaberry tree; maybe a mule tethered and the light hitting its hide just so. Anything could stir him and he tried hard not to love it." By emphasizing Paul D.'s schizoid attraction to and dissociation from the land, Morrison forces us to consider how the impulse to possess land may be more complex for historically marginalized people.[6]

Paul D. reminds one of Ralph Kabnis, a character in Toomer's *Cane*. Toomer's Georgia is a place of "pain and beauty," a "land of cotton" where the white folks get the boll and blacks get the stalk. Southern nights entice northern intellectual Kabnis. The hills and valleys are "heaving with folk-songs," "a radiant beauty in the night that touches and tortures." He is attracted to the deep-rooted African culture and simultaneously repulsed by a place where humans burn and hang other humans. Rural Georgia offers "the serene loveliness of . . . autumn moonlight," but also "loneliness, dumbness, [and] awful, intangible oppression" that can drive one to insanity. Eldridge Cleaver summed up such African American ambivalence to rural landscapes thirty years ago in an essay entitled "The Land Question and Black Liberation":

> From the very beginning, Afro-America has had a land hang-up. The slaves were kidnapped on their own soil, transported thousands of miles across the ocean and set down in a strange

land. They found themselves in a totally hostile situation and America became a land from which black people wanted only to flee, to escape such evil soil and those vicious creatures who had usurped it.

During slavery itself, black people learned to hate the land. From sunup to sundown, the slaves worked the land: plowing, sowing, and reaping crops for somebody else, for profit they themselves would never see or taste. This is why, even today, one of the most provocative insults that can be tossed at a black is to call him a farm boy, to infer that he is from a rural area or in any way attached to an agrarian situation. In terms of seeking status in America, blacks—principally the black bourgeoisie—have come to measure their own value according to the number of degrees they are away from the soil.

Security and terror, sublimity and alienation—African American attitudes toward southern landscapes are packed with conflict.[7]

*   *   *

Literary critic Gurleen Grewal notes that *Song of Solomon* resonates alongside novels "that have documented and refashioned ethnic identities in the United States since the 1970s": Louise Erdrich's *Love Medicine*, Maxine Hong Kingston's *China Men*, Leslie Marmon Silko's *Ceremony*, and Peter Najerian's *Voyages*. In such novels, "characters' self-hatred and angry confusion are related to a historic dispossession and to a psyche cut off from ancestral or communal wellsprings; their narratives chart a moving and powerful repossession of selfhood, articulating personal well-being in terms of the collective." *Song of Solomon*, examines a similar theme through the character of Milkman Dead, a young midwesterner who travels alone to a rural community in the Blue Ridge Mountains, the locus of his paternal ancestry. Milkman's trip to the South has been the subject of a significant amount of critical inquiry. Most critics have focused on the final section of the novel, framed by Milkman's searching for mythical gold and his ultimate enthusiasm for discovering the oral history of his family. Stephanie A. Demetrakopoulos views Milkman's flight to the South in quest of gold as an "archetype of the hero leaving home to seek his fortune," and his subsequent "ego death" as a point of maturation. She writes, "Milkman can connect authentically and deeply with women and his own anima only through and after this ego death." Gurleen Grewal points out that Milkman is raised with little historical perspective and is thus "representative of every person's existential predicament: that of being born to a time and place in medias res. . . . Milkman has grown up within the specific cultural discontinuity created by migration from the South to the urban north and by the black middle-class's repudiation of a stigmatized past." His trip to Virginia brings a reversal of this existential condition through a newfound awakening to family history and through his connection to a human community. "The entire novel is about the interdependence of individuals and the insurance of mutual life; redemption cannot be individual," Grewal writes. This statement brings to mind farmer-writer Wendell Berry's emphasis on holistic health care, his belief that "the community—in the fullest sense: a place and all its creatures—is the smallest unit of health and that to speak of the health of an isolated individual is a contradiction in terms."[8]

Milkman Dead certainly undergoes a change in attitude while visiting his ancestral homeland, and yes, this shift is linked to his establishing roots—an understanding of familial cultural continuity—where none existed before. My intrigue, however, lies in the echoes of American "nature writing" that I detect in Morrison's prose. To what extent is Milkman's "regenerative moment" in the Virginia woodlands a sincere expression of natural mysticism or, conversely, a parody of the American gesture of escaping into the wilds to soothe the wounds of the soul?[9]

Milkman is a dynamic character whose growth Morrison charts by illustrating his progressive awareness of the landscapes he moves within. Scenes that immerse Milkman in unfamiliar territory, that show him struggling as an uninitiated visitor to sylvan lands, are reminiscent of literature in the American naturalist tradition. Like ecologist Anne LaBastille—who details in her memoir *Woodswoman* how she fronts harsh, dangerous winters while relocating to a remote cabin in the Adirondack National Park, gaining a heightened awareness of her own limitations and strengths[10]—Milkman becomes more self-aware through his encounters with the "other" realm of woods, streams, and caves. During the early stages of Milkman's southbound journey, he is a passive observer of his surroundings. On a Greyhound bus approaching Danville, Pennsylvania, Milkman tries to appreciate the scenery he has heard his father rave about, "but Milkman saw it as merely green, deep into its Indian summer but cooler than his own city, although farther south. . . . For a few minutes he tried to enjoy the scenery running past his window, then the city man's boredom with nature's repetition overtook him. Some places had lots of trees, some did not; some fields were green, some were not, and the hills in the distance were like the hills in every distance. . . . His eyes were creasing from the sustained viewing of uneventful countryside."[11] A few pages earlier, at the beginning of the second section of the novel, Morrison emphasizes the disjunction or radical shift from urban space to rural by showing Milkman bungling through this strange territory, blind to the multiple species and local life surrounding him. In the countryside outside of Danville, Milkman "was oblivious to the universe of wood life that did live there in layers of ivy grown so thick he could have sunk his arm in it up to the elbow. . . . Life that burrowed and scurried, and life so still it was indistinguishable from the ivy stems on which it lay. Birth, life, and death— each took place on the hidden side of a leaf" (220). But of course, Milkman is not concerned about what occurs on the underbelly of a leaf, the "universe" of wood life—insect and animal communities—because he is forever moving, negligent of even the human communities he encounters.

We first encounter Milkman's lack of interest in the landscape early in Part II of the novel as he rides the bus into Danville, and we appropriately perceive the first stages of his heightening perception as he rides the Greyhound bus away from that place. After his uncomfortable experience in the country, Milkman has a changed vision: "The low hills in the distance were no longer scenery to him. They were real places that could split your thirty-dollar shoes" (256). Milkman's excursion through the fields and woodlands of Pennsylvania in quest of gold provides substantial comic relief. He falls into a creek, tears the sole of a leather dress shoe, agitates bats in a cave with his "hollering," and is thereafter driven, shoe sole flapping, from the cave. This disjunction between the protagonist and the landscapes he encounters forces him to reevaluate his character and opens him to new possibilities. Or, as ecocritic Scott Slovic writes about literary naturalists, "it is only by testing the boundaries of self against an outside medium (such as nature) that many nature writers manage to realize who they are and what's what in the world."[12]

Milkman's rejuvenation involves much more than a bonding with so-called "nature"; it also involves his growing respect for a human community and its history. Before making the trip to Pennsylvania, Milkman "had never had to try to make a pleasant impression on a stranger before, never needed anything from a stranger before, and did not remember ever asking anybody in the world how they were" (229). His compassion for human others has been slight, as evidenced by his careless attitude toward members of his family. For example, he breaks his long-term relationship with Hagar by sending her a terse note and some money. He steals from his aunt Pilate. He has been the recipient of a privileged childhood, without having to give much in return. His older sister Magdalene chastises him for his selfishness, suggesting that he has "peed" on people since childhood: "'You've been laughing at us all your life. Corinthians. Mama. Me. Using us, ordering us, and judging us: how we cook your food; how we keep your house. . . . You have yet to wash your own underwear, spread a bed, wipe the ring from your tub, or move a fleck of your dirt from one place to another. And to this day, you have never asked one of us if we were tired, or sad, or wanted a cup of coffee. You've never picked up anything heavier than your own feet, or solved a problem harder than fourth-grade arithmetic'" (215). Milkman's southbound journey places him in difficult situations—for instance, his bungling excursion into the Pennsylvania countryside—that force him to reevaluate his attitudes toward others.

After his initiation into the rugged Pennsylvania countryside, Milkman travels to the Blue Ridge Mountains. The journey ultimately liberates Milkman, allowing him a sense of independence from the long arm of his wealthy, domineering father. Before he adopts a newfound responsibility to self and others, however, Milkman encounters and overcomes multiple challenges. For instance, upon arriving in the town of Shalimar, Virginia—a "no-name hamlet ... so small nothing financed by state funds or private enterprise reared a brick there" (259)—Milkman confronts economic need and the violence stemming from it. He is a conspicuous stranger: "His manner, his clothes were reminders that they [the poor locals] had no crops of their own and no land to speak of either. Just vegetable gardens, which the women took care of, and chickens and pigs that the children took care of. He was telling them that they weren't men, that they relied on women and children for their food. And that the lint and tobacco in their pants pockets where dollar bills should have been was the measure" (266). Shalimar is not the "home" that Milkman expects. He assumes the locals will treat him with respect, as they have in other small towns en route to Shalimar. Indeed, his positive experiences with people in the early stages of his journey prompt him to wonder why black people ever left the South: "Where he went, there wasn't a white face around, and the Negroes were as pleasant, wide-spirited, and self-contained as could be" (260). In the impoverished hamlet of Shalimar, however, Milkman encounters men who challenge him to a knife fight. His ancestral "home" appears to offer little more than a dilapidated service station and easily offended, unemployed rustics.

Some local men invite Milkman on a nighttime hunting trip, an episode that sets up the ego dissolution that several critics associate with growth or maturity.[13] Morrison seems to be intentionally pushing readers to connect Milkman's experience with the motif of relinquishment common in American literary naturalism, by using a language of land-based mysticism familiar to the genre. Before examining a key passage, however, I wish to consider for a moment Annie Dillard's discourse on "seeing" in her staple of American nature writing, *Pilgrim at Tinker Creek*. Like Wordsworth in his poems on childhood, Dillard romanticizes infancy as a time of hypersensitive perception. She accordingly laments the passage of innocence that accompanies adult knowledge and the consequent loss of "newly sighted" vision that follows our immersion in language systems. "Form is condemned to an eternal danse macabre with meaning," she writes. Dillard therefore desires to see "the world unraveled from reason, Eden before Adam gave names." She is unable as an adult to see the "color patches" she believes she saw as an infant. "My brain then must have been smooth as any balloon," she reflects. "I'm told I reached for the moon; many babies do. But the color-patches of infancy swelled as meaning filled them. . . . The moon rocketed away." To be able to reclaim this rare privileged vision, one must relinquish one's ego, Dillard suggests. One must "hush the noise of useless interior babble." But of course few individuals are privy to this gift, because "the mind's muddy river, this ceaseless flow of trivia and trash, cannot be dammed. . . . Instead you must allow the muddy river to flow unheeded in the dim channels of consciousness. . . . The secret of seeing is to sail on solar wind. Hone and spread your spirit till you your-self are a sail, whetted, translucent, broadside to the merest puff." Dillard's prose is fanciful—the skeptical reader may call it ridiculously abstract, akin to Emerson's metaphor of the transparent eyeball—but nevertheless it conveys the idea that dissolution of the ego is a necessary stage toward an experience of natural mysticism.[14]

Bearing in mind Dillard's words, consider Toni Morrison's description of Milkman when he falls behind on the nighttime hunting trip in the Blue Ridge Mountains. The other hunters, in pursuit of a bobcat, leave Milkman behind. He is winded. He cannot keep up with their pace. He wants to rest a while under a sweet gum tree, long enough at least to allow his heart to drop back down into his chest. There he rests, his mind filled with existential ponderings, when suddenly, without warning, he experiences a momentary reprieve from his ego: "Under the moon, on the ground, alone, with not even the sound of baying dogs to remind him that he was with other people, his self—the cocoon that was his 'personality'—gave way. He could barely see his own hand, and couldn't see his feet. He was only his breath, coming slower now, and his thoughts. The rest of him had disappeared" (277). Milkman's thoughts, however, remain. Indeed, unlike with Dillard, who views spiritual perception as the world detached from language and reason, Milkman's mys-tical moment is bound up with language. It is for him a new language—the voices of people and animals tied to their regional landscape.

As with Ike McCaslin in Faulkner's "The Bear," Milkman's material possessions will not help him in the woods, but hamper him. "His watch and his two hundred dollars would be of no help out here, where all a man had was what he was born with, or had learned to use. And endurance." Like young McCaslin, Milkman must abandon his material possessions before he can learn the language of the woods—the distinctive, complicated commu-nications between hunting dogs and men, and the subtle tracks on tree bark and the ground that hunters read. He thinks there may be an ur-language shared by rustics, "[l]anguage in the time when men and animals did talk to one another, when a man could sit down with an ape and the two converse; when a tiger and a man could share the same tree, and each understood the other; when men ran *with* wolves, not from or after them" (278). Milkman feels a sudden rush of brotherly love under the sweet gum tree in the Blue Ridge, and believes he may finally understand his country companions and his friend Guitar's nostalgia for the South. He admires for the first time these bobcat hunters, men like Calvin who can communicate with dogs and "read" the earth: "It was more than tracks Calvin was looking for—he whispered to the trees, whispered to the ground, touched them, as a blind man caresses a page of Braille, pulling meaning through his fingers" (278).

Withdrawing from the hunt for just a brief time opens Milkman to this flood of thoughts and raises his awareness of these alternate modes of perception; Milkman therefore reminds one of Thoreau, Dillard, Edward Abbey, Barry Lopez, and other naturalists who believe one may discover rare perception when distancing oneself from the white noise of dominant society. Lopez, for instance, suggests that places like the Inner Gorge of the Grand Canyon offer incomparable respite from the pain of the world. Down in the belly of the canyon, an individual may experience a "stripping down, an ebb of the press of conventional time, a radical change of proportion, an unspoken respect for others that elicits keen emotional pleasure, a quick, intimate pounding of the heart."[15] In like manner, while alone in the bucolic quiet of the Virginia night, Milkman begins to "merge" with the woodlands of his ancestors: "Down either side of his thighs he felt the sweet gum's surface roots cradling him like the rough but maternal hands of a grandfather. Feeling both tense and relaxed, he sank his fingers into the grass" (279).

However, for Milkman there is no escape to the "original garden," for his moment of "union" with the dirt and sweet gum is interrupted when a man tries to strangle him. Morrison bursts Milkman's pastoral moment with violence: "He tried to listen with his fingertips, to hear what, if anything, the earth had to say, and it told him quickly that someone was standing behind him and he had just enough time to raise one hand to his neck and catch the wire that fastened around his throat" (279). Milkman's childhood friend Guitar, having tracked him from the city, unleashes on Milkman his history of racial frustration. As Grewal notes, "Guitar's problem is a baneful race politics sowing discord with hate." Earlier in the novel, we learn how Guitar attempts to check hate crimes against black people by murdering white people. He wants to keep the ratio of black to white in balance. Before Milkman begins his trip south, Guitar reminds him about the links between racial oppression and the control of land holdings: "The earth is soggy with black people's blood. And before us Indian blood . . . and if it keeps on there won't be any of us left and there won't be any land for those who are left. So the numbers [the ratio of black to white people] have to remain static" (158). Guitar's statement recalls Eldridge Cleaver's point about the "deep land hunger" of African Americans: "Suffice it to say that Afro-Americans are just as land hungry as were the Mau Mau, the Chinese people, the Cuban people; just as much so as all the people of the world who are grappling with the tyrant of colonialism now, trying to get possession of some land of their own." Both Guitar's and Cleaver's remarks remind us that unbuilt landscapes and "wild" places are far from being ahistorical. Morrison seems to be emphasizing this point, forcing readers to consider Milkman's potential regeneration in the woods within the context of black-on-black crime, or, perhaps, to connect the wire around his neck with the lynchings that have bloodied southern ground.[16]

In *Ride Out the Wilderness: Geography and Identity in Afro-American Literature*, Melvin Dixon reads Milkman's experience with the southern landscape as authentic regeneration. He believes Milkman "develops a more effective relation to the land when he confronts the wilderness. . . . Milkman's participation in the hunt gains . . . fraternity and friendship [of local men]. . . . Milkman has to earn kinship by enduring the woods, the wilderness. Like the fugitive in slave narratives, he has to renew his covenant with nature to secure passage out of the wilderness that had invited him in." Dixon reads the southern woodlands he calls "wilderness" as a proving ground for meaningful livelihood. Similarly, in *Reclaiming Community in Contemporary African American Fiction*, Philip Page notes that Milkman's night in the woods serves the function of connecting him with his heritage: "Milkman is guided not only by ancestor figures but also by Calvin, Small Boy, Luther, and Omar, who initiate him during the hunt and offer him the bobcat's heart, thereby inducting him into his past and his racial identity and midwifing his rebirth in harmony with himself, his family, his community, and nature." These evaluations seem apt, for after Milkman's interrupted merging with the southern woodlands, he appears renewed. Walking along with the local hunters, Milkman "found himself exhilarated by simply walking the earth. Walking it like he belonged on it; like his legs were stalks, tree trunks, a part of his body that extended down down down into the rock and soil, and were comfortable there—on the earth and on the place where he walked" (281). Perhaps the exhilaration he feels is a case of "death makes life sweet," a type of euphoria expressed by those who have recovered from life-threatening cancers and car wrecks, or even by those awakening from realistic nightmares to find their bodies warm and breathing; or maybe Milkman's elation is the result of a real transformation, a shift in attitude from one who feels disconnected from other people and places to one who, for the first time in his life, understands a sense of membership in a community. In the land of his ancestry, Milkman appears to experience rootedness, a sense of connection with the locals "as though there was some cord or pulse or information they shared. Back home [in the city] he had never felt that way, as though he belonged to anyplace or anybody" (293). One cannot, of course, neatly separate from "culture" to escape into "wilderness." Morrison recognizes this and accordingly brings Guitar, a stalking history of racial bigotry who confounds the archetypal moment of ego dissolution in the wilderness, back into the story.[17]

Is Morrison parodying conventional nature writing by suggesting that the archetypal "flight" into the woods and wilderness is much more complex for historically oppressed people? Consider, furthermore, how early in his travels Milkman hears from the local men in Pennsylvania stories about his grandfather, the magnificent Macon Dead—a model example of one who turned a piece of land into a profitable farm and therefore strived to establish a sense of history where none existed before. The farm owned and worked by Milkman's grandfather served as an inspiration for how to establish a sense of place and worth. It spoke "like a sermon" to the other poor men in Montour County:

> "You see?" the farm said to them. "See? See what you can do? . . . Here, this here, is what a man can do if he puts his mind to it and his back in it. Stop sniveling," it said. "Stop picking around the edges of the world. Take advantage, and if you can't take advantage, take disadvantage. We live here. On this planet, in this nation, in this country right here. Nowhere else! We got a home in this rock, don't you see! Nobody starving in my home; nobody crying in my home, and if I got a home you got one too! Grab it. Grab this land! Take it, hold it, my brothers, make it, my brothers, shake it, squeeze it, turn it, twist it, beat it, kick it, kiss it, whip it, stomp it, dig it, plow it, seed it, reap it, rent it, buy it, sell it, own it, build it, multiply it, and pass it on—can you hear me? Pass it on!" (235)

For these newly freed ex-slaves, the land is a commodity, property with which one needs to forge an identity and family history rather than to escape it. Furthermore, after this "sermon" on the land, in a descent from the sublime moment that is even more poignant than Milkman's interrupted merging with the sweet gum tree, the narrative shifts. In the next paragraph following the command to "Pass it on!" we read: "But they shot the top of his head off and ate his fine Georgia peaches. And even as boys these men began to die and were dying still" (235). White men murder Milkman's grandfather and take his farmland, thereby destroying not only a family's longevity in the place but also the will of the male progenitors who would shape the future of African American existence in that particular region. These African American subjects are deprived of agency unwillingly, in contrast to the tradition of ego dissolution in American nature writing, where subjects *desire* relinquishment of self-hood.

Where does Milkman's experience of "self" giving way under the sweet gum tree stand in relation to these violent, involuntary removals of self-hood? Where does his potential regeneration stand vis-à-vis the "classic" dissolutions of ego in American wilderness writing? Milkman's ego dissolution in/on unowned land provides a marked contrast to his father's attitude toward property as the material to confirm one's societal status. Macon Dead promises to Milkman an inheritance of property: "You'll own it all. All of it. You'll be free. Money is freedom. . . . The only real freedom there is" (163). Milkman's journey southward begins is a quest for such material prosperity, before he realizes spiritual benefits from intense interaction with a local culture and undeveloped woodlands. In place of his father's version of freedom, Milkman discovers he can be rejuvenated through nonmaterial means, or as Valerie Smith puts it, "through [Milkman's] story, Morrison questions Western conceptions of individualism and offers more fluid, destabilized constructions of identity."[18]

The quest for a destabilized or alternative mode of identity from that offered by dominant Western culture is shared by writers of American naturalism. I have noted how Annie Dillard seeks to experience "the world unraveled from reason." In *Desert Solitaire*, Edward Abbey describes a kindred desire to escape Western modes of perception. About his self-imposed isolation in a Utah wilderness area, Abbey claims: "I want to be able to look at and into a juniper tree, a piece of quartz, a vulture, a spider, and see it as it is in itself, devoid of all humanly ascribed qualities, anti-Kantian, even the categories of scientific description. To meet God or Medusa face to face, even if it means risking everything human in myself. I dream of a hard, a brutal mysticism in which the naked self merges with a nonhuman world and yet somehow survives still intact, individual, separate. Paradox and bedrock."[19] Milkman's climactic moment of "merging" with the sweet gum is just that—a "moment" of ego-dissolution, after which he must mobilize his mental and physical capacities to repel/thwart his would-be murderer. Abbey's merging with the desert landscape is likewise tentative. Perhaps he drops some of his civilized mannerisms during his season in the wilderness, while getting closer to the more-than-human world, as when he crawls on his belly in an attempt to observe two gopher snakes entwined together in a courtship dance; but Abbey nevertheless remains intact, of (arguably) sane mind, or as he puts it, "individual, separate." Even though the experience with more-than-human nature is temporary, it nevertheless seems worthwhile to consider, as Abbey, Dillard, and Morrison do, these moments when an individual can sample a mode of "being" not grounded in material culture.

*   *   *

Interesting questions arise when we consider a hybrid literature such as *Song of Solomon* that illuminates the lives of African American subjects while making use of British and Anglo-American narrative conventions, or, conversely, literature by writers of the dominant culture that appropriates the conventions of, say, Native American or African American art.[20] We may ask such questions as: How innocent (or not) is a writer's use of the themes, subjects, and narrative forms of the other culture? To what extent does a writer appropriate the conventions of the other uncritically? Is the writer sincere in the use of these conventions, or is she merely co-opting them for parodic effect? Lawrence Buell raises such questions when he notes how Native American poet Simon Ortiz mixes both "Native" and "Anglo" narrative conventions in his verse and therefore practices a "hybridized art." It would be wrongheaded, Buell asserts, to think of Ortiz as having been "colonized" by the time he spent at a writing program at Iowa or as "using western lyric conventions of persona and aesthetic distance to deconstruct them."[21] My initial reading of *Song of Solomon* was, perhaps, wrongheaded in this sense: I believed Morrison's use of such conventions as the moment of ego dissolution in the woods to be a parody of the mystical "nature writing" dominated by Anglo-American writers. A more constructive approach to Morrison's fiction, however, may ask how her "hybrid" art takes risks by placing an African American protagonist in a situation where he "finds" himself after losing his material well-being, after his magnificent ego is broken down, and is therefore a shift from what we expect from African American writers—namely, narratives that reinforce the importance of asserting and gaining subjectivity.[22] By echoing emphatically the language of ego dissolution in such canonical environmental texts as *Desert Solitaire* and *Pilgrim at Tinker Creek*, Morrison may be giving voice to a progressive "nature writing"—one that sincerely considers the spiritual possibilities of human interaction with more-than-human life-forms, but that does so within a complex web of cultural and historical contexts.[23]

NOTES

1. Gracious thanks to Ann Fisher-Wirth and Jay Watson for reading drafts of this essay and offering skillful criticism.

2. Elizabeth Dodd, "Forum on Literatures of the Environment," *PMLA* 114 (1999): 1094; Alice Walker, *Living By the Word* (San Diego: Harcourt, 1988); Eddy L. Harris, *Mississippi Solo: A River Quest* (New York: Harper, 1988).

3. John Tallmadge, "Beyond the Excursion: Initiatory Themes in Annie Dillard and Terry Tempest Williams," in *Reading the Earth: New Directions in the Study of Literature and Environment*, ed. Michael P. Branch et al. (Moscow, Id.: University of Idaho Press, 1998), 197; Jean Toomer, *Cane* (1923; rprt., New York: Norton, 1988); Zora Neale Hurston, *Their Eyes Were Watching God* (1937; rprt., New York: Harper, 1990); Dori Sanders, *Her Own Place* (New York: Fawcett Columbine, 1993); Gloria Naylor, *Mama Day* (New York: Vintage, 1988); Lawrence Buell, *The Environmental Imagination: Thoreau, Nature Writing, and the Formation of American Culture* (Cambridge: Harvard University Press, 1995), 7.

4. William Cronon, "The Trouble with Wilderness: or, Getting Back to the Wrong Nature," in *Uncommon Ground: Toward Reinventing Nature*, ed. William Cronon (New York: Norton, 1995), 79–80; Richard Slotkin, *Regeneration Through Violence: The Mythology of the American Frontier, 1600–1860* (Hanover, N.H.: Wesleyan University Press, 1973); Walter Inglis Anderson, *The Horn Island Logs of Walter Inglis Anderson*, ed. Redding S. Sugg Jr. (Rev. ed.; Jackson: University Press of Mississippi, 1985); Philip Lee Williams, *Crossing Wildcat Ridge: A Memoir of Nature and, Healing* (Athens: University of Georgia Press, 1999); Barry Lopez, *Crossing Open Ground* (London: Picador, 1989), 82.

5. Richard Wright, *Uncle Tom's Children* (1940; rprt., New York: Harper-Perennial, 1993), 28, 55; Eddy Harris, *South of Haunted Dreams: A Ride Through Slavery's Old Back Yard* (New York: Simon and Schuster, 1993).

6. Hurston, *Their Eyes Were Watching God*, 17–18; Toni Morrison, *Beloved* (New York: Plume, 1988), 268.

7. Toomer, *Cane*, 107, 84–86; Eldridge Cleaver, *Eldridge Cleaver: Post-Prison Writings and Speeches*, ed. Robert Scheer (New York: Random House, 1967), 57–58. Granted the apparent shortage of African American narratives of regeneration through landscape, if landscape is understood in the traditional sense of wilderness, still there is another subgenre where regeneration is achieved through what Wendell Berry calls "kindly use" of the land. Here the pattern is not so much one of escape and relinquishment as it is one of "settling in," of domestic cultivation and farming. Dori Sanders's *Her Own Place*, a novel tracing the life of Mae Lee Barnes, a female farmer in South Carolina who is loyal to her farm and community, is one contemporary African American novel modeling this alternate mode of regeneration through work and benevolent use of the land.

8. Gurleen Grewal, *Circles of Sorrow, Lines of Struggle: The Novels of Toni Morrison* (Baton Rouge: Louisiana State University Press, 1998), 63, 66, 73; Karla F. C. Holloway and Stephanie A. Demetrakopoulos, New *Dimensions of Spirituality: A Biracial and Bicultural Reading of the Novels of Toni Morrison* (New York: Greenwood, 1987), 93; Wendell Berry, *Another Turn of the Crank* (Washington, D.C.: Counterpoint, 1995), 90.

9. Ann E. Imbrie, "'What Shalimar Knew': Toni Morrison's *Song of Solomon* as a Pastoral Novel," *College English* 55, no. 5 (1993): 473–90, addresses how the novel develops patterns of such archetypal pastoral literature as *The Winter's Tale* and *As You Like It*, and thus is likewise concerned with the excursion motif—the restorative sojourn from the "civilized" place and into the "natural" world.

10. Anne LaBastille, *Woodswoman* (New York: Penguin, 1976).

11. Toni Morrison, *Song of Solomon* (New York: Plume, 1987), 226–27. Subsequent references to this work are given parenthetically in the text.

12. Scott Slovic, *Seeking Awareness in American Nature Writing: Henry Thoreau, Annie Dillard, Edward Abbey, Wendell Berry, Barry Lopez* (Salt Lake City: University of Utah Press, 1992), 4.

13. In addition to Stephanie A. Demetrakopoulos's psychoanalytical reading of Milkman's "ego death," Joyce Irene Middleton's "From Orality to Literacy: Oral Memory in Toni Morrison's *Song of Solomon*," in *New Essays on "Song of Solomon,"* ed. Valerie Smith (Cambridge: Cambridge University Press: 1995), focuses on how the scene highlights Milkman's initiation into African American "cultural oral memory": "Milkman's immersion in this auditory experience awakens his dormant listening skills to new language experiences and ways of knowing." His experience in the woods "move[s] him to use his preliterate imagination to reclaim his unlettered ancestors' skill for listening," an ability that saves his life by enabling him to sense Guitar's presence and thus avoid being strangled by him (35).

14. Annie Dillard, *Pilgrim at Tinker Creek* (1974; Toronto: Bantam, 1975), 31–32, 34, 35.

15. Lopez, *Crossing Open Ground*, 52–53.

16. Grewal, *Circles of Sorrow*, 71; Cleaver, *Eldridge Cleaver*, 63.

17. Melvin Dixon, *Ride Out the Wilderness: Geography and Identity in Afro-American Literature* (Urbana: University of Illinois Press, 1987), 167; Philip Page, *Reclaiming Community in Contemporary African American Fiction* (Jackson: University Press of Mississippi, 1999), 15.

18. Valerie Smith, "Introduction," in *New Essays on "Song of Solomon,"* 13.

19. Edward Abbey, *Desert Solitaire: A Season in the Wilderness* (1968; New York: Touchstone, 1990), 6.

20. Writing about Third World literary traditions, particularly those of the Maori of New Zealand, C. Christopher Norden in "Ecological Restoration and the Evolution of Postcolonial National Identity in the Maori and Aboriginal Novel," in *Literature of Nature: An International Sourcebook*, ed. Patrick D. Murphy (Chicago: Fitzroy Dearborn, 1998), notes the critical richness of cross-cultural intertextuality. Noting that Maori writer Witi Ihimaera's novel *Tangi* may evoke in some readers echoes of Emerson, Whitman, and other American transcendentalists, Norden writes: "An interesting question regarding Native novelistic and poetic traditions concerns the degree to which particular writers have intentionally evoked and played off of either transcendentalist rhetoric, for models of spiritual connectedness, or . . . Anglo-American modernist writers for models of alienation from nature, community, and traditional culture" (274). Inquiries about the extent of such intertextual influences may, as I hope this essay has, continue to reveal fresh ways of viewing nature writing and the position of minority writing against or within it.

21. Buell, *The Environmental Imagination*, 20.

22. Demetrakopoulos's affirmative reading of Milkman's "ego death" in *Song of Solomon*, for instance, deviates from the focus upon ego consolidation often emphasized in African American literature and scholarship. Consider *Their Eyes Were Watching God*, which foregrounds the growth of Janie into a confident, independent woman. Through her oral autobiography to Phoeby, Janie affirms the value of her sexuality, voice, and sense of self-worth. Likewise, a primary concern of Alice Walker's *The Color Purple* is Celie's acquisition of voice, her ability to assert

her selfhood after years of forced silence and abuse by violent men. With the help of Shug, Celie realizes she is a valuable inhabitant of this earth.

23. Rachel Stein's *Shifting the Ground: American Women Writers' Revisions of Nature, Gender, and Race* (Charlottesville: University Press of Virginia, 1997) is one of a growing body of texts offering provocative criticisms of minority literature and its position in relation to canonical American nature writing. Stein's study includes discussions of textual production by Emily Dickinson, Zora Neale Hurston, Alice Walker, and Leslie Marmon Silko, as she explores her fundamental question: "[H]ow do their revisions of the intersections of nature, gender, and race shift the ground of problematic aspects of American identities and allow the writers to rei-magine more fertile social/natural interrelations?" (4). Other texts considered to be a "new wave" of American literary ecology—shifting the focus of nature writing from the "pastoral impulse" to considerations of complex social problems bound up with our conceptualizations and use of what we call "nature"—include Karen J. Warren, ed., *Ecofeminism: Women, Culture, Nature* (Bloomington: Indiana University Press, 1997) and Greta Gaard and Patrick D. Murphy, eds., *Ecofeminist Literary Criticism: Theory, Interpretation, Pedagogy* (Urbana: University of Illinois Press, 1998).

LORIE WATKINS FULTON

William Faulkner Reprised:
Isolation in Toni Morrison's Song of Solomon

A critical discussion of almost any author in conjunction with modernist giant William Faulkner risks treating Faulkner's work as a master text. This potential for privilege perhaps accounts for Toni Morrison's sensitivity to such comparisons early in her writing career. One can practically hear the irritation in her voice when she stated in a 1983 interview with Nellie McKay, "I am not *like* James Joyce; I am not *like* Thomas Hardy; I am not *like* Faulkner. I am not *like* in that sense" (152). Morrison has elsewhere said, "I'm not sure that he [Faulkner] had any effect on my work" and "I don't really find strong connections between my work and Faulkner's" ("Faulkner and Women" 296–97). However, Morrison has also expressed praise and admiration for Faulkner's work, particularly for his unique style.[1] She once described teaching a class in which she traced for her students the way that Faulkner's *Absalom, Absalom!* forces readers "to hunt for a drop of black blood [by trying to ascertain Charles Bon's lineage] that means everything and nothing." Morrison elaborated, "No one has done anything quite like that ever. So, when I critique, what I am saying is, I don't care if Faulkner is a racist or not; I don't personally care, but I am fascinated by what it means to write like this" ("Art of Fiction" 101). She developed that fascination early on; as she told the audience at the 1985 Faulkner and Yoknapatawpha Conference, "in 1956 I spent a great deal of time thinking about Mr. Faulkner

From *Mississippi Quarterly* 58, nos. 1–2 (Winter 2004–Spring 2005): 7–24. © 2004–2005 by *Mississippi Quarterly*.

because he was the subject of a thesis that I wrote at Cornell." Morrison added, "there was for me not only an academic interest in Faulkner, but in a very, very personal way, in a very personal way as a reader, William Faulkner had an enormous effect on me, an enormous effect" ("Faulkner and Women" 295–96).

Critics have already identified several facets of Morrison's Faulknerian influence. Typical comparisons point out structural similarities such as syntax and cadence, and thematic similarities centering in historical concerns and social codes. Two pairings repeatedly emerge as scholars generally read *Beloved* with *Absalom, Absalom!* and *Song of Solomon* with *Go Down, Moses*.[2] However, Morrison's thesis, "Virginia Woolf's and William Faulkner's Treatment of the Alienated," also provides the basis for drawing thematic comparisons between Quentin Compson's story in the two Faulkner novels that it considers, *Absalom, Absalom!* and *The Sound and the Fury*, and Morrison's own bildungsroman, *Song of Solomon*.[3] Only Alessandra Vendrame has made a concerted effort to connect Morrison's interpretation of Faulkner in the thesis to her own body of work and I would argue that doing so affords valuable insight into her fiction, and into Faulkner's as well.[4] Morrison begins her thesis by defining "alienation," which she seems to use interchangeably with "isolation," as the predominant literary theme of the twentieth century ("Treatment" 1). After establishing this working definition, she analyzes Woolf's *Mrs. Dalloway* and the Faulkner novels in light of their differing approaches to isolation. Essentially, Morrison determines that Woolf's characters can only become self-aware and honest with themselves in isolation, and that Faulkner's characters can never attain this sort of self-knowledge when isolated (2–3). That her thesis privileges Faulkner's insistence on the need for communal connection becomes apparent when she reads Faulkner's stance as the "antithesis" to Woolf's position, rather than vice-versa (4). Her chapter on Faulkner also seems more fully developed than the one on Woolf, and, after all, Morrison's later writings reveal where her sympathies lie. In her thesis introduction she writes, "Alienation is not Faulkner's answer" to the problems of modernity (3). Nor is it Morrison's.

While Morrison has since, most certainly, revised many of the ideas and opinions that her thesis explores, she remains constant on the dangers of isolation, and even told Elizabeth Farnsworth in a 1998 *Online Newshour* interview concerning *Paradise* that isolation "carries the seeds of its own destruction." Indeed, Richard Misner says in that novel, "Isolation kills generations. It has no future" (*Paradise* 210). Morrison's thesis carefully chronicles the destruction wrought by isolation in the lives of both Quentin Compson and Thomas Sutpen, two protagonists that she feels Faulkner "doomed to a tragic failure" (3); this failure stemming from isolation later becomes one of the major Faulknerian themes that her own work acts against. In *The Signifying Monkey*, Henry Louis Gates, Jr. suggests that African American writers often revise Western texts with what he describes as "a compelling sense of difference based on the black vernacular" (xxii). By keeping this process in mind, readers can resist privileging either author and simply ask how these sorts of interpretations add to our understanding of each writer's work. Guitar even implicitly calls for such revision in *Song of Solomon* when he tells Milkman that white people "know they are unnatural. Their writers and artists have been saying it for years. Telling them they are unnatural, telling them they are depraved. They call it tragedy" (157). Morrison's third novel seems to "naturalize," as Guitar might say, what Morrison deems problematic in the two Faulknerian tragedies that her thesis addresses. Morrison reworks, with regard to the specific theories that she articulates in her thesis, the isolation that dooms Quentin and Sutpen, and she transforms it to create the conditions that allow Milkman to triumph in *Song of Solomon*. Morrison, consciously or unconsciously, reprises Faulkner's original theme and makes it her own in this novel that celebrates community and vanquishes the destructive isolation that she sees as the dark heart of Faulkner's fiction.

2

Milkman's and Quentin's stories parallel most obviously in that both characters engage in a quest centered in history. Morrison once described *Song of Solomon* as "my own giggle (in Afro-American terms) of the proto-myth of the journey to manhood" ("Unspeakable" 29), so she freely admits that this novel deliberately alters the idea of the masculine quest, a theme Faulkner held sacrosanct. The tales also resemble each other in that they both reveal the past through multiple layers of meaning, and Quentin and Milkman respectively reconstruct history based upon the various versions of it that they hear. Morrison states, "Faulkner puts Quentin through a thorough learning process and gives him the task of assimilating, under the eye of an outsider, Shreve, all he has been exposed to in the South" ("Treatment" 26). Morrison shows that Quentin doubts his neighbor's, Miss Rosa Coldfield's, version of Sutpen's story because he recognizes that it lacks objectivity, and he similarly doubts his father's, Mr. Compson's, nihilistic version because it lacks faith in anything at all (26–27). Furthermore, Morrison articulates how Shreve, Quentin's roommate at Harvard, forces Quentin to make an uninformed choice in responding to his famous question about why Quentin hates the South: "Shreve forces him [Quentin] into an oral confirmation that he has here-to-fore evaded" (28). According to Morrison, Quentin's anguished cry of "I dont hate it!" necessarily becomes his "acceptance of

Rosa Coldfield's loyalty to the South as more valid than his father's negativism" (28).

In *Song of Solomon* Morrison puts Milkman through the same sort of historical reconstruction that Quentin attempts, but she gives him far more to work with and allows him to make a more informed decision than the one that Shreve abruptly forces upon Quentin.[5] Milkman's community also provides him with more reliable sources of information, and from that community he gets a much more solid sense of the past, in various ways, than Quentin ever can. Milkman's first confirmation comes from Circe. When he visits her, she fills in many of the blank and confused areas of the family history that he has begun to assemble based on Pilate's and his father's partial revelations. From her, Milkman learns the names of Sing and Jake Dead (*Song* 243, 248), and that someone "dumped" the elder Macon's body in Hunters Cave after his original shallow grave eroded (244). Susan Byrd later significantly verifies and augments this information. She confirms that the full version of Sing's name is indeed Singing Bird, identifies Sing's adopted brother (Susan's father) as Crow Bird, and verifies the names of Jake, Ryna, and Heddy. Moreover, Susan clears up Milkman's misconception that Jake was the only son of Solomon and explains the legend of the flying African (321–23). Although one might argue that these multiple verifications also derive from a human memory subject to the same sort of error and partiality that Quentin distrusts, Morrison provides yet another level of verification in the actual song of Solomon. The song functions as an oral history, one much more vital than any written historical record or artifact, because it continues to live. When Milkman finally discerns the significance of the song, he becomes "as eager and happy as he had ever been in his life" as all the pieces fall into place and the historical story finally fits into the living story of the song (304).[6] Furthermore, Morrison illustrates Milkman's accommodation to this oral history when she forces him to rely on memory to record the song; in this scene, the written word remains conspicuously absent (303). In contrast, the only sort of tangible proof of the past that Faulkner allows Quentin to consult resides in the unkempt Sutpen graveyard (*Absalom* 156). Quentin can hardly extract the same sort of affirmation from epitaphs written on the cracked slabs and crumbling vaults that Milkman can from Morrison's living oral historical record.

Just as he cannot make sense of the historical artifacts, Quentin fails to understand the full import of Sutpen's story as it concerns the need for human connection because he dehumanizes both the players in it and the people in his own life. Morrison writes that Quentin sees others as "forms of behavior or reactions to various elements of the South" ("Treatment" 28), and elaborates that Sutpen's story "has no human value to him [Quentin], for it has become the tale not of people suffering and needing pity, but of values and abstract ideas which have failed" (29).[7] Morrison works against just this sort of dehumanization in Milkman's saga. Early in *Song of Solomon*, Milkman describes his mother as "too insubstantial, too shadowy for love." As a result, he has never thought of her as "a person, a separate individual, with a life apart from allowing or interfering with his own" (75). Milkman's attitude later changes drastically, and a large part of his understanding evolves from his learning not simply to hear but to listen and, more importantly, to understand. During their conversation in chapter ten, Circe tells Milkman, "You don't listen to people. Your ear is on your head, but it's not connected to your brain" (247). Milkman appears to take this admonition to heart because shortly thereafter he begins to treat people quite differently. Nancy Ellen Batty convincingly argues that when Circe teaches Milkman to hear, she acts as a revision of Faulkner's Clytie, Sutpen's mulatto daughter whom Quentin finds guarding the crumbling Sutpen mansion when he escorts Rosa upon her fateful return to that house. Batty points out that Quentin does not listen to Clytie in *Absalom, Absalom!* (84–85), and she feels that Morrison reworks the Clytie figure by having Circe successfully teach Milkman how to listen (89). During the hunt in Shalimar, Circe's lesson takes hold as Milkman realizes the self-centered nature of his attitude and begins to see things from the viewpoint of others. For instance, he thinks, "why shouldn't his parents tell him their personal problems? If not him, then who?" and muses that Hagar "had a right to try to kill him" for the way he betrayed her (*Song* 276–77). In the dark of the hunt, Milkman searches for self-knowledge, and "the thoughts came, unobstructed by other people, by things, even by the sight of himself" (277). When Milkman begins to listen in response to Circe's criticism, he finally begins understanding people instead of simply objectifying them.

In preparation for this impending connection to his distinctly oral history, Milkman begins to listen carefully to the hunter's signals, sounds he likens to "what there was before language. Before things were written down" (*Song* 278). As he begins to reflect upon his own life with greater clarity, the import of what Guitar earlier said about the peacock becomes clear: "Can't nobody fly with all that shit. Wanna fly, you got to give up the shit that weighs you down" (179). In the dark of the hunt, Milkman begins to give up the metaphorical shit that weighs him down and prepares for his own upcoming flight. As Marilyn Sanders Mobley notes, Milkman begins to respond to "the very voices he had been conditioned to ignore under the discipline of patriarchal hegemony" (61). As he learns to hear those voices, the ones his misunderstanding with Circe taught him to listen for, he becomes capable of the sort of reciprocal behavior that he displays with Sweet in the bath scene (*Song* 285). This capacity for genuine feeling and reciprocity ultimately culminates in the connection that he feels to Pilate at novel's end. And Morrison gently guides her readers through a similar process by forcing them to shed their dehumanizing tendencies as Milkman sheds his. Morrison spoke to this when she said in an interview with Thomas LeClair, "I feel that I do play to the gallery in *Song of Solomon*, for example, because I have to make the reader look at people he may not wish to look at. You don't look at Pilate. You don't really look at a person like Cholly [Breedlove]" (123). However, Morrison forces her readers to look, to humanize characters they might otherwise consider defective or even monstrous. In doing so, she extends her literary resistance to dehumanization to her readers and forces them, as she does Milkman, to recognize the humanity of others on a level she thinks Quentin Compson incapable of even approaching.

3

Morrison connects most of Quentin's problems to his attempts to "manipulate reality as God would or could" as he rails against fate in a battle that Faulkner depicts as futile ("Treatment" 32). Quentin most dramatically tries to do this by controlling time, and Morrison notes that Quentin breaks his grandfather's watch in an effort to stop time and thus escape reality (33). She adds that Quentin also tries to play God when he attempts to convince his father that he had an incestuous relationship with his sister, Caddy. With this false admission, he attempts to "make his own sin and arrange its due punishment, relying on God simply to carry out the terms of the contract he himself has drawn up" (29). Morrison characterizes the imagined incest itself as an act of isolation, a "sin" by which Quentin tries "to create out of nothing a private and living hell" (32). Although Morrison does not explicitly state it, this hell that Quentin proposes would, of course, never end. As such, it amounts to another of Quentin's attempts to play God by controlling time, the metaphysical equivalent of breaking his grandfather's watch.

Milkman engages in a similar battle with time, but he fares more successfully. He begins *Song of Solomon* existing only in the lived moment. Until he learns something of his history from his father and Pilate, the future and, by implication, the past do not exist for Milkman; rather, as Morrison writes, "the present did extend itself" (35). As Milkman becomes aware of his past, he comes to realize first that "You can't do the past over" when his father tells his version of the events surrounding Ruth's father's death, how he supposedly found Ruth lying next to her father's newly dead body, naked "as a yard dog, kissing him" (76, 73). Milkman becomes angry when this knowledge of the past threatens him, for the first time, in a personal way. He seethes with resentment because his father came to him "with some way-out tale" to explain the high level of animosity between himself and Ruth (76). In short,

Milkman initially resists engaging with his past in any critical, meaningful way, and by chapter eight, he actually runs from it when he feels the need to "beat a path away from his parents' past, which was also their present and which was threatening to become his present as well" (180).

However, after Circe teaches Milkman how to listen *and* hear, and the "shit" that weighs him down begins to fall away, Milkman stops running and begins to cultivate an understanding of his past. Morrison charts this constructive change by employing Milkman's watch as a symbol of it. When he realizes that Grace failed to give his watch back to him during that initial visit with Susan Byrd, he remarks, "Damn, ... I'm losing everything" (294). Milkman then determines, "a watch was not worth worrying about. All it could do was tell him the time of day and he really wasn't interested" (295). After the second meeting, during which Susan confirms many of Milkman's speculations about his family history, she offers to get his watch back for him and he replies, "Never mind" (325). As he begins to learn about the past, his interest in the measurement of present time begins to wane, and Morrison, through Milkman's conspicuous indifference to his watch, establishes the distinct difference between his approach to time and Quentin's. Quentin remains obsessed with time, particularly as he prepares for his suicide in *The Sound and the Fury*. From his grandfather's watch to the clock in the square's watchtower, Quentin never manages to escape time, save in suicide. Milkman, conversely, learns to take control of time by surrendering to it as he accepts his past and integrates it into his present. As Morrison says of Faulkner and time in her thesis, "Faulkner believes that time should be neither conquered as Quentin would like, nor ignored as Mr. Compson would. He believes that man has a responsibility to time and must endure it" (33). Morrison, unlike Faulkner, lets Milkman learn this lesson and gives him the means by which to accept his past and its inevitable influence on the present.

Quentin ends his quest to preserve the Compson family honor when he finally escapes time by committing suicide, an act Morrison defines as "the solution of the truly alienated" ("Treatment" 34). Morrison rightly reads Quentin's suicide as a highly desirable form of self-punishment; essentially, Quentin validates his cause by suffering for it. For Quentin, then, suicide becomes "a method of striking back" (34), yet Morrison interprets Quentin's suicide as a hollow victory, if not an outright defeat, because it defies the characteristics of humility and endurance that she feels Faulkner's work espouses. Quentin's failure "to adequately expiate the guilt of his family is Faulkner's statement that the reconciliation of man to his position is at hand when he learns to live outside of self and within time" (35). Milkman's leap toward Guitar at the conclusion of *Song of Solomon* might, at first, seem similar to Quentin's willful act of self-destruction; however, Morrison pointedly constructs Milkman's leap as another submissive triumph.[8] Rather than defying fate as Quentin does, Milkman submits to whatever consequences his landing might hold. And readers can logically assume that Milkman will likely emerge victorious from the encounter with Guitar because Pilate's earlier prediction, "Ain't nothin goin to kill him but his own ignorance" (*Song* 140), has thus far held true. By novel's end, Milkman has overcome much of that ignorance and has become empowered through his connection to his African heritage. However, Milkman can only obtain this power through submission. When he takes his leap, which symbolically connects him to the ancestral Solomon, he definitively embraces this knowledge of his heritage. That acceptance also extends the earlier lesson that Milkman learned about time to include the future. As he jumps, Milkman reflects that he now knows what Solomon knew, "If you surrendered to the air, you could ride it" (337). Milkman's ride, with all its attendant cultural and historical associations simply must, on some level, represent his submission to whatever destiny awaits him. His fate, though, ultimately becomes irrelevant because he acquires, along with the knowledge of his past, a connection to his ancestors that renders true, final death an impossibility according to the African religious beliefs which inform that ancestral knowledge. Like Solomon, Milkman will presumably one day survive, even thrive, indefinitely as an ancestor himself. In direct contrast to Quentin's desire to suffer eternally in a hell of his own creation, Milkman's spirit will live on in the collective cultural memory of his family.

<h2 style="text-align:center">4</h2>

The nuclear family that surrounds Milkman, however, seems highly problematic. Like many of the fathers in Faulkner's fiction, Macon Dead simply cannot provide the sort of emotional support that his son requires. In her thesis, Morrison says that Quentin "is estranged from his father because of the great distance between their points of view" (30). Although one might say the same of Macon and Milkman Dead, and Ruth Dead likewise exists as a shadow that rivals Mrs. Compson's ephemeral nature, Morrison provides Milkman with an alternative familial figure of authority in his aunt, Pilate. Her influence most usefully guides Milkman as he quests after the specifics of his history, possibly because Morrison makes her representative of that history. She introduces him to the knowledge that allows him to "fly" and, as John N. Duvall notes, this kind of flying involves "the ability to transcend self and self-love" (111). Pilate, then, teaches him this lesson by establishing a connection with his past, and in her powerful role as guide, she stands in stark opposition to Macon Dead.[9] Pilate exists as part conjure woman, part rebel, and part original woman. Like the Eve of the creation story, she has no navel, and Circe further establishes that Pilate "Borned herself" when she struggled free from her dead mother's womb after Circe had given up any hope of saving either mother or child (*Song* 244). In keeping with Morrison's characterization of Pilate as a living embodiment of antiquity, Gay Wilentz reads Pilate as a traditional African ancestral figure and convincingly traces the variety of ways that Pilate embodies that tradition as a cultural custodian (63–69), and Joyce Irene Middleton likewise reads Pilate as a "culture bearer" in the tradition of the African *griotte* (35).

Such a view of Pilate as the bearer of culture and history might seem unwarranted because, after all, Milkman gains most of his historical knowledge from other sources. However, Pilate teaches him more about how to interact with that history than simple facts ever could. She instructs him in the lessons about responsibility that he must learn before he can understand both other people and his heritage, lessons she learned from her father's ghost when he appeared and told her, "You just can't fly on off and leave a body" (147). Readers later discover that in this scene Pilate misinterprets Jake's lament that his own father, Solomon, left him behind as a statement about responsibility (333). However, this misunderstanding does not invalidate the lesson that she learns.[10] She takes this notion of responsibility to heart and lives her life according to its precepts. For years, Pilate drags around the bones of a man whose death she feels accountable for (readers later learn that they are actually her father's bones) in homage to the debt she thinks she owes him. This belief also extends to Pilate's relationship to society, because unlike Morrison's other pariah characters, Pilate feels a social responsibility and connection; she does not possess the brand of absolute freedom that characterizes Sula or Cholly Breedlove. Pilate's notions of responsibility temper the myth of the utterly free flying African in ways that significantly affect Milkman's understanding of his own obligation to others and to history. Wilentz shows that Morrison "is quick to remind us that the man flying away leaves people behind, most often women and their children" (72). Morrison does this, in part, by constructing Pilate's life as the antithesis to Solomon's flight. Because Pilate knows that you "just can't fly on off and leave a body" (147), she learns to fly within her body by freeing her mind and soul. When she dies, Milkman finally realizes that he loved her because "Without ever leaving the ground, she could fly" (336). As he cradles her dying body, Milkman realizes that Pilate taught him how to fly in a similar fashion by teaching him how to appreciate and interact with his familial legacy. He assumes control of that history and demonstrates both his mastery of it and debt to it by acknowledging his responsibility to Pilate when he revises her "Sugarman" lament into a tribute for her, the "Sugargirl" he continues to sing for even after she dies, his voice rising "louder and louder as though sheer volume would wake her" (336).

Morrison focuses a significant portion of her thesis on another of Faulkner's fathers, Thomas Sutpen. Faulkner hardly characterizes Sutpen as the sort of ineffectual father embodied by Mr. Compson; instead, Sutpen seems an overpowering patriarchal figure who has little, if any, regard for his children outside of his own interests. Morrison asserts that Sutpen lived a life "without love or need of it," and maintains that his "early acts of inhumanity return to plague him and his family" ("Treatment" 36–7). Moreover, she determines that in his state of alienation, Sutpen never even realizes that he acted wrongfully because isolation impairs his "moral sense" (38). In "Eruptions of Funk," Susan Willis reads Pilate as a "mythic hero" similar to Sutpen as a type, yet different in that Morrison "invests her . . . with utopian aspirations" (39); while this interpretation offers one possibility, a composite of the first two Macon Deads seems a more likely parallel. As Philip Weinstein points out, the original Macon arrived in Montour County in the same state of ignorance and poverty that marked Sutpen's entrance to Jefferson (120). A specific phrase that suggests a further connection between the two characters concerns the establishment of their estates. In her thesis, Morrison quotes the line from *Absalom, Absalom!* in which Quentin imagines how Sutpen "dragged house and gardens" out of a "virgin swamp" ("Treatment" 36, *Absalom* 32); she describes the way the elder Macon established his farm, using very similar terms when Milkman thinks of how he "tore a farm out of a wilderness" (*Song* 293). Milkman's father also feels a Sutpen-like materialistic desire. He advises Milkman that the most important thing in life is to "Own things," and thus reveals that his father's death and the loss of the family farm instilled in him a desire for worldly possessions that rivals even Sutpen's (55). Unlike Sutpen, however, Macon realizes what a high price he paid for that material comfort. Readers first sense this awareness as he longingly stands outside Pilate's window. Pilate, his "first caring for," draws him to the house, and the genuine emotion he expresses when thinking of her contrasts starkly with his thoughts of returning home to "his wife's narrow unyielding back; his daughters, boiled dry from years of yearning; his son, to whom he could speak only if his words held some command or criticism" (28). Macon's deliberate disassociation from his family appears even more devastating when juxtaposed with the three-part harmony that Pilate's family creates as he watches "the effortless beauty of the women singing in the candlelight" (29). Milkman later notices that talking about the past softens his father somehow, and Macon's childhood becomes the subject of the first genuine conversation the two men ever have (52). Morrison may create Milkman's father in the image of Sutpen, but when the past returns to haunt Macon, unlike Sutpen, he realizes that he sold out by trading human connection for respectability and security; Macon longs for the early familial affinity that he threw so carelessly away, if only for a moment as he walks away from Pilate's window, "resisting as best he could the sound of the voices that followed him" (28).

5

Macon's awareness of his loss makes it apparent that when viewed through the lens of Morrison's earlier work, *Song of Solomon* marks a turning point in her exploration of the theme of isolation. Readers can see Morrison working though the problems she associates with isolation in her first two novels, in which abusive, emotionally distant fathers and communities simply refuse to acknowledge the ugliness of the reality that exists in their midst. In *The Bluest Eye*, neither an entire community nor a single family, trapped by Cholly's domination, can save Pecola Breedlove. In Morrison's second novel, the community of Medallion refuses Sula a similar salvation in this life, though Morrison intimates that she likely achieves it in the next one. *Song of Solomon* finally shows readers a protagonist who becomes intimately connected to a communal and historical knowledge and grows through that relationship. In this novel, readers can see Morrison working towards the powerful communal saving force that will later rescue Denver, and perhaps even Sethe, in *Beloved*.

Some critics, though, believe that Milkman's gender makes that growth problematic and criticize *Song of Solomon*'s apparently careless treatment of women.[11] While women certainly do not fare well in Morrison's text, I would argue that Milkman's increasing valuation of Pilate and the responsibility he comes to feel for Hagar's death somewhat answer such claims. As Milkman points out, "You can't do the past over," and, in the end, he can offer those he has wronged only his regret (*Song* 76). It also seems important to note that rather than reducing the women in this novel at Milkman's expense, the way that Morrison reworks Faulkner's theme of isolation with Milkman's sisters, First Corinthians and Magdalene called Lena, significantly empowers these female characters. At the end of chapter nine, Milkman attempts to control Corinthians's sexuality in a scene highly reminiscent of the sort of sexual control that Quentin tries to establish over Caddy. Morrison's thesis interprets Caddy quite passively and concludes that she "submits to the doom without question or reflection" (25). Caddy ultimately runs away from home in *The Sound and the Fury*; in *Song of Solomon*, however, Morrison offers Corinthians another option via her sister. When Milkman attempts to prevent Corinthians from dating Henry Porter, Lena comes to her rescue. Lena practically attacks Milkman on her sister's behalf, questioning, "Where do you get the right to decide our lives?" (*Song* 215). She then assaults Milkman's own sexuality by referring to his penis as a "little hog's gut," and tells him that he has "pissed" his "last in this house," meaning, of course, that he can no longer "piss" on her or Corinthians. Finally, Lena whispers "get out of my room," and, probably in a state of shock, Milkman complies (216). Lena acts powerfully on her sister's behalf in a way that directly contrasts the passivity and aloneness that Morrison reads in Caddy. Instead of forcing Corinthians to leave home in order to gain control of her sexuality, Morrison has Lena order Milkman to stop manipulating Corinthians. One can only speculate how Faulkner's novel might have differed if Caddy had had a sister, and in her "Conversation" with Gloria Naylor, Morrison speaks of great fiction in a way that suggests such an agenda:

> for me there's nothing like reading a really, really fine book; I don't care who wrote it. You work with one facet of a prism, you know, just one side, or maybe this side, and it has millions of sides, and then you read a book and there is somebody who is a black woman who has this sensibility and this power and this talent and she's over here writing about that side of this huge sort of diamond thing that I see, and then you read another book and somebody has written about another side. And you know that eventually that whole thing will be lit—all these planes and all of the facets. . . . That's so gratifying, so exciting. That eliminates the feeling I had at the beginning [of her writing career]—that of solitude. (214–15)

Morrison's description of this literary diamond illustrates perfectly Gates's articulation of how African American authors revise Western texts with a distinct difference. Given that Morrison makes her interest in reinterpreting Western texts very clear in *Playing in the Dark*, the extension of that interest from her reading to her writing seems inevitable. In the end, perhaps we might most usefully regard Morrison and Faulkner as two Nobel laureates, separated by both time and circumstance, yet writing towards the same goal from different sides of that diamond. In reworking Faulkner's theme of isolation, Morrison takes her readers a step closer to the sort of literary illumination that she so desires as she brings to light yet another facet of that figurative literary gem.

Notes

1. At the 1985 Faulkner and Yoknapatawpha Conference, Morrison said of Faulkner's fiction, "My reasons, I think, for being interested and deeply moved by all his subjects had something to do with my desire to find out something about this country and that artistic articulation of its past that was not available in history, which is what art and fiction can do but sometimes history refuses to do" ("Faulkner and Women" 296). In that same speech, she went on to admire what she called

Faulkner's unique gaze, or "refusal-to-look-away approach in his writing" and his ability to "infuriate you in such wonderful ways" (297). Later, in the Elissa Schappell interview, Morrison praised Faulkner for his "brilliant" imagining of African American characters (100), and in an interview with Thomas LeClair she said, "Faulkner wrote what I suppose could be called regional literature and had it published all over the world. It is good—and universal—because it is specifically about a particular world. That's what I wish to do" (124).

2. For examples of the first pairing, see Kodat, Novak, and Hogan in *Unflinching Gaze*. For examples of the second pairing, see Cowart, MacKethan, Weinstein, and Duvall.

3. A few critics have connected elements of *Song of Solomon* with *The Sound and the Fury* and *Absalom, Absalom!*. For example, Willis contrasts Pilate's exclusively female household with the one formed in *Absalom, Absalom!* by Clytie, Judith, and Rosa during the Civil War (41). Batty also compares Faulkner's Clytie to Morrison's Circe and maintains that "Morrison perhaps 'hears' Clytie in a different register than most other critics of the novel, and that Clytie's voice can somehow be heard coming out of the mouth of Circe in *Song of Solomon*" (89).

4. This essay owes an enormous debt to Alessandra Vendrame's "Toni Morrison: A Faulknerian Novelist?" Vendrame describes Morrison's thesis as both "the most reliable source for discovering what Faulknerian features most impressed her in 1955, and the most appropriate jumping-off point for attempting to sketch out some elements in common between their [Faulkner's and Morrison's] narratives." Vendrame adds, "A close reading of *Song of Solomon* (1977) and of the thesis of 1955 reveals that in the novel, there is a very original revoicing of central Faulknerian motifs and themes—such as alienation, incest, and the impact of the past on the present—which were also at the core of Morrison's argument in the Faulkner chapter of her thesis" (679).

5. As Vendrame points out, "In Morrison's work, history emerges as a nurturing cultural foundation from the dialogic interaction between Milkman's search for himself and an obscure mythical past. While Faulkner in his treatment of Southern history seems willing to maintain uncertainties and constantly evades closure, Morrison establishes a point of intersection between the different voices in a commitment to recover and rewrite Milkman's family history. Thus, Milkman Dead not only repossesses his past, but also restores its meaning through the re-actualization of his family's mythical heritage" (684).

6. In the Neustadt interview at Bryn Mawr, Morrison explained the significance of Solomon's song as a personal oral history: "The song of Solomon: there's a song like that in my family. I don't know all the lyrics but it starts with a line like 'Green, the only son of Solomon,' and then some words I don't understand, but it is a genealogy" (90).

7. Morrison's thesis describes the characters in the Sutpen saga as "ghosts" which Quentin has "no feeling of affinity for" (28). She then asserts that Quentin sees his own family in much the same way. Caddy embodies family honor to Quentin, and he sees Benjy only as a duty. The other family members, Jason and Mr. and Mrs. Compson, seem too far removed from Quentin's mindset to share any sort of common ground (30).

8. In a 1977 interview with Pepsi Charles, Morrison classified *Song of Solomon* as an "absolute triumph" because "a man learns the only important lesson there is to learn. And he wins himself, he wins himself. And the quality of his life improves

immeasurably. Whether its length improves or lengthens is irrelevant" (50). Morrison elaborated on the final scene in her interview with Charles Ruas, "I really did not mean to suggest that they kill each other, but out of a commitment and love and selflessness they are willing to risk the one thing that we have, life, and that's the positive nature of the action. I never really believed that those two men would kill each other. I thought they would, like antelopes, lock horns" (111).

9. It testifies to Pilate's power as a character that when Schappell asked Morrison if she had ever had to tell any of her characters to "shut up," Morrison replied, "Pilate, I did. Therefore she doesn't speak very much. . . . I had to do that, otherwise she was going to overwhelm everybody. She got terribly interesting; characters can do that for a little bit. I had to take it back. It's *my* book; it's not called *Pilate*." (106).

10. MacKethan asserts that such misunderstandings actually create meaning: "this fluidity of language is consistent with the nature of the world. it is what gives life its creativity, and for Morrison, it is a literally lifesaving attribute of words" (106).

11. For example, Weinstein argues that, "Milkman's triumphant recovery of Solomon is ringed round with female suffering and exclusion." He then points out the negativity associated with the women in the text. He refers to elements such as Ruth's exclusion from the text, Hagar's tragic death, and Sweet's function as a sexual reward for Milkman, and concludes that "something in the internal binary logic of this text understands the saved life of a black man in terms of the yielded life of a black woman" (122–23).

WORKS CITED

Batty, Nancy Ellen. "Riff, Refrain, Reframe: Toni Morrison's Song of Absalom." Kolmerten 77–90.

Cowart, David. "Faulkner and Joyce in Morrison's *Song of Solomon*." *American Literature* 62.1 (1990): 87–100.

Duvall, John N. "Doe Hunting and Masculinity: *Song of Solomon* and *Go Down, Moses*." *Arizona Quarterly* 47.1 (1991): 95–115.

Faulkner, William. *Absalom, Absalom!* 1936. *William Faulkner: Novels 1936–1940*. Ed. Joseph Blotner and Noel Polk. New York: Library of America, 1990. 1–316.

Gates, Henry Louis, Jr. *The Signifying Monkey: A Theory of Afro-American Literary Criticism*. New York: Oxford UP, 1988.

Hogan, Michael. "Built on the Ashes: The Fall of the House of Sutpen and the Rise of the House of Sethe." Kolmerten 167–80.

Kodat, Catherine Gunther. "A Postmodern *Absalom, Absalom!*, A Modern *Beloved*: The Dialectic of Form." Kolmerten 181–98.

Kolmerten, Carol A., Stephen M. Ross, and Judith Bryant Wittenberg, eds. *Unflinching Gaze: Morrison and Faulkner Re-Envisioned*. Jackson: UP of Mississippi, 1997.

MacKethan, Lucinda H. "The Grandfather Clause: Reading the Legacy from 'The Bear' to *Song of Solomon*." Kolmerten 99–114.

Middleton, Joyce Irene. "From Orality to Literacy: Oral Memory in Toni Morrison's *Song of Solomon*." Smith 19–39.

Mobley, Marilyn Sanders. "Call and Response: Voice, Community, and Dialogic Structures in Toni Morrison's *Song of Solomon*." Smith 41–68.

Morrison, Toni. "The Art of Fiction CXXXIV." Interview with Elissa Schappell. *Paris Review* 128 (1993): 83–125.

———. "A Conversation: Gloria Naylor and Toni Morrison." Interview with Gloria Naylor. *Southern Review* 21.3 (1985): 567–93. Rpt. in Taylor-Guthrie 188–217.

———. "Faulkner and Women." *Faulkner and Women: Faulkner and Yoknapatawpha*, 1985. Ed. Doreen Fowler and Ann J. Abadie. Jackson: UP of Mississippi, 1986. 295–302.

———. Interview with Pepsi Charles. *NIMROD* 21 & 22 (1977): 43–51.

———. Interview with Elizabeth Farnsworth. *Online Newshour.* 9 March 1998. 30 June 2002 <www.pbs.org/newshour/bb/entertainment/jan-june98/morrison_3–9.html>.

———. Interview with Nellie McKay. *Contemporary Literature* 24.4 (1983): 413–29. Rpt. in Taylor-Guthrie 138–55.

———. Interview with Charles Ruas. *Conversations with American Writers.* New York: McGraw-Hill, 1984. 215–43. Rpt. in Taylor-Guthrie 93–118.

———. "The Language Must Not Sweat: A Conversation with Toni Morrison." Interview with Thomas LeClair. *New Republic* 184 (21 March 1981): 25–29. Rpt. in Taylor-Guthrie 119–28.

———. *Paradise.* 1997. New York: Plume, 1999.

———. *Playing in the Dark: Whiteness and the Literary Imagination.* 1992. New York: Random House, 1993.

———. *Song of Solomon.* 1977. New York: Plume, 1987.

———. "Unspeakable Things Unspoken: The Afro-American Presence in American Literature." *Michigan Quarterly Review* 28.1 (1989): 1–34.

———. [Chloe Ardellia Wofford]. "Virginia Woolf's and William Faulkner's Treatment of the Alienated." MA Thesis, Cornell, 1955.

———. "The Visits of the Writers Toni Morrison and Eudora Welty." Interview with Kathy Neustadt. *Bryn Mawr Alumnae Bulletin* (Spring, 1980): 2–5. Rpt. in Taylor-Guthrie 84–92.

Novak, Phillip. "Signifying Silences: Morrison's Soundings in the Faulknerian Void." Kolmerten 199–216.

Smith, Valerie, ed. *New Essays on Song of Solomon.* Cambridge: Cambridge UP, 1995.

Taylor-Guthrie, Danille, ed. *Conversations with Toni Morrison.* Jackson: UP of Mississippi, 1994.

Vendrame, Alessandra. "Toni Morrison: A Faulknerian Novelist?" *Amerikastudien* 42.4 (1997): 679–84.

Weinstein, Philip M. *What Else But Love?: The Ordeal of Race in Faulkner and Morrison.* New York: Columbia UP, 1996.

Wilentz, Gay. "Civilizations Underneath: African Heritage as Cultural Discourse in Toni Morrison's *Song of Solomon.*" *African American Review* 26.1 (1992): 61–76.

Willis, Susan. "Eruptions of Funk: Historicizing Toni Morrison." *Black American Literature Forum* 16.1 (1982): 34–42.

JUDY POCOCK

"Through a Glass Darkly": Typology in Toni Morrison's Song of Solomon

In a 1981 interview, Morrison told Charles Ruas that "the Bible wasn't part of my reading, it was part of my life" (97). In her use of structure, language, and concepts—her use of metaphor, repetition, and reiteration—the Bible resonates throughout Toni Morrison's novel, *Song of Solomon*. Erich Auerbach describes the Bible as a text "fraught with background" (qtd. in Alter, "The Old Testament" 22); the *Song of Solomon* is a text fraught with the background of the Bible. Here, I concentrate on Morrison's use of biblical names. The novel's epigraph—"The fathers may soar and the children may know their names"—signals the central role names will play in the novel. Over and over again, characters and places are named, renamed, or misnamed, and more often than not, the Bible is at the centre of this process. The title of the novel and the names of almost all the women and some of the men come from the Bible. Each one of these names evokes complex biblical characters, allusions, metaphors, and narrative cycles that resonate back and forth throughout the text, and each name signals a parallel with, reversal of, or contradiction with a given biblical allusion.

Buried in the text is a hint that those who know their Bible well will have special access when they read Toni Morrison's *Song of Solomon*. When Pilate goes to the police station to get her nephew, Milkman, and his friend, Guitar, out of jail, she impresses Milkman and the jail guards with her knowledge of

From *Canadian Review of American Studies* 35, no. 3 (2005): 281–298. © 2005 by the University of Toronto Press.

the Bible by quoting verbatim Matthew 21.2: "Bible say what so e'er the Lord hath brought together, let no man put asunder" (207). A reader well-versed in the Bible would realize that the verse Pilate is referring to is not the verse she quotes out loud. Matthew 21.2 actually quotes Jesus directing his followers to "Go into the village and . . . straightway ye shall find an ass tied, and a colt with her: loose them and bring them unto me,"[1] a Bible verse implying a far more appropriate metaphorical allusion to the matriarch's demand that the guards hand over the two reckless and selfish young men. In this playful example, we can see how Morrison uses the Bible to juxtapose implied narratives, images, and symbolic motifs to heighten contradictions and conjure up meaning. In the way that she uses biblical imagery and combines this with African and Afro-American folkloric elements, Morrison engages in what African American theologian Osayande Obery Hendricks describes as "guerrilla exegesis":

> *Exegesis*, from the Greek term signifying a narrative, a description, an explanation, an interpretation; a process of bringing out/leading out/teasing out meanings and significance heretofore obscured or hidden from view. *Guerrilla exegesis*, then, is the bringing or leading out of oppressed/ suppressed/don't-get-no-press meanings by sabotage subversion or other non-traditional appropriations of hegemonic renderings . . . a theology of new categories and old (and emergent) structures of feeling: a double-voiced theology. (2–3)

In operating as a guerrilla exegete, Morrison appropriates the methodology of Christian typology, and her primary strategy is to mobilize the typological power of biblical names. Typology, throughout the history of Christian exegesis, has been used as a key to clarifying the meaning of the Bible. This is how Northrop Frye explains typological interpretation of the Bible:

> The general principle of interpretation is traditionally given as "In the Old Testament the New Testament is concealed; In the New Testament the Old Testament is revealed." Everything that happens in the Old Testament is a "type" or adumbration of something that happens in the New Testament . . . Paul speaks of Adam as a *typos* of Christ (Romans 5:14). . . . What happens in the New Testament constitutes an "antitype," a realized form, of something foreshadowed in the Old Testament. In 1 Peter 3:21 Christian baptism is called the *antitypos* of the saving of mankind from the flood of Noah. Typology . . . moves in time: the type exists in the past and the antitype in the present, or the type exists in the

present and the antitype in the future ... Typology points to future events that are often thought of as transcending time, so that they contain a vertical lift as well as a horizontal move forward. The metaphorical kernel of this is the experience of waking up from a dream as when Joyce's Stephen Dedalus speaks of history as a nightmare from which he is trying to awake ... [I]t is essentially a revolutionary form of thought and rhetoric. We have revolutionary thought whenever the feeling 'life is a dream' becomes geared to an impulse to awaken from it. (79–83)

However, Toni Morrison's "guerrilla" use of typology and the power typology invests in names is not Frye's traditional Christian one. In her hands, typology can move back and forth at the same time and her types are sometimes not restricted to the biblical canon. Typology becomes a tool to reveal her own personal vision, a vision that speaks to the fate and condition of African American people.

In her use of typological names and the biblical narratives they evoke, Morrison is not simply interested in mobilizing the power of analogy. Typology in her hands becomes a vehicle for revealing contrast and contradiction as well as unity and the universal. Robert Alter's discussion of the way the Bible utilizes contradiction "as a guide for contemplating the dense tangle of human fate" (*Canon* 20) is a useful tool for understanding Morrison's use of a biblical subtext to set opposites in motion and create the ambiguity and play of contradictions that are so central to her novel. In examining the two conflicting biblical versions of the creation of woman, Alter argues that placing these stories side by side is evidence of "a strong synthesizing imagination" (*World* 7) that sought wholeness out of complexity, and that the author of Genesis "chose to combine these two versions of creation precisely because he understood that his subject was essentially contradictory" (*Art* 145).[2] He goes on to elaborate:

> The decision to place in sequence two ostensibly contradictory accounts of the same event is an approximate narrative equivalent to *the technique of post-Cubist painting* which gives us ... juxtaposed or superimposed, a profile and a frontal perspective of the same face. The ordinary eye could never see these two at once ... analogously, the Hebrew writer takes advantage of the composite nature of his art to give us a *tension of views* ... first woman as man's equal ... then, woman as man's subservient. (146; emphasis added)

Morrison, in her mobilization of biblical typology and the narratives this typology evokes, steals from both the Hebrew and the Christian traditions, insisting, like a post-Cubist artist, on a vision that incorporates the "tension of views" that encompasses the ambiguous and the contradictory.

It is impossible to separate Morrison's use of typology from the experience of African American people with Christianity. According to Lerone Bennett, "the Antebellum black was not converted to God, but converted God to himself" (qtd. in Lawrence-McIntyre 394). Vincent Wimbush, in "Reading Darkness, Reading Scripture," his introduction to the book *African Americans and the Bible*, explores this phenomenon:

> Almost from the beginning of their engagement with it, African Americans interpreted the Bible differently from those who introduced them to it, ironically and audaciously seeing in it—the most powerful of the ideological weapons used to legitimize their enslavement and disenfranchisement—a mirroring of themselves and their experiences, seeing in it the privileging of all those who like themselves are the humiliated, the outcasts and powerless ... African Americans' engagement of the Bible points to the Bible as that which both reflects and draws unto itself and engages and problematizes a certain complex order of existence associated with marginality, liminality, exile, pain, trauma....
>
> [The Bible] was seen as a sort of rhetorical paint brushing of their existence and a virtual manifesto for their redemption and triumph. So for African Americans to read scriptures is to read darkness. (17)

Toni Morrison appropriates, reverses, and extends typology to read darkness.[3]

Morrison signals her typological use of naming in the title she gives her novel, *Song of Solomon*. Controversy has surrounded the biblical book, Song of Solomon, since the origins of Hebrew and Christian exegesis. Certainly, this is a peculiar work to find in a religious book. This explicit poem of romantic and sexual love, placed in an idyllic setting full of vivid images of nature, never mentions God and seems to have no religious significance. As early as 90 CE, Rabbi Aqiba felt called upon to defend its place in the canon: "The whole world is not worth the day on which the Song of Songs was given to Israel, for all Scriptures are holy, but the Song of Songs is the Holy of Holies" (qtd. in Pope 19). Certainly, its enigmatic nature has always been acknowledged. Another early Hebrew exegete described it as "a lock to which the key has been lost" (qtd. in Pope 101). Because the literal meaning of the poem did not fit either a Jewish or a Christian paradigm, religious scholars were forced to read the poem as an allegory. Some read it as an allegory of the quest for salvation and the promised land, others as an allegory of God's relationship to human beings, and still others as an allegory of Jesus's relationship to the church. Try as they might, these scholars were never able to obliterate the sensual physicality of the poem or overcome its subversive, contradictory relationship to imposed canonical readings of the biblical text. Because the "beloved" of the poem has long been considered a black woman—"I am black but comely"—the "Song" has also been seen as God's gift to African American women. The title of the novel might lead one to expect a love story centred around a black woman. Instead, the title is part of the novel's enigma—its riddle—and, rather than explicitly pointing to an interpretation, it hints, through its evocation of types, at the meaning and the contradictions that underlie the novel.

The setting of the poem is pastoral—a garden that is a type of Eden, but a garden where there is no fall and no expulsion. Nature merges with the body of the lovers, just as Milkman feels his body merge with the land as he travels deeper and deeper into the fields and forests of the south: "Milkman rubbed the back of his head against the bark ... He felt a sudden rush of affection for them all ... down either side of his thighs he felt the sweet gum's surface roots cradling him ... he tried to listen with his fingertips, to hear what, if anything, the earth had to say" (278–9). The Song's garden is permeated with sexuality and the mutual passion of a woman and a man. It provides a type for the antitype scene of Sweet and Milkman's lovemaking. In these brief scenes, Milkman is able for the first time to really give himself to—love—a woman. And, in turn, these two scenes provide types for Milkman's final flight. Morrison describes this flight as sexual: "Milkman is able to surrender to the air and ride it at the same time ... it's the sexual act" (qtd. in Koenen 76). Morrison sees the orgasmic rhythm of sexuality that is so evident in the biblical poem as saturating the whole novel: "The rhythm of the book has this kind of building up, sort of in and out, explosion. There's this beat in it ... something in the blood, in the body, that's operating underneath the language" (76), the same rhythm that operates underneath the language of the Song o. Solomon.

By using the Song of Solomon as a type to frame her novel, Morrison emphasizes the central role that song, especially the song that Pilate sings at the beginning of the novel and that the children chant at the end, plays in her story. Lawrence-McIntyre argues in her essay "Double Meanings of Spirituals" that "slaves used Bible stories to retain aspects of their traditional religions in the form and structure of their songs" (383). To support her argument, she quotes Quincy Jones's observation in *Downbeat Magazine*:

We didn't have writers, but we did have music, and the music was the vehicle to carry the remnants of black history. The true history of blacks is not in our history books, but in the music. Our history

is all locked in the music and is passed down in its different forms
through that music. (399)

History is locked in Milkman's grandmother's name Sing, and in his great-
grandmother's name, Ryna, the ancient Hebrew word for song of rejoicing,
and, of course, in his great-grandfather Solomon's song ("Ryna"). Solomon
is associated with wisdom and he was the last king of a united Jewish king-
dom, a type of the New Jerusalem. The song reaches outside the Hebrew
and Christian canons to include traditional African and Islamic types.
Yoruba images are evoked, and in one version of the song, Solomon's Ara-
bic name, Sulieman, is used. Mohammed is named, as is Mecca, the city
where the angel Gabriel began to dictate the Koran to the prophet. Bilal,
a slave freed from a cruel master by Mohammed to become the first to call
believers to prayer and the first black Muslim, is also named. The baby that
is abandoned recalls Moses, a type of Jesus and a metaphor of liberation
for black American slaves. And the baby's name is Jacob, another type of
Jesus and—renamed by God, Israel—a patriarch, along with his grandfather Abraham, of the Jewish people. All Milkman's ancestors—actual and
mythic—are merged in this one song. Locked in the song are the history
and identity that Milkman is seeking.

The poem's allegorical implications also provide a typological frame for
the novel. To one degree or another, all the allegorical interpretations allude to
the biblical, epic journey of people toward salvation. The whole biblical story,
beginning with the journey of Jews toward a promised land and ending with
eschatological liberation, is encompassed in the allegories. From the early
days of slavery, this trope has been adopted by African Americans as a type
of their own struggle out of bondage toward liberation. This biblical journey,
a progressive journey, is also a type of Milkman's journey from the world of
sin and confusion toward a promised land of liberation. But his journey is
a regressive journey, back to origins. Morrison reverses the type. To move
forward, Milkman must move backward, into the south, toward rediscovery
and re-appropriation. In adopting this type to emphasize Milkman's journey
back to the south, Morrison not only appropriates but also subverts the common African American vision of how this biblical type has been particularly
reflected in the life of their own community. In African American Christian
typology, the "great migration," the mass migration of freed black slaves out
of the south into the north, is one of the main experiences associated with
the Jews' escape from Egypt (Sernett 448). However, this escape from bondage entailed loss as well as gain, epitomized in the sterility of Macon Dead's
existence. In their northward quest in search of political and economic justice,
African Americans lost, for the second time, connection with origins and

ancestors. Morrison argues that if you "kill your ancestors, you kill all. There's no future, there's no past, there's just an intolerable present" (qtd. in Koenen 73). Milkman's backward journey, at the same time as it subverts the materialistic north as a type of the promised land, celebrates another traditionally African American type of the promised land, Africa. In her integration of fragmentary allusions to a mythic African past, Morrison incorporates this significant African American antitype of the biblical journey into her vision of Milkman's search for salvation.

In the south, Milkman not only discovers his family origins, he experiences a unity with the land, respect for his family and fellow human beings, and a visceral sense of his African origins. When Milkman takes flight, he is "born again," but his rebirth is one not of redemption or salvation but of restoration. Flight re-establishes the umbilical cord to Africa. This rebirth is not a movement forward into a new world but a birth backward, a re-entry into the womb of history and origins. With her focus on flight, Morrison again expands her typology to include types outside the biblical canon. People do not fly in the Bible. Generally, even angels do not fly. But flight is a central image of black American and African folklore. Morrison comments that "flying was one of our gifts" (qtd. in LeClair 122), and by establishing flight as central to her typology, Morrison merges the biblical tradition with the African.

Just as the title provides a typological frame for the novel, Morrison's choice of biblical names for her individual characters resonates with typological significance. On the surface, none of these characters appears to have much in common with their types. Some critics believe that the purpose of the biblical names is simply to provide a contrasting image to highlight characteristics that are the exact opposite of the qualities of their namesakes. Certainly, characters like Ruth, Hagar, First Corinthians, and Pilate seem to have little in common with their biblical namesakes. However, to ignore the typological significance of these names and the biblical narratives that these types evoke is to lose whole layers of meaning that can enrich our reading of the novel. To borrow from the metaphor that Alter uses to describe the artistry of the author of Genesis, Morrison mobilizes a biblical subtext to create "post-Cubist" portraits of her characters that juxtapose or superimpose apparently contradictory qualities to produce an encompassing whole.

Ruth is a character who seems to have little in common with her type. It is true that the biblical Ruth is known for her loyalty and that Morrison's Ruth is loyal to the memory of her father; however, the loyalty of the biblical Ruth is of a very different nature. Blood does not define it; she *chooses* to be loyal to her poverty-stricken and helpless mother-in-law, Naomi. By juxtaposing the two loyal Ruths, Morrison uses biblical subtext to emphasize the dead end of misplaced loyalty. Ruth's loyalty to her father, Dr. Foster, chains her to the power of patriarchy, materialism, and assimilation into the dominant culture of racism.

However, a closer look at the biblical Ruth's narrative and her typological role provides clues to a deeper reading of Milkman's mother's character and her part in Morrison's text. All the biblical Naomi's sons are dead and she has no grandson, so her ancestral line has been destroyed. Alone, without a husband, Naomi faces a future of poverty and loneliness. Her widowed daughter-in-law defies convention to stay with her mother-in-law, uttering the famous words that have become a trope of loyalty: "For whither thou goest, I will go; and where thou lodgest, I will lodge: thy people shall be my people, and thy God my God" (Ruth 1.16). Together, the widow Ruth and her mother-in-law Naomi conspire to ensure that Ruth will marry a man with wealth and power and, in this way, ensure Ruth's own security as well as Naomi's. Ruth's marriage and the birth of a son, who, through levirate tradition, is considered her dead husband's son, ensures the survival of Naomi's line and the line that goes on to produce King David and then Jesus. Ruth, an alien who has chosen to throw her lot in with the Jewish people, becomes one of the "mothers of Israel" and, for Christians, a type of Mary (Jeffrey 669). Her great-grandson David, the greatest Jewish king and the protector of the Ark, the repository of memory, is a type of Jesus.

Ruth Dead is also an alien. Her light skin and her inherited bourgeois aspirations separate her from the black community. Her husband is symbolically dead, having abandoned his ancestry for the pursuit of materialism. Although Ruth Dead's hesitant steps pale in comparison to the biblical Ruth's bravery, she does turn at crucial times to her sister-in-law, Pilate. Together they do everything they can to ensure a son. Pilate, here an antitype of Naomi, uses her magic to revive her brother's sexual desire and thus preserve her ancestral line. Milkman's conception resonates with the immaculate conception of Jesus. In his final flight, he becomes the true descendant of his aunt Pilate and the ancestral line that she has spent her life striving to keep alive. Like David, he becomes the guardian of the ark of memory that Pilate has struggled, with her bag of bones, to preserve. David's Ark is lost in wars and confusion but, since Milkman's flight is a flight backward to origins, the "ark" entrusted to him by Pilate will only grow in meaning and memory. Ruth, like her biblical type, becomes an unlikely mother of revival and restoration.

Morrison's Hagar in some ways evokes her biblical type more explicitly than the novel's Ruth. The biblical Hagar, like Pilate's haunted and rejected daughter, is used sexually and then abandoned. She is the Egyptian handmaid of Abraham's wife Sarah. The barren Sarah, believing that, at seventy-six, she is too old ever to provide an heir to her eighty-six-year-old husband, gives

Hagar to Abraham as a surrogate to ensure that Abraham's family line does not die. But once Hagar is pregnant, Sarah becomes jealous and, with Abraham's complicity, forces Hagar into exile in the wilderness. God intervenes and Hagar is returned to Abraham and Sarah, only to be abandoned once again when Sarah miraculously becomes pregnant at ninety with Isaac, who becomes Abraham's official heir and one of the great Hebrew patriarchs. This time, Hagar's abandonment is permanent, but once again God takes pity on here and saves Hagar and her son Ishmael from certain death by creating a well of pure water in the arid desert.

Like her biblical type, Morrison's Hagar is a misfit, lost in the wilderness of the materialistic north and unable to find her way back to the comfort of origins. Like the Bible's Hagar, her life is destroyed by a man who uses her sexually and then abandons her. Both Hagars' destinies are marked by loss. But there is one glaring difference in the fate of the two women: Morrison's Hagar is alone and childless, while the Bible's Hagar has her son, Ishmael. For those who know the Bible, Hagar's barrenness and her obsessive sense of loss is emphasized by the missing Ishmael, an absence that haunts the novel. Paul's typological interpretation of this story intensifies the poignancy of the missing Ishmael. In his letter to the Galatians, Paul reads this story as an allegory. Hagar's son Ishmael, the son of a slave, represents the people of the old covenant, excluded from the new Christian covenant with God and thus spiritually enslaved, while Isaac, although born second, is the son of a free woman and represents the "children of promise" who, through Christ, are the rightful heirs of the new Jerusalem (Gal. 4.22–31). Hagar and her absent son Ishmael are types of the novel's Hagar and the excluded African American people of the United States.

In the Bible, Hagar is a relatively minor character and just as, for people who know the Bible, Ishmael's absence haunts *The Song of Solomon*, for those that know the Koran, the missing links of Hagar's story haunt the Bible. The Koran's Hagar is a central character and her son Ishmael plays a pivotal role, much like the one Isaac plays in the Bible. It is Ishmael, not Isaac, who escapes sacrifice at the hand of his father through divine intervention, and he then goes on to found the ancestral line that produces the prophet Mohammed. The matriarch Hagar's triumph in the face of adversity is commemorated every year by thousands of devote Moslems who are obliged, once in a lifetime, to complete the Hajj pilgrimage, a journey that retraces Hagar's wanderings in the wilderness. By robbing her Hagar of Ishmael, Morrison draws attention to the obliteration of most of Hagar's story from the Christian Bible and to the way the forces of slavery robbed the African American people of their Islamic heritage. But just as traces of this tradition survive in Solomon's song, Hagar, the courageous matriarch of the Koran, is a type who lurks in the background of the untold history of the African American people.

One of the most intriguing biblical names in the novel is that of Milkman's sister, First Corinthians. Corinthians, throughout most of the novel, seems to be part of the "dead" world of her father. She is educated, but her education does not provide her with a way forward and she seems doomed to spend the rest of her life in the tomb of the old house on No Doctor Street. In spite of her education, the only job she is able to get is as a maid. As hopeless as her life seems to be throughout most of the novel, Corinthians is one of the few secondary characters in the book who achieves a form of liberation, and her liberation is a product of one of the most perplexing events in the novel. Afraid that she will lose her lover, Porter, "Corinthians climbed up on the fender and lay full out across the hood of [Porter's] the car. . . . She lay there, stretched across the car, her fingers struggling for a grip on steel. She thought of nothing. Nothing except what her body needed to do to hang on, to never let go" (199). In an ironic parody of romantic novel tropes, Porter, a most unlikely romantic hero, responds by sweeping her up in his arms and carrying her off to bed. Corinthians is redeemed through love and redeems Porter, in turn, through her love for him. She debases herself, stripping herself of all traditional notions of self-respect, and becomes, paradoxically, empowered. Her way forward is not to emulate strong independent female figures like her Aunt Pilate, but it is a way forward, nonetheless. Morrison has created in Corinthians a testament to the unexpected, unorthodox, and surprising ways human beings find their own path to freedom. She is reminiscent of one of the post-Cubists portraits that Alter refers to. She is full of contradictions but is characterized by an underlying coherence that is satisfying at the same time as it is unsettling.

Corinthians' problematic character is emphasized by her biblical name, First Corinthians. Unlike the other biblically named characters in the novel, Corinthians is named for a whole book of the Bible. Unlike the parts of the Bible that Morrison draws her other allusions from, this book does not include heroic types or dramatic narrative. First Corinthians is a letter written by the Apostle Paul to the small struggling congregation of early Christians at Corinth and is ideological in nature. In this letter, Paul lays out the explicit rules and regulations that should govern the young congregation. The book, along with the other Pauline letters, has proved problematic for many African Americans. Howard Thurman, in his book *Deep River*, recalls what Grey Gundaker considers a typical experience:

When I was a boy, it was my responsibility to read the Bible to my Grandmother, who had been a slave. She would never permit me

to read the letters of Paul, except on occasion the 13th Chapter of
First Corinthians.... When at length I asked for the reason, she
told me that during the days of slavery, the minister (white) on the
plantation was always preaching from the Pauline letters—"Slaves,
be obedient to your masters," etc. "I vowed to myself," she said,
"that if freedom ever came and I learned to read, I would never read
that part of the Bible!" (qtd. in Gundaker 757)

Not only can First Corinthians be read as a justification of slavery and class
(1 Cor. 12.18), but in this letter, Paul condemns sex—"[I]t is good for a man
not to touch a woman" (7.1)—even as he grudgingly accepts marriage—[I]t
is better to marry than to burn" (7.9). He goes on to insist that "the head
of the woman is the man" (11.3) and that it is forbidden and a "shame for
woman to speak in church" (14.35). This one biblical book includes many
of the oppressive qualities of Christian ideology that African Americans,
and especially African American women, have had to contend with as they
appropriate the Bible for their own use. However, one chapter, chapter
thirteen, stands out in sharp contrast to the rest of Paul's diatribe. In this
chapter, with some of the most beautiful poetry in the Bible, Paul proclaims
the supremacy and healing power of love: "Though I speak with the tongues
of men and of angels, and have not love, I am become as sounding brass or
a tinkling cymbal . . . and now abideth faith, hope and love; but the greatest
of these is love" (13.1–13). Corinthians has grown up internalizing the racism, misogyny, and class prejudice that surround her. Her internal struggle
is instinctive and unthinking but ideological nonetheless. Her victory, like
Milkman's, is to "dominate and surrender," and her liberation lies in the play
of contradictory ideological fragments that are intrinsic to the biblical book,
First Corinthians. She surrenders, but on her own terms, following Paul's
advice to "become a fool, that [s]he may be wise" (3.18). She is determined
to see "through a glass darkly" (13.12) to insist on her own personally paradoxical liberation.

Milkman too suggests biblical types. He has the same name as his grandfather, and near the end of the novel, we learn that his grandfather's name is
not Macon Dead but Jacob. Jacob is a type of Jesus and, in Milkman's story,
we can see echoes of the life, sacrifice, and resurrection of Jesus. However,
Jacob, one of the most complex and contradictory biblical characters, provides
a more interesting type for the hero of Morrison's novel. Like Ruth, Jacob's
mother Rachel is barren for many years, until God, like Pilate, intervenes and
"open[s] her womb" (Gen. 29.31). Milkman, like Jacob, is privileged. Jacob's
grandfather Abraham is picked by God to be the patriarch of the chosen people and Jacob's mother favours and protects him. And again, like Milkman,

Jacob, who cheats his brother out of his birthright and his father's blessing, is a hero but often not a very *nice* man. In the southern wilderness, Milkman's struggles for life against his friend Guitar are a mirror of Jacob's night-long struggle with God or the angel. In one of the most perplexing incidents in the Bible, Jacob prevails over God and, through the struggle, gains a new name, Israel (Gen. 32.24–8). Milkman too, against all odds, survives his struggle with Guitar, who has appropriated the power of life and death. Guitar is an angel powered by the wrath of a righteous, avenging God. Roland Barthes, in his famous essay "The Struggle with the Angel," sees in this struggle a reflection of Jacob's struggle with his brother Esau (90). Milkman and Guitar, like Jacob and Esau, are both brothers and enemies. Their connection and enmity reflect that of Jacob and Esau, but the deep love they have for each other reflects another type in the Bible, the passionate love of David[4] and Jonathan, a male love "passing the love of women" (2 Sam. 1.26). Like Jacob, Milkman is transformed by this struggle and is able to rejoin the men of Shalimar with a new humility and appreciation. Like Jacob, he has seen "the face of God" (Gen. 32.30), but he sees it in the face of his fellow human beings.

Pilate's name conjures up the most perplexing type in the whole novel. Pilate in the Bible is the Roman governor who orders the crucifixion of Jesus—the killer of Christ. Pilate seems to have nothing in common with her type. She is the heroine of the novel. She, alone of all the characters, consistently keeps faith with the past, preserves traditions, and protects the next generation as best she can. Morrison sees Pilate as coming the closest of all her female characters to being an ideal woman: "The woman that is most exciting ... is Pilate, only because she has a kind of ferocity, that's very pointed, astute, and she's also very generous and wide-spirited; she has fairness and braveness, you know, in a way I'd like to be" (qtd. in Koenen 69). Few critics have commented on the significance of Morrison's choice of the biblical name Pilate for her heroine. Some see it as a straightforward pun on the word pilot, pointing to her role as a guide in facilitating Milkman's search and his final flight; others see it as a condemnation of the arbitrary way in which African Americans were given their names. However, all the other characters with biblical names connect, in one way or another, directly with their namesakes; Morrison's choice of Pilate as a name for her heroine is so shocking and perplexing it demands more attention. By choosing Pilate as her heroine's name, Morrison travels into uncharted typology and extremely subversive territory. The biblical Pilate is a type of Morrison's Pilate because her Pilate also kills Christ.

When Pilate sacrifices her life for Milkman, she usurps Christ's role. It is through her death, not Jesus's, that Milkman is saved. The truth that will set Milkman free is not the truth of Jesus but the truth that is "locked in music," the truth that Pilate preserves in her bag of bones. Jesus is not the "way"; Pilate is. The biblical Pilate is not the only biblical type of the novel's Pilate. Born without a navel, Pilate is an antitype of Eve, who in turn is a type of Mary, who in turn is an antitype of all the powerful matriarchs of the Old Testament. Pilate is Rachel as she steals and hides away her father's household gods, in that way—in a paradoxical, biblical way—preserving paganism in the heart of patriarchal monotheism. But Pilate has gone a step further than the matriarchs of the Bible. She has given birth to herself and used her magic to bring about the birth of at least one other. Like the biblical Pilate, she has power; but his power is a temporal power—the power of the oppressor over the oppressed. Morrison's Pilate has a much stronger power. Hers is the power of the matriarchy, of the traditions that women preserve, and of the spiritual force of paganism—the gods of her ancestral Africa. Jesus is not only the Christian Saviour; he is the direct descendant and the antitype of all the patriarchs of the Old Testament. In burying the bones of her father and usurping Christ's role, she murders the patriarchy. In her sacrifice, the matriarchy dies too, but matriarchal power is regenerative and will be born again in some new form.

With her sacrifice, she allows Milkman to be reborn, to re-appropriate the magic of his ancestor Shalimar—to fly. After all, as Morrison has said, this novel is about men, and Milkman, in flight, is the type of his antitype, the new African American man. His name, first earned through ridicule, incorporates the male and the female principle of milk—maternal nourishment and a powerful biblical type of promise, mercy, and the final salvation. He is a new Everyman. In flight, Milkman surrenders to the air:

> I want him to learn how to surrender, and to dominate—dominion and surrender ... women already know that surrender part, and can easily learn how to dominate.... But what I wanted was a character who had everything to learn.... This man, Milkman, has to walk into the earth—the womb—in that cave, then he walks on the surface of the earth and he can relate to its trees—that's all very maternal—then he can go into the water ... then he can bathe and jump in the air. (Morrison, qtd. in Koenen 75–6)

In murdering the patriarchy and usurping the role of Jesus, Pilate allows Milkman to be reborn to become the promise—the type—of the new man.

His rebirth, however, is problematic. Morrison marks Milkman's final flight with contradiction: "[T]he ambiguity is deliberate because it doesn't end, it's an ongoing thing" (Morrison, qtd. in Davis 232). On the one hand, Milkman can fly because he relinquishes part of his maleness and embraces the female. As long as "Milkman is in a male, macho world and can't fly, [he] isn't human, [he] isn't complete until he realizes the impact that women have made on his life. It's really a balance between classical male and female force that produces, perhaps a kind of complete person" (Morrison, qtd. in Ruas 107). On the other hand, when Milkman flies, he leaves Hagar's broken body behind. His is an individual rather than a collective liberation. Morrison is acutely aware of the contradictions implicit in her appropriation of the flight metaphor:

> I used it not only in the African sense of whirling dervishes and getting out of one's skin, but also in the majestic sense of a man who goes too far, whose adventures take him far away ... black men travel, they split, they get on trains, they walk, they move.... It's a part of black life, a positive, majestic thing, but there is a price to pay—the price is the children. The fathers may soar, they may triumph, they may leave, but the children ... remember, half in glory and half in accusation. (qtd. in Watkins 46)

And, as Milkman flies toward Guitar, is his liberation a freedom from death or a freedom in death, a form of revolutionary suicide? We are left with the feeling that the dialectical tension between the male and the female, the past and the future, struggle and reconciliation, is just beginning to be played out. Although Milkman's journey is the central narrative of *Song of Solomon*, by superimposing his story on the tangled narratives of all the other characters in the novel, on the mythic and historical past of African America, and on the subtext of the Bible, Morrison is able to create a complex picture that includes both divergence and unity. Like the authors of the Bible, Morrison uses "composite narrative as a purposeful technique" (Alter, *Art* 147) to capture the dynamism of the contradictions facing African Americans as they face the future. In setting these contradictions in motion, she points to the possibility of some resolution but leaves other possibilities in the hands of her readers and the future.

At the end of *The Great Code*, Frye observes that "man is constantly building anxiety-structures, like geodesic domes, around his social and religious institutions." He goes on to say that the Bible is written in "a language that would smash these structures beyond repair, and let some genuine air and light in" (232). Toni Morrison, with her unique use of biblical typology, has done just that.

Notes

I would like to thank my friend Shahram Kholdi for his assistance in understanding the Islamic references and their significance in the Solomon's song. Kholdi, a graduate student in Political Science at the University of Toronto and a graduate of the University of Theran was able to draw on his background to explain references and point me to relevant sections of the Koran.

1. All biblical references are to the Authorized Version. However, in the reference to 1 Cor. 13.1–13, the word "charity" has been replaced with the word "love." This translation occurs in versions of the Bible that have appeared since the Authorized Version, including the New King James Version.

2. In Gen. 1.27 God creates, "in his own image," man and woman simultaneously. In Gen. 2.22, God creates woman after the creation of Adam, out of one of Adam's ribs.

3. In developing her own interpretation of typology Morrison builds on the African American tradition of "figuralism." Chanta M. Haywood, in her article "Prophesying Daughters: Nineteenth-Century Black Religious Women, the Bible and Black Literary History," cites Theophus Smith's definition of this critical approach: "a hermeneutic or interpretative tradition in which a person or place, object or event [in the Bible] is connected to a second entity in such a way that the first signifies the second and the second fulfills or encompasses the first" (362). Haywood describes how nineteenth-century black women preachers used this approach to argue for political change.

4. Guitar's name itself also evokes David, the composer of the Psalms, whose skilful playing of the lute comforts Saul. David, born in Bethlehem, provides an ancestral link between the Hebrew patriarchs and Jesus and, in traditional biblical typology, is considered a type of Jesus. Guitar, with his association with the vengeful secret society Seven Days, is another type of Jesus. However, the Jesus he evokes is not the Jesus of redemption but the Jesus of the Second Coming, who judges and condemns those who have sinned. The name of his organization not only provides an ironic reversal on the seven days of creation of the Bible and a nod to the cleansing destruction of the seven days of Noah's flood but also alludes to the numerous references to seven that occur in Revelation (seven churches, seven candlesticks, seven stars, seven seals, seven trumpets, seven vials, seven plagues, seven kings, seven angels, and the beast with seven heads).

Works Cited

Alter, Robert. *The Art of Biblical Narrative*. London: Allen, 1981.

———. *Canon and Creativity*. New Haven: Yale UP, 2000.

———. "The Old Testament." Introduction. *The Literary Guide to the Bible*. Ed. Robert Alter and Frank Kermode. Cambridge: Harvard UP, 1987. 11–35.

———. *The World of Biblical Literature*. New York: Basic, 1992.

Barthes, Roland. "The Struggle with the Angel: Textual Analysis of Genesis 32:22–32." Trans. Stephen Heath. *Modern Critical Views: The Bible*. Ed. Harold Bloom. New York: Chelsea, 1987.

Davis, Christina. "An Interview with Toni Morrison." Taylor-Guthrie 223–32.

Frye, Northrop. *The Great Code*. Toronto: Academic, 1981.

Gundaker, Grey. "The Bible *as* and *at* a Threshold." Wimbush, *African Americans* 754–72.

Taylor-Guthrie, Danille, ed. *Conversations with Toni Morrison*. Jackson: U of Mississippi P, 1994.

Haywood, Chanta M. "Prophesying Daughters: Nineteenth-Century Black Religious Women, the Bible, and Black Literary History." Wimbush, *African Americans* 355–66.

Hendricks, Osayande Obery. *Guerrilla Exegesis—Struggle as a Scholarly Vocation: A Postmodern Approach to African-American Biblical Interpretation.* 29 Jan. 2004. <http://www.payne.edu/guerrilla_exegesis.pdf>.

Jeffrey, David Lyle, ed. *A Dictionary of Biblical Tradition in English Literature.* Grand Rapids, MI: Eerdmans, 1992.

Koenen, Anne. "The One Out of Sequence." Taylor-Guthrie 67–83.

Lawrence-McIntyre, Charlotte Charshee. "Double Meanings of Spirituals." *Journal of Black Studies* 17.4 (1987): 384–401.

LeClair, Thomas. "The Language Must Not Sweat: A Conversation with Toni Morrison." Taylor-Guthrie 119–27.

Morrison, Toni. *Song of Solomon.* New York: Knopf, 1977.

Pope, Marvin P. *The Anchor Bible: Song of Songs.* New York: Doubleday, 1978.

Ruas, Charles. "Toni Morrison." Taylor-Guthrie 93–118.

Sernett, Milton. "The Great Migration and the Bible." Wimbush, *African Americans* 448–63.

Watkins, Mel. "Talk With Toni Morrison." Taylor-Guthrie 43–7.

Wimbush, Vincent L., ed. *African Americans and the Bible.* New York: Continuum, 2000.

———. "Reading Darkness, Reading Scripture." Introduction. Wimbush, *African Americans* 1–48.

JUDITH FLETCHER

Signifying Circe in Toni Morrison's Song of Solomon

Toni Morrison's *Song of Solomon* shares with Homer's *Odyssey* a profound concern with naming. Names are obscured, replaced, and eventually revealed in both epic poem and novel.[1] They possess a transformative power at times: Odysseus does indeed become No Man, the name he uses to trick the Cyclops, when he arrives home as a nameless beggar; in Morrison's novel the man whose name is changed to Macon Dead is murdered, and his descendants transfixed in a spiritual death. Names in *Song of Solomon* are deeply implicated in issues of narrativity: this is a story *about* naming, and its characters frequently bear names which denote their narrative function, for example Pilate, who acts as a guide to the protagonist Milkman Dead, or Sweet, the woman he wins after completing his ordeal in Shalimar. Certain names allude to other stories: Hagar, Ruth, Rebecca, and First Corinthians have obvious biblical associations in keeping with the novel's title. The midwife, Circe, a pivotal figure in the puzzles of naming and narrative around which the novel is structured, is the only character to bear a name from Greek mythology. Yet while she so obviously signifies a Homeric intertext and the patrilineal literary history that is its legacy, Circe simultaneously subverts this tradition, sending the protagonist on a journey that resembles the master narrative, but is destabilized by other discourses. The integrity of the narrative is accordingly stretched between a system of dualities: men's

From *Classical World* 99, no. 4 (2006): 405–418. © 2006 by the Classical Association of the Atlantic States.

and women's stories compete for authority, Western mythic traditions are contested by African folklore, and the myth of the catabis, the descent to the Underworld, is challenged by a fantasy of ascent manifested in the folktale of the man who could fly.

In this essay I focus on how Morrison employs the figure of Circe to position her novel both within and beyond the classical tradition of the catabatic narrative. Toni Morrison graduated with a minor in classics from Howard University in 1953, and it is obvious that her academic training informed *Song of Solomon*.[2] This, her third novel, is distinguished from much of her other work, which explores the experience of black American women, by its focus on a central male character, Milkman Dead. Milkman, the son of a prosperous slumlord in an unnamed Michigan city, is set on a quest for his history and identity that leads him back to Virginia and the Gullah traditions of his ancestors. That *Song of Solomon* is structured as an archetypal heroic saga was immediately recognized when it made its debut in the late 1970s. In an early essay on the novel, A. Leslie Harris identified a mythic structure that conforms to the male initiatory pattern. Harris' analysis was exclusively concerned with Milkman's role as an archetypal hero whose childhood is narrated as a series of events "resonating with symbolic and archetypal significance,"[3] beginning with a miraculous birth (the first black baby to be born in Mercy Hospital), proceeding to a period of alienation from his family, and culminating in a quest ostensibly for gold, but also for his genealogy. Other characters in the novel can be mapped onto this mythic grid. Milkman's childhood friend and eventual antagonist, Guitar, functions as an alter ego, while women such as Pilate and Circe correspond to the positions of helpers and threshold guardians.[4]

This early literary criticism identified Milkman's quest as an exponent of a Rankian mythic structure, which valorizes the male initiation pattern. This is a completely legitimate reading of the text, but one with limitations. The resolution of the novel, which implicates a female oral tradition and African folktale, suggests a more subversive approach to the familiar mythic structure. Later scholarship posits that Morrison manipulates the male initiation theme to expose it as problematic. Gerry Brenner and Michael Awkward recognized that Morrison employs the mythic archetype to articulate a male narrative which allows women to function only as a supplement in the androcentric narrative of a hero's quest.[5] I would like to expand upon this reading by providing a closer inspection of the novel's classical antecedents with special emphasis on Circe. My objective here is to facilitate a better understanding of how Morrison manipulates and subverts the catabatic traditions connected with coming of age or initiation narratives and how she situates the obligatory descent to the Underworld with relation to the story of flight.

The catabasis of Odysseus functions as a prototype for this narrative tradition, and as a model for Morrison's novel: the hero experiences a death of identity which is symbolized by his trip to Hades, where he encounters the shades of figures from the heroic past.[6] He is symbolically reborn when he is cast ashore, naked and alone, at Scheria, and he works towards recuperating his identity when he finally arrives home in Ithaca.[7] Circe plays an important role in Odysseus' visit to the Underworld. After spending a year of indolence on her island, the hero prepares to leave, only to be told by Circe that he must make the descent. She provides information about how to accomplish the catabasis, and is an integral part of the *Nekyia*.[8] Although her role in *Song of Solomon* is obviously modeled on this Homeric tradition, Morrison scholars have not fully explored and accounted for her origins outside the novel.[9] Essays which recognize the novel's mythical underpinnings seldom look to the classical texts themselves, but tend to rely on popular works by Robert Graves or Joseph Campbell, which provide generalized schemata of the "monomyth."[10] Although Marilyn Sanders Mobley presents a compelling and informed analysis of how Morrison revises myth and folktale, even she designates Circe as "more like a prophetess or sibyl,"[11] without considering how her role in the development not only of Milkman, but also of his father, Macon Dead, and his aunt Pilate, resonates with her role in the *Odyssey*. Mobley, however, does make an important point when she cautions:

> The temptation throughout the entire novel ... is to make a series of one-to-one correspondences between [Morrison's] text and classical texts. But in the irony, complexity, and multiplicity of mythopoesis, this temptation is thwarted and the reader must acknowledge a variety of ways to interpret the names, to read the signs, to understand the rituals.[12]

Morrison's Circe is by no means simply a carbon copy of Homer's, but she does invite the reader to recall the traditional heroic saga from which she seems to be imported. It is by examining how she both signifies that narrative tradition and operates as an agent of its rupture that we understand the full implications of her presence and power.

Let us turn now to the story. Like the *Odyssey* it features a complex narrative structure, with numerous embedded tales which fill in the past and which even sometimes contradict one another. The protagonist, nicknamed "Milkman," is the third in his line to carry the name of Macon Dead, his father's name, and his father's before him. Yet the first Macon Dead, an illiterate ex-slave, had another name (Jake Solomon), lost to his progeny, and it will be Milkman's project to recover the name and story of his forebears. As the second Macon Dead recounts, when his father registered with the Freedman's Bureau in Virginia, the man behind the desk was drunk:

He asked Papa where he was born. Papa said Macon. Then he asked him who his father was. Papa said, "He's dead." Asked him who owned him, Papa said, "I'm free." Well, the Yankee wrote it all down, but in the wrong spaces . . . and in the space for his name the fool wrote, "Dead" comma "Macon."[13] (53)

It is as if death displaces and thus conceals the name of Milkman's forefather, who kept this misnomer because his wife, Sing, "Liked the name. Said it was new and would wipe out the past" (54). It does indeed wipe out the past, but it also becomes a prediction of the untimely demise of Macon Dead, who is murdered right in front of his two young children by a white neighbor who covets his farm. Macon the second and his little sister Pilate hide until they see the smoke from a cook stove—just as the smoke from her cottage had signified Circe's presence to Odysseus and his companions (10.196–197). The children are concealed and fed by Circe; in this version she is a black woman who works for the wealthy white family who murdered Macon Dead. After several weeks in seclusion, yearning for fresh air and simple food, they return to the wild, and eventually hide in a cave where young Macon, surprised and frightened by an old prospector, stabs him in the back. Brother and sister part company here, permanently alienated with their characters firmly set. Macon wants to take the old man's gold, Pilate understands the danger and immorality of such an action. Macon is depicted as anything but heroic—the assault of the old man in the cave hardly seems justified, and his wrangle with his sister sets the tone for his future relationships with women. Pilate spends the next night alone in the cave, and then sets out on her journeys. The process has been her initiation,[14] and she will develop into a doublet of Circe, a griot or wise woman of the African folk tradition.

Pilate travels throughout the South collecting rocks and lovers along the way, until she settles with her daughter Reba and granddaughter Hagar outside the Michigan town where her brother has established himself. In contrast to his sister's life on the margins of society, Macon becomes an entrepreneur who marries respectably and has three children: two daughters, First Corinthians and Lena, and a son, Milkman. Spiritually annihilated by the trauma of his father's murder, Macon Dead the second is undone by his compensating lust for money and property. His family life is sterile and repressive, and he continues to ignore his sister. Pilate's life is more emotionally rich, but still she experiences tragedies and sorrows directly related to the fragmentation of family. As Philip Page observes: "Without their name (Solomon) and the wisdom it implies, the Deads are ignorant of their ancestry, and hence of themselves, and they are alienated from their community, each other, and themselves."[15]

Although he is the third man in his family to inherit the name of Macon Dead, his grandfather's misnomer, Milkman acquires his life name, which replaces his patronymic, through his protracted connection to his mother's body. The neurotic Ruth, starved for intimacy, breastfeeds her son long into his early boyhood, a secret which, when discovered, provides the child with his new name. The maternal body is thus imposed on the already displaced name of the father which is correlative with the story itself. This matronymic, as it were, contributes to the initiatory theme by pinioning Milkman in a maternal world from which he must break free, a common element in such narratives.[16] Ruth even tries to appropriate the naming of her son more completely when she suggests that he become a doctor like her father, and adopt his name, becoming Dr. Macon Foster. But once he learns how he acquired his nickname, Milkman begins to move away from his suffocating mother, and starts his journey of self-discovery, which is unfortunately complicated and forestalled by Milkman's identification with his father. Milkman's quest for his true name is his story; it becomes a process that involves considerable stripping away of his masculine ego and social identity, and a renunciation of his father's solipsism and materialism.

The dead must be named in order for the story to be put to rest. Yet the power of naming, despite the strong patrilineal surface narrative, resides to a very large extent within the bodies and knowledge of women: Sing, wife of the first Macon Dead, determines that he will keep his name; Circe and the women of Shalimar reveal the names of Milkman's ancestors. Responding to the ghost of her father (Macon Dead the first), Pilate and her family unknowingly enact the name of her mother. "Sing, Sing," says the ghost, and understanding his revelation to be a command, Pilate and her family do indeed sing. Their song about Sugarman contains the vestigial name of their forefather, Solomon or Shalimar, who flew away from slavery—and family. It will guide Milkman to the truth about his origins. The song, which recurs with variations throughout the narrative like a refrain, is first sung in the opening chapter by a shabby and eccentrically dressed woman (presumably Pilate) who is part of the crowd watching the insurance agent's failed attempt to fly from the roof of Mercy Hospital:

> O Sugarman done fly away
> Sugarman done gone
> arman cut across the sky
> Sugarman gone home.... (6)

Pilate's song contextualizes an apparently foolish suicide within a larger narrative framework, the folktale of the slave who flew back to Africa; her voice provides meaning and continuity for a death performed before an audience. The event corresponds with the birth of Milkman, who will later hear the song performed by his aunts and cousin, with Solomon replacing Sugarman, providing the key to his patrimony. Naming and narrativity are inextricably woven together in this instance, and it is the voices of women (and later children) who transmit this patrimony, and who contest its significance and meaning. For Milkman the tale is self-affirming and heroic, but the wise women of Shalimar read it differently. Susan Byrd (Milkman's great-aunt) focuses more on Ryna, Solomon's wife, and their twenty-one children, abandoned when Sugarman flew to freedom. It would seem that the discovery of Milkman's true name requires him to burrow through layers or distortions of names—Sugarman, Charlemagne, Solomon, Shalimar—that also signify an absence of narrative fixity or certitude; versions of stories change according to who tells them.

The relationship between names and narrative is established early in the novel by the subversive processes that bring about the designation of "Not Doctor Street." The black community had a different name for what was officially Main's Avenue. Since the only black doctor in town, Dr. Foster, lived there, it became Doctor Street; when city officials insisted that it was not Doctor Street, the black population responded by calling it Not Doctor Street. This contest of naming and renaming is symbolic of "a conflict between two kinds of narrative authority"[17] which prevails throughout the novel. There is a corresponding competition for narrative control between Milkman's mother and father. As I have noted, Ruth's inappropriate intimacy with her son challenges the patrilineal system of naming her son. Her attempt to make him adopt her father's name and profession is a pathetic attempt to revive her dead father. Ruth's obsession becomes the subject of her husband's confidence to Milkman, a version that she challenges. The tension between Macon and Ruth is most forcefully realized in their competing narratives regarding Ruth's relationship with her dead father. Ruth's morbid adulation of Dr. Foster (after whom Not Doctor Street was named) extinguishes any desire Macon ever felt for her. Explaining his contempt for and abuse of his wife to Milkman, Macon recounts a scene of incestuous necrophilia—his naked wife sucking the fingers of her father's corpse. But Ruth's account of the event differs substantially; although she admits to such a longing for her dead father that she surreptitiously visits his grave at night, she represents her yearning in more natural terms, and accuses Macon not only of trying to poison her father, but also of trying to cause a miscarriage of her unborn son, Milkman.

Milkman hears the contesting tales of both his parents, uncertain of the truth. Yet he chooses to privilege one particular story of his father: that after Macon and his sister Pilate, as children, spent the night in a cave, he left his sister with the corpse and three bags of gold. Convinced that Pilate has the gold in a bag tied to her ceiling, he sends Milkman and Guitar to steal it. The counter-narrative is told by Pilate to Ruth, in a story never circulated among the men: that the sack contains rocks from different places Pilate had visited, and, as Milkman finally discovers after he and Guitar are picked up by the police, human bones. But whose bones? For when the skin has melted from a body, it is impossible to tell if a man was black or white. The bones that Pilate carries with her are not those of a lost husband, Mr. Solomon, as she tells the police, or even those of the white prospector, as she believes, but those of her own father, whom she unconsciously names. The narrative without this missing name is incomplete. This search for a name and a story becomes Milkman's quest. It is his function to fill in the spaces of the form properly, to slide the elements of his grandfather's history into their original positions, and thus to discover the names of his forefathers and foremothers: Jake and Singing Bird, his grandparents, and his great-grandparents, Shalimar and Ryna. The momentum for this quest for knowledge, however, is his father's greed; Macon Dead still lusts for the prospector's gold, so does Guitar, Sunday hit man for the Seven Days, and so at first does Milkman, who sees the gold as freedom from the overpowering unhappiness of his family. His quest, however, will evolve into a search for personal and cultural identity, an identity that individuates him from the father who bullies his wife and daughters, neglects and repudiates his only sister, and turns an old woman and her family out of her home. Given his father's misogyny, Milkman's treatment of women is hardly surprising. He callously dumps his cousin Hagar, after a long-term relationship, with a thank-you note and a gift, he interferes in his sister's love affair, and he robs his aunt. Milkman's quest for knowledge and identity, then, is a gradual movement toward a more decent relationship with women, and a value system more in line with that of Pilate rather than his father. The figure at the threshold of his development is the uncanny Circe.

Circe is first named by Macon when he starts to recount his history to Milkman. The narration is in response to Milkman's forbidden visit to Macon's estranged sister Pilate, and to her version of their shared childhood experience. The name of Circe surfaces like a specter, as Macon reminisces about life on his father's farm. He remembers the animals named after humans, and significantly, a pig named General Lee, who was delicious.

> Circe made up the best pot of maws she ever cooked. Huh! I'd forgotten that woman's name. That was it, Circe. Worked at a big farm some white people owned in Danville, Pennsylvania. Funny how things get away from you. For years you can't remember nothing. Then just like that, it all comes back to you. (52)

In chapter 10 Milkman encounters Circe for himself when he visits Danville in search of the gold that he believes is in the prospector's cave. His investigations lead him to the Butler mansion, where Circe concealed Macon and Pilate. Although his grandfather's old friends have vivid memories of Circe, they assume she is dead, since she was "a hundred when I was a boy" (237). The accent on her extreme old age is suggestive of the antiquity of the tale from which Circe is imported (book 10 of the *Odyssey*). And even if her Homeric associations have not been emphasized at this point (although General Lee the pig should give us pause), Milkman's encounter with her will be infused with that ancient narrative. Her home, the decaying Butler mansion, is hidden behind bushes, much like the lush greenery of Aeaea; indeed the inaccessibility of the place makes it a veritable island.

Circe is a strange combination of appalling decrepitude and sexual power. Like the ancient tale she is in decline, but still possessed of a compelling allure. As she embraces Milkman, mistaking him for his father, the young man finds himself simultaneously aroused and disgusted. Deathless she may be, but she is by no means ageless. Nonetheless Milkman's first encounter with her is sexually charged; she is like a figure from a dream, a sexual power which is again reminiscent of the Homeric Circe who keeps Odysseus for a year as her lover. Like her epic predecessor, who supplicates the hero soon after meeting him (after failing to enchant him with her potions, *Od.* 10.323), Circe immediately makes close physical contact with Milkman. Their embrace is only interrupted by her throng of dogs. Circe is also mistress of the animals; her strange Weimaraners with human eyes recall the men turned into wolves, who fawned on Odysseus' companions "like dogs fawn on their masters" (*Od.* 10.215–216). Whether they are in fact her former masters is never specified. Reverend Cooper had advised Milkman that "any evening up left to do, Circe took care of" (233); readers are left to make their own conclusions about the full details of her retribution.

Circe's association with animals is suggestive of her origins as a fertility goddess.[18] She is, after Odysseus has overpowered her, benevolent and nurturing, attributes she passes down to her twentieth-century counterpart who succors Macon and Pilate after the murder of their father. Associated with her fecundating qualities is her role as a midwife; she delivered most of the people in Denford, including Macon and Pilate. It is Circe to whom Odysseus returns after his visit to the Underworld, so in a sense she too functions as a midwife in his rebirth. Her nurturance extends to her tutelary capacity: she not only tells Odysseus that he must make his trip to Hades, but also, once he returns, explains what he must do for the remainder of his voyage. Milkman similarly learns important information from Circe:

the names of his ancestors and their history. She directs the course of his journey to his ancestral home, Shalimar, a Gullah town on the coast of Virginia.

From Circe he hears the strange history of his grandfather's corpse, which his father had buried in a shallow grave. The body had been dislodged, washed upstream, and eventually put in the cave, without a proper burial. The unburied corpse is a feature of *Odyssey* 11 and *Aeneid* 6. It is as if Elpinor and Palinurus open a portal for the heroes' trips to the Underworld. Milkman declares that he will bury the bones, unaware that they are in Pilate's possession. Circe, like her namesake, gives him instructions on how to locate the cave where he expects to find his grandfather's remains. Like Odysseus, Milkman must travel through water to arrive at his destination, struggling through a stream and a thicket of trees to reach the hill he must then climb. And here is where things start to go askew for the reader anticipating a hero's descent. Milkman sees the cave, but it is fifteen or twenty feet *upwards*. His climb to the cave's entrance is arduous; he rips his clothes and exhausts himself scrambling up the rocky slope. Once there he notices another path (perhaps implying alternate narrative possibilities), one that would have made this part of the trip far easier. Now inside the cave, he manages to find the pit, but it does not contain the gold that he set out to find, nor does it hold the bones that he claimed to want to bury. Frustrated and exhausted, Milkman emerges from this cavern with a ravenous hunger, as if his spiritual starvation has been physically manifested, and with a damaged watch, its hands twisted as if time has somehow become distorted.

Circe seems to be able to change the quality of time. Milkman's episode with her has been, despite his disappointed expectations, a transformative experience. She is a liminal figure who mediates between death and life, but she also sits at the portal between two stories, not only the two sections of the novel, but also the novel and the epic tradition. Under her direction time for Milkman has folded in on itself: he experiences a reversal of the birth process and is then reborn. Milkman has of course been in the Underworld all his life, existing as one of the dead under the control of a Hades figure, his father.[19] He is climbing out of death into life.[20] Although the trip to the cave occupies the same position as the catabasis in the master narrative, it seems instead to be an *anodos*, a "going up." As he makes his difficult passage through the stream, another citation of mythic prototypes, he is like a newborn traveling through a birth canal. His destination, however, is curiously womb-like, a cave so dark that he is blinded by the absence of light. He has embarked on the hero's journey away from his mother but now crawls back symbolically into the maternal body—a striking variation of the traditional catabasis, and a decided temporal inversion.

If Milkman's damaged watch signifies a departure from linear chronology, it also announces his release from quotidian temporality. He has been sent forth from a mundane existence as his father's minion into an epic landscape where his identity will be transformed. And transformation is what Circe is all about. When she dispatches Milkman to the cave, she effectively sends him into a narrative matrix, a loaded symbol of other stories. The cave evokes the Odyssean tradition, which gave birth to Aeneas' descent to the Underworld (also through a cave, *Aen.* 6.237–242),[21] and those of Dante and Milton. Milkman will emerge from the cave reborn into a different world than the one he left behind; he will enter a mythic continuum in which his view of the world and of himself will be drastically changed. His voyage from here will be deeper south, which represents, as it so often does in Morrison's fiction, the past, correlative to his return to the womb. His encounter with Circe has emphasized a different sense of time, what Julia Kristeva has called "Women's Time," circular and eternal, a temporality which circumscribes a landscape strongly inflected as feminine but which is also deeply resonant of established mythology.[22] In her revision of the catabasis Morrison has emphasized the strong connection between the midwife Circe and the womb-like earth, and set aside the wise old man, Teiresias, whom Odysseus had to consult.[23]

As Mobley recognizes, the cave has ritualistic significance as "a turning point in Milkman's journey because it begins his series of encounters with life-threatening situations."[24] These initiatory tests appear to be sequenced as a linear "phallic" (to use Kristeva's terminology) temporal progression. Milkman's experience in Shalimar, the home and name of his great-grandparents, is represented as a continued citation of the *Odyssey*. He arrives in Shalimar without recognizing it, as Odysseus does in Ithaca. Yet like Odysseus, he has found his true home, where he encounters hostile males (first in Solomon's store) who insult and assault him. After his trials are over, and once he has achieved the self-knowledge that has been his true quest, he has a romantic affair with a Penelope-like woman named Sweet with whom he shares a mutually satisfying intimacy. This refashioning of the epic poem accentuates the initiatory aspects of Milkman's experience: his aggressive badinage with Saul in Solomon's store is a form of ritual insult or *aischrologia*, a frequent component of initiation rites. Other features include the change of clothing (his city suit for battle fatigues), his bath in the sea with Sweet, and most significantly, the nighttime hunting expedition with the elders of the town.[25] It is during the last that Milkman experiences his epiphany in the woods, and comes to understand how thoughtlessly he had treated various women in his life, and how valuable his cultural heritage is to his sense of identity. He comes of age, and anticipates a new sense of integration with his family which will include bringing Pilate back to Shalimar to give Jake's bones a proper burial.

While Milkman's experience is charted along a narrative axis that corresponds to a male *Bildungsroman*, there is a calculated twist in the narrative journey. We have noted how the encounter with Circe marks the landscape as feminine, the very landscape where Milkman will undergo his rite of passage as a hunter. His initial impression of Shalimar, an isolated coastal village, emphasizes the women who are unencumbered by pocketbooks, bags, or any baggage: "These women walked as if they were going somewhere, but they carried nothing in their hands" (259). Yet the chapter which begins with a description of women quickly turns to the archetypal myth in which a youth proves his masculinity by hunting with the men. While this tale is completed within the compass of chapter 11, the remainder of the novel contests this apparently heroic resolution. The mythic subtext is interleaved with the narratives of Hagar and Guitar. As Milkman is putting the pieces of his story together, the jilted Hagar dies of a broken heart. Unlike him she has not successfully completed her coming of age.[26] Instead she corresponds to Ryna, the woman whom Milkman's great-grandfather left behind when he flew away, and whose story offered by Susan Byrd serves to devalue Solomon's flight. It is during his visit with Susan that Milkman finally loses his watch; the reader is alerted that the linear time of the *Bildungsroman* is not what structures this tale after all.

The second to last chapter of the novel is permeated with the voices of women, Pilate in particular, who sings a song of lamentation at her granddaughter's funeral. This tragic turn of events intersects with the heroic resolution of Milkman's coming of age—and as it so often is in Classical Greek literature, women's lamentation is a disruptive energy.[27] Moreover, as Milkman is going through his initiation process, hunting with the elders at night and bathing in the sea with Sweet, he is being stalked by the murderous Guitar. The heroic resolution and citational practices that connect his story to European literary history are further compromised when Guitar's bullet misses Milkman and kills Pilate as they are burying Jake's remains. The novel ends with Milkman's revision of the Song of Solomon as he sings to Pilate, naming her as "Sugargirl" and then leaping off a cliff in a reenactment of his great-grandfather's flight. The linear tale with its teleology of the heroic quest is now circumscribed by a ring composition, suggesting eternal repetitions of flight and song. We can choose to think that Milkman has plunged to his death, like Icarus and Robert Smith, whose suicide flight opened the novel, or that he has replicated the flight of his great-grandfather Shalimar, and flown away. However our imagination completes the tale for us, two related structural qualities are obvious: first, the story is a ring composition, coming back to where it began with a man leaping into the air; second, the story ends in mid-air, that is to say, it does not end.

This circularity, identified by Cedric Gael Bryant as a "trope of resistance,"[28] obviates the concept of a linear conclusion. Bryant observes that Morrison uses the circle as a "unifying principle of closure" in much of her fiction, and that this circularity "informs Morrison's method of interconnecting narrative elements by reversing causality."[29] I have already identified this cyclical temporality as "Women's Time," described by Kristeva as "a specific measure that essentially retains repetition and eternity from among the multiple modalities of time known through the history of civilizations . . . cycles, gestation, the eternal recurrence of a biological rhythm."[30] This brings us back to the midwife Circe, who stood at the threshold of this part of the story, and whose name relates her to this cyclical quality.[31] In his optimistic reading of her role Page suggests that Milkman "reaches the womb of his family (the cave) by embracing the terrifying but guiding Circe who models Milkman's quest by fusing Western and African-American cultural traditions, life and death, and present and past."[32] From Page's critical perspective Milkman is able to fuse and integrate his fragmented family, his position in the diaspora and the two cultural traditions, African and European, which are in harmony at the end of the tale. But from the perspective of a feminist classicist, the synthesis is perhaps not so well knit. There are significant fissures in the text which remain unresolved at its conclusion, fissures which are opened by Circe, who signifies the mythic narrative of the hero's quest, but who simultaneously deconstructs it. On one level of meaning, as the careful citations of the sojourn on Aeaea make clear, Circe functions as she does in the *Odyssey*: she is an initiatrix who sets the hero on his path to symbolic rebirth—but not death, for he is already dead. Her name alone, singular in its Homeric allusion, denotes the male heroic pattern with its linear androcentric emphasis. Yet because she has existed in other narratives, including epics, poetry, and novels, she also represents a never-ending cycle of stories. Within the compass of the novel Circe is linked with other female voices who convey Milkman's history: Pilate who sings the Song of Solomon and recounts her family history, and Susan Byrd who completes the tale. Circe's position in this respect is dually coded. Her name denotes the androcentric myth, yet she is an agent who allows the hero to seek for something more than his masculine identity, his place in the parade of heroes who make the necessary trip to the Underworld with the help of female guardians. This dualism is connoted in part by her gorgeous voice, the voice of a sexy young woman. As narrator, Odysseus mentions Circe's voice several times; she sings in a sweet or clear voice as she goes about her weaving (*Od.* 10.221 and 254). Correspondingly, Morrison's Circe is possessed of a "strong young cultivated voice" (242), the "mellifluent voice of a twenty year old girl" (240). In the Homeric context female voices denote danger; the Sirens are the most obvious example of this.[33] But in a novel that reverberates with the voices of women, Circe's voice has a different timbre. One way of accounting for the discrepancy between her corpse-like appearance and youthful tones might be that her seductive voice betokens a new story enclosed within an ancient tradition.

Circe's activities in the Butler mansion contribute to the sense that the old must be disassembled before the new can take its place. It had been her job to clean and maintain the opulent household with its priceless tapestries and imported marble. Now that the family is extinct, and she alone survives, her self-appointed task has been to dismantle and tear apart the edifice room by room. This deconstruction of the master's house is a fitting symbol for Circe's function in the story. Her name suggests that she will maintain the master narrative, and to a certain extent she does, but she also disrupts that narrative, which is replaced by deconstructive reading of a literary edifice, the hero's quest.

NOTES

1. On the implications of names in the *Odyssey* see J. Peradotto, *Man in the Middle Voice: Name and Narration in the* Odyssey (Princeton 1990). The significance of naming in *Song of Solomon* is discussed at length by M. S. Mobley, *Folk Roots and Mythic Wings in Sarah Orne Jewett and Toni Morrison* (Baton Rouge 1991) 102–8.

2. Morrison herself has identified the influence of Classical Greek literature on her work. See Mobley (above, n.1) 41, n.119.

3. A. L. Harris, "Myth as Structure in Toni Morrison's *Song of Solomon*," *MELUS* 7.3: *Ethnic Women Writers* 1 (1980) 70.

4. Accordingly, Milkman is like "Aeneas, like Ulysses" (Mobley [above, n.1] 74).

5. G. Brenner, "*Song of Solomon*: Morrison's Rejection of Rank's Monomyth and Feminism," *The New England Quarterly* 15.1 (1987) 13–24; M. Awkward, "'Unruly and Let Loose': Myth, Ideology and Gender in *Song of Solomon*," *Callaloo* 13 (1990) 482–98.

6. Odysseus of course does not descend into Hades like Aeneas, but his trip to the Underworld is clearly modeled on myths of the catabasis and functioned as a model for later versions. See A. Heubeck and A. Hoekstra, *A Commentary on Homer's Odyssey: V.II, Books IX–XVII* (Oxford 1989) 75–77.

7. For a reading of the birth symbolism in Odysseus' voyage from Calypso's island to the Phaeacians see R. M. Newton, "The Rebirth of Odysseus," *GRBS* 25 (1984) 5–20.

8. See D. Ogden, *Greek and Roman Necromancy* (Princeton 2001) 139–41. Ogden records Circe as being the first of a line of female necromancers in literature. As he points out, her knowledge of Odysseus' consultation with Teiresias in the Underworld suggests that she accompanied him unseen. Furthermore, her association with the Underworld seems to predate the *Odyssey*. Siduri, a Circe-like figure in the Akkadian *Gilgamesh*, directs the hero to Utnapishtim (the land of the dead)

through a forest and water. N. Marinatos ("Circe and Liminality: Ritual Background and Narrative Structure," in M. Dickie and O. Anderson, eds., *Homer's World: Fiction, Tradition, and Reality* [Bergen 1995] 133–40) draws comparisons with Babylonian Ishtar and Asherah. For further folktale parallels, discussion, and bibliography see Heubeck and Hoekstra (above, n.6) 50–52.

9. In her survey of the manifestations of Circe in literary history, Judith Yarnell (*Transformations of Circe: The History of an Enchantress* [Urbana and Chicago, 1994] 183) devotes only a paragraph to *Song of Solomon* which aptly identifies her as "keeper of true names and pointer of true directions." For an excellent discussion of how Circe appears throughout classical literature including Apollonius, Vergil, Ovid, and Petronius, and her iconographic tradition in the plastic arts see R. Brilliant, "Kirke's Men: Swine and Sweethearts," in B. Cohen, ed., *The Distaff Side: Representing the Female in Homer's* Odyssey (Oxford 1995) 165–74.

10. P. Page (*Dangerous Freedom: Fusion and Fragmentation in Toni Morrison's Novels* [Jackson, Miss., 1995] 98), for instance, relies on "the monomyth of the hero's quest as delineated by Joseph Campbell and Otto Rank."

11. Mobley (above, n.1) 120.

12. Mobley (above, n.1) 119.

13. All quotes from the novel are from T. Morrison, *Song of Solomon* (New York 1977).

14. See J. S. Bakerman, "Failures of Love: Female Initiation in the Novels of Toni Morrison," *American Literature* 52.4 (1981) 541–63. Bakerman does not discuss female initiation as a mythic pattern in *Song of Solomon*, but nonetheless makes some valuable observations about the initiatory themes in the novel. Hagar is an example of a failed initiation, First Corinthians, Milkman's sister, individuates from her father by seeking employment and taking a lover, but this is a delayed initiation (taking place when she is in her forties). Only Pilate goes through an initiation when she is an adolescent, "as is traditional." (554). As Bakerman points out, the device indicates "the extreme difficulty of the black woman's search for self-determination" (554).

15. Page (above, n.10) 86.

16. Telemachus must leave the home of his mother, or, to give a more trenchant example, Orestes must kill Clytemnestra.

17. T. O. Mason, "The Novelist as Conservator: Stories and Comprehension in Toni Morrison's *Song of Solomon*," in H. Bloom, ed., *Toni Morrison's Song of Solomon* (New York and Philadelphia, 1990) 177.

18. "So Homer's Circe, whose attributes of the *potnia theron* connect her in part with the Great Mother, goddess of sexuality, death, and rebirth in the cycles of vegetation, has both life-giving and destructive functions: she holds the key to both love and death" (C. Segal, "Circean Temptations: Homer, Virgil, Ovid," *TAPA* 99 [1968] 427). For her possible origins as a Near Eastern fertility goddess, e.g., Ishtar, see also D. Page, *Folktales in Homer's* Odyssey (Cambridge, Mass., 1973) 51–69.

19. Mobley (above, n.1) 102 points out the similarities between Macon Dead the second and Hades: his wealth in particular, symbolized by his black hearse-like car.

20. In this respect Milkman differs from (but alludes to) the hero of another African-American novel. In Ralph Ellison's *Invisible Man* (1952) the protagonist remains underground. See the remarks of H. Bloom, "Two African-American Masters of the American Novel," *The Journal of Blacks in Higher Education* 28 (2000) 89–93.

21. See Ogden (above, n.8) 62–69 on the necromantic associations of the cave at Avernus.

22. J. Kristeva, "Women's Time," in R. R. Warhol and D. Price Herndl, eds., *Feminisms: An Anthology of Literary Theory and Criticism* (New Brunswick, N.J., 1993) 445.

23. Mobley (above, n.1) 121 over-interprets the blinding darkness of the cave as an allusion to Teiresias. The motif of blinding, and the suggestion of a return to the womb in the cave sequence, resonates with the Oedipal myth, especially since Milkman walks with a limp. The Oedipal imagery is beyond the scope of my essay, but for a nuanced psychoanalytical reading of the motif see E. B anch, "Through the Maze of the Oedipal: Milkman's Search for Self in *Song of Solomon*," *Literature and Psychology* 41 (1995) 52–84.

24. Mobley (above, n.1) 121.

25. See Page (above, n.10) 103, who synthesizes approaches which interpret the men's collective skinning of the bobcat, Milkman's initiation into the black male community, as an induction into "his racial identity and past." The hunting, flaying, and evisceration of the animal are reminiscent of the atrocities performed on black men. Milkman receives the heart of the bobcat, a symbol of his "new heart in communion with the natural world of the bobcat, and implying his rebirth as a new man and his penetration to the heart of himself, his ancestry, his community, and his universe."

26. Bakerman (above, n.14) 558.

27. In this respect Pilate is aligned with Demeter. For the disruptive potential of women's lamentation throughout Greek culture see M. Alexiou, *The Ritual Lament in Greek Tradition* (Cambridge 1974).

28. C. G. Bryant, "'Every Goodbye Ain't Gone': The Semiotics of Death, Mourning, and Closural Practice in Toni Morrison's *Song of Solomon*," *MELUS* 24 (1999) 98.

29. Bryant (above, n.28) 99.

30. Kristeva (above, n.22) 445.

31. The usual etymology of her name associates her with the hawk or falcon, *kirkos*. Douglas Frame (*The Myth of Return in Early Greek Epic* [New Haven and London, 1978] 50), however, makes the very appealing suggestion that associates her name with the Greek word for "ring," *krikos*, which is also attested as *kirkos*. Frame notes that Hesiod and other authors situate Circe in the west (*Theog.* 744), but Odysseus and his crew meet her in the east after their visit to the Underworld (*Od.* 12.1–4). As a child of Helios, she is associated with the sun, and her role in the *Odyssey* is "both to usher the hero into the underworld and to receive him back again from it. When Odysseus and his men 'return to life and light,' she is naturally equated with the dawn. The complement to this would be that she is equated with sunset when Odysseus and his companions venture into 'death and darkness'" (48).

32. Page (above, n. 10) 100.

33. For further discussion on the baneful effects of women's voices in the *Odyssey*, see V. Wohl, "Standing by the Stathmos: The Creation of Sexual Ideology in the *Odyssey*," *Arethusa* 26 (1993) 19–50.

Chronology

1931	Toni Morrison born Chloe Anthony Wofford on February 18 in Lorain, Ohio, the second child of George Wofford and Ramah Willis Wofford.
1953	Graduates with B.A. in English from Howard University. Changes name to Toni during years at Howard.
1955	Receives M.A. in English from Cornell University.
1955–57	Instructor in English at Texas Southern University.
1957–64	Instructor in English at Howard University.
1958	Marries Harold Morrison, a Jamaican architect.
1964	Divorces and returns to Lorain with her two sons.
1965	Becomes editor for textbook subsidiary of Random House in Syracuse, New York.
1970	First novel, *The Bluest Eye*, is published. Takes editorial position at Random House in New York, eventually becoming a senior editor.
1971–72	Associate professor of English at the State University of New York at Purchase.
1973	*Sula* published.
1975	*Sula* nominated for National Book Award.

1976–77   Visiting Lecturer at Yale University.

1977   *Song of Solomon* published; receives National Book Critics Circle Award and the American Academy and Institute of Arts and Letters Award.

1981   *Tar Baby* published.

1984–89   Becomes Schweitzer Professor of the Humanities at the State University of New York at Albany.

1986–88   Visiting Lecturer at Bard College. In 1986, her play *Dreaming Emmett* first produced in Albany.

1987   *Beloved* published and nominated for National Book Award and National Book Critics Circle Award.

1988   *Beloved* awarded Pulitzer Prize in fiction and the Robert F. Kennedy Award.

1989   Becomes Robert F. Goheen Professor of the Humanities at Princeton University.

1992   Publishes *Jazz* and *Playing in the Dark: Whiteness and the Literary Imagination*.

1993   Receives Nobel Prize in literature.

1996   Publishes *The Dancing Mind*, the text of her Nobel Prize acceptance speech.

1998   *Paradise* published.

1999   With her son Slade, publishes first children's book, *The Big Box*.

2002   Publishes with Slade *The Book of Mean People*.

2003   Publishes *Love*. Publishes with Slade *The Ant or the Grasshopper?* and *The Lion or the Mouse?*

2004   Publishes with Slade *The Poppy or the Snake?* Also publishes *Remember: The Journey to School Integration*.

2005   Opera *Margaret Garner*, which Morrison wrote the libretto for with composer Richard Danielpour, premieres in Detroit.

2006   Retires from full-time teaching at Princeton.

2008   Publishes *What Moves at the Margin: Selected Fiction* and *A Mercy*.

Contributors

HAROLD BLOOM is Sterling Professor of the Humanities at Yale University. He is the author of 30 books, including *Shelley's Mythmaking, The Visionary Company, Blake's Apocalypse, Yeats, A Map of Misreading, Kabbalah and Criticism, Agon: Toward a Theory of Revisionism, The American Religion, The Western Canon*, and *Omens of Millennium: The Gnosis of Angels, Dreams, and Resurrection. The Anxiety of Influence* sets forth Professor Bloom's provocative theory of the literary relationships between the great writers and their predecessors. His most recent books include *Shakespeare: The Invention of the Human*, a 1998 National Book Award finalist, *How to Read and Why, Genius: A Mosaic of One Hundred Exemplary Creative Minds, Hamlet: Poem Unlimited, Where Shall Wisdom Be Found?*, and *Jesus and Yahweh: The Names Divine*. In 1999, Professor Bloom received the prestigious American Academy of Arts and Letters Gold Medal for Criticism. He has also received the International Prize of Catalonia, the Alfonso Reyes Prize of Mexico, and the Hans Christian Andersen Bicentennial Prize of Denmark.

TRUDIER HARRIS is a professor at the University of North Carolina at Chapel Hill. She has written several titles, including *South of Tradition: Essays on African American Literature*, and coedited several titles, including *The Literature of the American South: A Norton Anthology* .

PATRICK BRYCE BJORK is Web Development Specialist at Bismarck State College, where he had been an assistant professor of English. He authored *The Novels of Toni Morrison* and *Reading, Writing and the World Wide Web*.

J. BROOKS BOUSON is a professor in the English department at Loyola College in Chicago; since 2002 she has also been assistant department chair. She is the author of a book on Jamaica Kincaid and another on Margaret Atwood.

JOHN N. DUVALL is an English professor at Purdue University and the editor of *Modern Fiction Studies*. He has written on such authors as William Faulkner, Flannery O'Connor, John Barth, Don DeLillo, and John Updike. He is the author of *Race and White Identity in Southern Fiction* and other titles, and the editor or coeditor of four titles as well.

DANA MEDORO is an assistant professor in the English department at the University of Manitoba. She has published *The Bleeding of America: Menstruation as Symbolic Economy in Pynchon, Faulkner, and Morrison*.

WES BERRY is an assistant professor at Western Kentucky University. His published work includes short stories, creative nonfiction, and critical essays on authors such as Wendell Berry and Cormac McCarthy. He is completing a book, *Landscapes of Healing in Contemporary American Prose*.

LORIE WATKINS FULTON taught undergraduate classes in basic composition and American literature at the University of Southern Mississippi. She is a contributor to the *Student's Companion to American Literary Characters* and is working on a book-length manuscript that examines William Faulkner's critique of the Cavalier myth.

JUDY POCOCK is a retired teacher and a representative of teaching assistants and sessional lecturers at the University of Toronto. She has contributed to *Papers of the Bibliographical Society of Canada* and *Arachne: An Interdisciplinary Journal of the Humanities*.

JUDITH FLETCHER is an associate professor at Wilfrid Laurier University in Ontario, where she was Women's Studies Coordinator from 2004–2007. She is the coeditor of two titles and has contributed essays to books and journals.

Bibliography

Bauer, Margaret Donovan. *William Faulkner's Legacy: "What Shadow, What Stain, What Mark."* Gainesville: University Press of Florida, 2005.

Bloom, Harold. "Two African-American Masters of the American Novel." *Journal of Blacks in Higher Education* 28 (Summer 2000): 89–93.

————, ed. *Toni Morrison.* Philadelphia: Chelsea House Publishers, 2005.

Bruck, Peter, and Wolfgang Karrer. *The Afro-American Novel since 1960.* Amsterdam: Grhuner, 1982.

Buehrer, David. "American History X, Morrison's *Song of Solomon*, and the Psychological Intersections of Race, Class, and Place in Contemporary America." *Journal of Evolutionary Psychology* 25, nos. 1–2 (March 2004): 18–23.

Chow, Karen. "'Stories to Pass On': Pedagogically Dialoging Maxine Hong Kingston and Toni Morrison." In *Crossing Oceans: Reconfiguring American Literary Studies in the Pacific Rim,* edited by Noelle Brada-Williams and Karen Chow, pp. 99–108. Hong Kong: Hong Kong University Press, 2004.

Cowart, David. "Faulkner and Joyce in Morrison's *Song of Solomon.*" *American Literature* 62 (March 1990): 87–100.

De Lancey, Dayle B. "Sweetness, Madness, and Power: The Confection as Mental Contagion in Toni Morrison's *Tar Baby, Song of Solomon,* and *The Bluest Eye.*" *Process: A Journal of African American and African Diasporan Literature and Culture* 2 (Spring 2000): 25–47.

Elia, Nada. *Trances, Dances, and Vociferations: Agency and Resistance in Africana Women's Narratives.* New York: Garland Publishing, 2001.

Ferguson, Rebecca Hope. *Rewriting Black Identities: Transition and Exchange in the Novels of Toni Morrison.* Brussels, Belgium: Peter Lang, 2007.

Frampton, Edith. "'You Just Can't Fly On Off and Leave a Body': The Intercorporeal Breastfeeding Subject of Toni Morrison's Fiction." *Women: A Cultural Review* 16, no. 2 (Summer 2005): 141–63.

Furman, Jan. *Toni Morrison's Fiction*. Columbia, South Carolina: University of South Carolina Press, 1996.

Furman, Jan, ed. *Toni Morrison's* Song of Solomon: *A Casebook*. Oxford; New York: Oxford University Press, 2003.

Guth, Deborah. "A Blessing and a Burden: The Relation to the Past in *Sula, Song of Solomon* and *Beloved*." In *Understanding Toni Morrison's* Beloved *and* Sula: *Selected Essays and Criticisms of the Works by the Nobel Prize-Winning Author*, edited by Solomon O. Iyasere and Marla W. Iyasere, 315–37. Troy, N.Y.: Whitston, 2000.

Hovet, Grace Ann, and Barbara Lounsberry. "Flying as Symbol and Legend in Toni Morrison's *The Bluest Eye, Sula*, and *Song of Solomon*." *CLA Journal* 27, no. 2 (December 1983): 119–140.

Ikuenobe, Polycarp. "Flying and Myth in *Song of Solomon*'s African Cultural and Philosophical Foundation." *International Journal of African Studies* 2, no. 2 (Spring 2001): 49–78.

Jordan, Margaret I. *African American Servitude and Historical Imaginings: Retrospective Fiction and Representation*. New York: Palgrave Macmillan, 2004.

Leak, Jeffrey B. "It's Time You Learned the Truth about a Few Things: Masculinity and the Myth of Cultural Depravation in David Bradley's *The Chaneysville Incident* and Toni Morrison's *Song of Solomon*." In *Racial Myths and Masculinity in African American Literature*. Knoxville: University of Tennessee Press, 2005.

Lee, Dorothy H. "*Song of Solomon*: To Ride the Air." *Black American Literature Forum* 16, no. 2 (Summer 1982): 64–70.

Loichot, Valérie. "Toni Morrison's Postplantation: *Song of Solomon*." In *Orphan Narratives: The Postplantation Literature of Faulkner, Glissant, Morrison, and Saint-John Perse*. Charlottesville: University of Virginia Press, 2007.

Marshall, Brenda. "The Gospel According to Pilate." *American Literature* 57 (October 1985): 486–549.

Mayberry, Susan Neal. "Flying without Ever Leaving the Ground: Feminine Masculinity in *Song of Solomon*." In *Can't I Love What I Criticize?: The Masculine and Morrison*. Athens: University of Georgia Press, 2007.

Murray, Rolland. "The Long Strut: *Song of Solomon* and the Emancipatory Limits of Black Patriarchy." *Callaloo* 22, no. 1 (Winter 1999): 121–33.

O'Reilly, Andrea. *Toni Morrison and Motherhood: A Politics of the Heart*. Albany: State University of New York Press, 2004

Otten, Terry. *The Crime of Innocence in the Fiction of Toni Morrison*. Columbia: University of Missouri Press, 1989.

Parrish, Timothy. "Off Faulkner's Plantation: Toni Morrison's *Beloved* and *Song of Solomon.*" In *From the Civil War to the Apocalypse: Postmodern History and American Fiction.* Amherst: University of Massachusetts Press, 2008.

Pendery, David. "Bringing Experience to Life and Life to Experience: Conscious Experience and Representation in Toni Morrison's *Song of Solomon.*" *Consciousness, Literature and the Arts* 7, no. 3 (December 2006).

Pollack, Harriet, ed. *Having Our Way: Women Rewriting Tradition in Twentieth-Century America.* Lewisburg, Pa.: Bucknell University Press; London: Associated University Presses, 1995.

Reid, Suzanne Elizabeth. "Toni Morrison's *Song of Solomon*: An African American Epic." In *Censored Books II: Critical Viewpoints, 1985–2000,* edited by Nicholas J. Karolides, pp. 387–94. Lanham, Md.: Scarecrow, 2002.

Rosenberg, Ruth. "'And the Children May Know Their Names': Toni Morrison's *Song of Solomon.*" *Literary Onomastic Studies* 8 (1981): 195–219.

Royster, Philip M. "Milkman's Flying: The Scapegoat Transcended in Toni Morrison's *Song of Solomon.*" *CLA Journal* 24 (June 1981): 419–440.

Schreiber, Evelyn Jaffe. *Subversive Voices: Eroticizing the Other in William Faulkner and Toni Morrison.* Knoxville: University of Tennessee Press, 2001.

Scott, Joyce Hope. "*Song of Solomon* and *Tar Baby*: The Subversive Role of Language and the Carnivalesque." In *The Cambridge Companion to Toni Morrison,* edited by Justine Tally, pp. 26–42. Cambridge, England: Cambridge University Press, 2007.

Smith, Valerie. "The Quest for and Discovery of Identity in Toni Morrison's *Song of Solomon.*" *Southern Review* 21 (Summer 1985): 721–32.

———, ed. *New Essays on* Song of Solomon. Cambridge [England]; New York: Cambridge University Press, 1995.

Spallino, Chiara. "*Song of Solomon*: An Adventure in Structure." *Callaloo* 8 (Fall 1985): 510–24.

Stave, Shirley A., ed. *Toni Morrison and the Bible: Contested Intertextualities.* New York, N.Y.: Peter Lang, 2006.

Thomas, H. Nigel. "Further Reflections on the Seven Days in Toni Morrison's *Song of Solomon.*" *Literary Griot: International Journal of Black Expressive Cultural Studies* 13, nos. 1–2 (Spring–Fall 2001): 147–59.

Thomas, Valorie D. "'1 + 1 = 3' and Other Dilemmas: Reading Vertigo in *Invisible Man, My Life in the Bush of Ghosts,* and *Song of Solomon.*" *African American Review* 37, no. 1 (Spring 2003): 81–94.

Tidey, Ashley. "Limping or Flying? Psychoanalysis, Afrocentrism, and *Song of Solomon.*" *College English* 63, no. 1 (September 2000): 48–70.

Wall, Cheryl A. *Worrying the Line: Black Women Writers, Lineage and Literary Tradition.* Chapel Hill: University of North Carolina Press, 2005.

Walters, Tracey L. *African American Literature and the Classicist Tradition: Black Women Writers from Wheatley to Morrison.* New York: Palgrave Macmillan, 2007.

Wang, Chih-ming. "The X-Barred Subject: Afro-American Subjectivity in Toni Morrison's *Song of Solomon.*" *Studies in Language and Literature* 9 (June 2000): 269–88.

Wardi, Anissa Janine. *Death and the Arc of Mourning in African American Literature.* Gainesville: University Press of Florida, 2003.

Wegs, Joyce M. "Toni Morrison's *Song of Solomon*: A Blues Song." *Essays in Literature* 9, no. 2 (Fall 1982): 211–23.

Acknowledgments

Trudier Harris, "Song of Solomon." From *Fiction and Folklore: The Novels of Toni Morrison*. © 1991 by Trudier Harris. Reprinted by permission.

Patrick Bryce Bjork, "*Song of Solomon*: Reality and Mythos Within the Community." From *The Novels of Toni Morrison: The Search for Self and Place Within the Community*. © 1992 by Peter Lang Publishing. Reprinted by permission.

J. Brooks Bouson, Reprinted by permission from *Quiet As It's Kept: Shame, Trauma, and Race in the Novels of Toni Morrison*, the State University of New York Press. © 1999, State University of New York. All rights reserved.

John N. Duvall, "*Song of Solomon*, Narrative Identity, and the Faulknerian Intertext." From *The Identifying Fictions of Toni Morrison: Modernist Authenticity and Postmodern Blackness*. © 2001 by John N. Duvall. Reproduced with permission of Palgrave Macmillan.

Dana Medoro, "Justice and Citizenship in Toni Morrison's *Song of Solomon*." From *Canadian Review of American Studies* 32, no. 1 (2002): 1–15. © 2002 by the University of Toronto Press, www.utpjournals.com. Reprinted by permission of Canadian Association for American Studies.

Wes Berry, "Toni Morrison's Revisionary 'Nature Writing': *Song of Solomon* and the Blasted Pastoral." From *South to a New Place: Region, Literature, Culture*, edited by Suzanne W. Jones and Sharon Monteith. © 2002 by Louisiana State University Press. Reprinted by permission.

Lorie Watkins Fulton, "William Faulkner Reprised: Isolation in Toni Morrison's *Song of Solomon*." From *Mississippi Quarterly* 58, nos. 1–2 (Winter 2004–Spring 2005): 7–24. © 2004–2005 by *Mississippi Quarterly*. Reprinted by permission.

Judy Pocock, "'Through a Glass Darkly': Typology in Toni Morrison's *Song of Solomon*." From *Canadian Review of American Studies* 35, no. 3 (2005): 281–298. © 2005 by the University of Toronto Press, www.utpjournals.com. Reprinted by permission of Canadian Association for American Studies.

Judith Fletcher, "Signifying Circe in Toni Morrison's *Song of Solomon*" by Judith Fletcher. From *Classical World* 99, no. 4 (2006): 405–418. © 2006 by Classical Association of the Atlantic States. Reprinted with permission of the editor of *Classical World*.

Every effort has been made to contact the owners of copyrighted material and secure copyright permission. Articles appearing in this volume generally appear much as they did in their original publication with few or no editorial changes. In some cases, foreign language text has been removed from the original essay. Those interested in locating the original source will find the information cited above.

Index

Page references followed by the letter *n* and a number refer to endnotes.

209